AF539471

Descriptive List of Acquired Documents

Volume VI (1831-1850)

Other Volumes in the Series:

1. *Calendar of Acquired Documents*, Vol. I (1402-1719), (New Delhi, 1982).
2. *Calendar of Acquired Documents*, Vol. II (1352-1754), (New Delhi, 1986).
3. *Descriptive List of Acquired Documents*, Vol. III (1356-1790), (New Delhi, 1992).
4. *Descriptive List of Acquired Documents*, Vol. IV (1559-1810), (New Delhi, 1995).

Descriptive List of Acquired Documents

Volume VI (1831-1850)

Edited by

Sanjay Garg

Compiled by

Nighat Shagufa

Muzaffar-e Islam

National Archives of India

2011

Descriptive List of Acquired Documents
Volume VI (1831-1850)
Edited by Sanjay Garg

First Published, 2011

ISBN 978-93-5002-127-9

Published by
AAKAR BOOKS
28 E Pocket IV, Mayur Vihar Phase I, Delhi 110 091
Phone : 011 2279 5505 Telefax : 011 2279 5641
info@aakarbooks.com; www.aakarbooks.com

in collaboration with
NATIONAL ARCHIVES OF INDIA
Janpath, New Delhi 110 001
archives@nic.in; www.nationalarchives.nic.in

Printed at
Mudrak, 30 Patparganj, Delhi 110 091

Contents

Preface

The National Archives of India plays a leading role in preserving the rich and varied documentary heritage of our country. With a view to enriching its collection it regularly acquires precious historical documents, manuscripts, rare books and other archival material through gifts, donations and purchase. Over the years a large collection has thus been built up which is being utilized by the scholars from far and wide. It had been our endeavour to facilitate the academic utilization of this valuable source material and therefore, we had been publishing the reference media of this material for the benefit of the scholar community. So far four volumes have been published in this series – Volumes 1 and 2 under the title of *Calendar of Acquired Documents* and Volumes 3 and 4 as *Descriptive Lists of Acquired Documents*. While another volume in this series (Vol. 5: 1811-30) is being compiled since long, I am extremely happy to place this latest volume in your hands.

This Volume contains 432 documents all of which are in Persian/Urdu. These documents are in the form of *farmans, parwanas, sanads, bainamas, tamliknamas, iqrarnamas, rahnnamas, rubakars, arzis, yaddashts, tamassuks,* etc. and cover a period of thirty years during the first half of the nineteenth century (i.e. from 1831 to 1850). All the dated documents have been arranged in a chronological order while the undated ones have been placed at the end. The original dates of writing the documents have been given on the left-hand margin of the documents along with its conversion in Gregorian era within brackets. Apart from the gist of the contents of each document, each entry also gives the physical description of the document, its style of writing, number of folios and the Accession Number. The illustrations of select documents have also been provided at the end of the Volume so that the readers may form an idea of the physical appearance and format of these documents. An indication of the documents thus illustrated is also given under the dates in the main listing. A detailed glossary of non-English and other technical terms used in the Volume has also been incorporated for the benefit of the advance users. A comprehensive index at the end is aimed to facilitate the quick retrieval of the desired information. Overall, diligent efforts have been put in to make this Volume an effective reference tool.

The documents included in this Volume contain a mine of information on the socio-economic and political conditions of India during 1831-1850. Though the subjects covered in these documents are as varied as the sources of their acquisition, even then some commonalities can be noticed since a majority of these documents represent the working of an agricultural economy in India. The effective working of the land deals was a result of an efficient judicial system, which in turn, was based on an elaborate system of records keeping. Thus there are documents which show as to how the *patta* or *ijara* (contract) of the agricultural land for a fixed period of years for cultivation worked (**1, 8, 13, 32, 68, 171, 318, 319,** and **324**). Amongst the documents included in this Volume one would also find *bainamas, hibanamas, tamliknamas, iqrarnamas, rahnnamas* and similar other documents dealing with land transactions. These documents were generally executed by the two parties in the presence of witnesses and later authenticated by getting the official stamp (*muhr*) of the *Qazi* (**42, 58, 87-8, 125, 165,** and **328)** or the *Mufti* (**104, 149,** and **333**) affixed on them. The use of land can also be seen as part of various religious endowments. Included in this Volume are certain documents pertaining to the family of Baba Ganeshgar of Dangawala (now in Punjab, Pakistan) who have been given land grants, *rasads* etc. on account of *dharmarth* (**18, 27, 51-2, 54, 63, 73, 81-2, 85-6, 118, 136, 154 etc.**). Likewise the *aimmadars* were given the land grants in recognition of their services to State (**16, 41, and 110**). Also included in this Volume are numerous Court Proceedings and the Judgments on cases contested between the individuals and the Government on the matter of land revenue on *lakhiraj* land (**17, 59, 69, 163, 180, 183, 195-6 etc.**). Besides, there are documents which are related to *khalsa darbar* etc. (**83, 126, 181, 240,** and **431-2**).

I am sure that the scholars would benefit from this reference medium and would be able to shed some new light on the history of this period. I shall look forward to your comments as to make these volumes more reader-friendly.

Lastly, I am extremely thankful to my colleagues, Km. Nighat Shagufa and Shri Muzaffar-e Islam, both Archivists for their diligent work in compiling the descriptive list of documents included in this volume. I would also like to record my gratitude towards Prof. Mushirul Hasan, Director General, National Archives of India for his guidance and encouragement to make the publication of this volume possible.

New Delhi
27 August 2010

Dr. Sanjay Garg
Deputy Director of the Archives

Descriptive List of Acquired Documents, Vol. VI (1831-1850)

1246 (AH?) (date in seal) (1830-31AD)	1.	Letter of Mirza Rustam Ali Beg to Mir Sahib (Mir Zakir Husain). Sends a sum of Rs. 90/- in cash and a receipt of Rs. 57/- of Muhammadpur and requests to make its entry as per schedule. Further requests for physical verification of the *sawars* who have come for and send them back to *chauki* to avoid inconvenience to the Government business. Expresses his inability to visit him at the moment as the peasants may make an excuse of not getting *patta* and that due to heavy rain cultivation suffered and thus would hamper the collection of revenue realization. Further says that the salary of the *sawars* which is due for the last four months would be paid very soon. Requests for the issuance of *Dastak-i Rasid*. The documents in Persian *shikasta* bears *sarnama Innahu* and seal of Mirza Rustam Ali Beg (the writer). **(ACC. NO. 1954; Original; f1).**
6 *Zilqada* (?) 1246 AH (18 April 1831)	2.	*Parwana* under the seal of Saiyid Muhammad Wali Khan Bahadur, *Nazim* of *sarkar* Khairabad etc. addressed to Chaudhari Mansab Ali of *pargana* Sandila.

Informs that Mir Kamil Ali Chaudhari of *pargana* Sandila, who is well wisher of the writer as well as the government has been assigned Rs. 51/- as *nankar* from the addressee's territory w.e.f. 1238 *Fasli* (1830 AD). Directs to pay him the aforesaid amount and may be entered in *wasilbaqi*.

The document in Persian *shikasta* bears *sarnama Alif*.

(ACC. NO. 1563; Copy; f1).

6 Zilqada 1246 AH (18 April 1831)

3. *Parwana* under the seal of Saiyid Muhammad Wali Khan, *Nazim* of *sarkar* Khairabad and Sandila to Mir Umaid Ali Khan *chakladar* of Sandila. Informs that in view of his loyalty Mir Kamil Ali Chaudhari of *pargana* Sandila has been assigned Rs. 51/- on account of *nankar* w.e.f. 1238 *Fasli*. Directs to pay him the amount from the territory of Chaudhari Mansab Ali attached to *pargana* Sandila, the receipt thereof obtained may be submitted in *wasilbaqi* which would be adjusted subsequently against the *wasilbaqi* of the said *pargana*.

The document in Persian *shikasta* bears *sarnama Alif*

(ACC. NO. 1562; Copy; f1).

20 April 1831/10 *Baisakh Sudi* 1888 *Samvat*

4. *Bainama* executed by Durga Dutt son of Lachman Singh resident of *qasba* Rewari in the suburbs of *dar al-khilafa* Shahjahanabad. States that he has sold his hereditary land along with the garden of Rao Shitab Rai, his grand father measuring 430 *ziras* by *gaz-i ilahi* situated in the aforesaid *qasba* to Nanak Ram and Tonghan sons of Naubat Ram residents of *qasba* Rewari for Rs. 145/- *(sikka-i kaldar)*.

Acknowledges the receipt of the amount in full.

The document in Persian *shikasta* executed on a two rupee punch marked paper, bears *sarnama Alif* and a seal of the executant and signatures of the witnesses in Devnagri and Persian.

(ACC. NO. 2657/13; Original; f1).

24 *Zilqada* 1246 AH/11 *Baisakh Budi* (5 May 1831)

5. *Tamassuk* executed by Pirthi Dubey and Durjan *zamindar* residents of *pargana* Sandila of village Alipur Handwa. Stands surety to Chunna *zamindar* of village Sarharipur who is imprisoned in the *sarkar* of Chaudhari Muhammad Daim. Promise to produce him whenever required by the *mutasaddis* of *sarkar* of Chaudhari Daim and if they fail to produce him they will be held responsible for this.

The document in Persian *shikasta* bears official endorsements in Persian and Hindi and signature of Moti Lal as witness.

(ACC. NO. 1565; Original; f1).

24 *Zilqada* 1246 AH/11 *Baisakh Budi* (5 May 1831)

6. *Tamassuk malzamin* executed by Pirthi Dubey resident of Sandila towards Ashraf Tola and Durjan *zamindar* of village Alipur, Handwa, *amla, pargana* Sandila. Stands surety of Rs. 77/- outstanding against Chunna Singh *zamindar* of village Sarharipur which is payable to Chaudhari Muhammad Daim. Promise to pay the amount in near future without hesitation.

The document in Persian *shikasta* bears endorsement in Hindi and signature of Moti Lal Patwati as witness.

(ACC. NO. 1564; Copy; f1).

9 *Zilhijja* 1238 *Fasli* (1246 AH)

7. Sale-deed of advance money executed by Shaikh Wajid Ali son of Nur Allah. States

(21 May 1831) that he has taken on lease 4 *annas* out of 8 *annas* of *dar-o-bast aimma malikana* of Abd al-Rashid Khan situated in *mauza* Saiyidpur against an annual jama of Rs. 50/- w.e.f. 1234 *Fasli* to 1240 *Fasli* and have paid Rs. 200/- as advance money out of which Rs. 50/- was sold to *Mst.* Bhikan the owner of the aforesaid *aimma* land. Further states that he has sold to *Mst.* Amiran another½ *anna* share i. e. Rs. 25/- and again has taken back from her half of the amount i. e. Rs. 12½ on lease. Furnishes other details of the sale of the remaining shares of the advance money to the leasee.

The document in Persian *shikasta* bears *sarnama Innahu* and signature of the witnesses and also contains a statement of *Mst.* Bhikan declaring that the sum of Rs. 50/-paid to her by the executant is due upon her.

(ACC. NO. 2531/ 8; Original; f1).

19 *Muharam* 1247 AH (30 June 1831)

8. *Qaul-o-qarar-i patta* executed in favour of Mir Tajammul Husain. Informs that taking into account the yield of 1239 *Fasli* (1831 AD) from *muhalla* Saiyidana Khurd the annual *jama* has been fixed as Rs. 301/- for which a *patta* has been given to him. Directs him to undertake cultivation whole-heartedly.

The document in Persian *shikasta* bears symbol of seal of Shaikh Mubarak Allah.

(ACC. NO. 2403/ 79; Copy; f1).

20 *Muharam* 1247 AH (1 July 1831)

9. *Parwana* under the seal of Anjha Singh *chakladar* of the *mahals* of Salon etc. to Abu al-Lais *tahsildar* of *qasba* Jais. Informs that as per the *sanad* of Padshah Begum and its confirmation through a *Parwana* issued to

him in 1237 *Fasli,* 25 *bighas* of measured land situated in *qasba* Jais excluded from revenue except Government dues has been assigned to Saiyid Haibat Allah son of Maulawi Saiyid Ali Akbar. Expressing anxiety on him for creating obstacles in the grant instructs him to relinquish the said land in his favour for 1238 *Fasli* as well and not to demand a fresh *sanad* every year.

The document in Persian *shikasta* bears *sarnma Alif* and the attestation seal of Qazi Saiyid Adil Husain.

(ACC. NO. 2096; Copy; f1).

15 *Safar* 1247 AH (26 July 1831)

10. *Iqrarnama/ Tamassuk/ Rahnnama* executed by Habib Allah son of Shaikh Abd Allah of zila Muradabad in respect of his ancestral 6 *bigha Kham* land situated at *mauza* Harevi *pargana* Kiratpur. States that he has mortgaged the aforesaid land in favour of Muhammad Bakhsh son of Muhammad Naim of *Qasba* Kiratpur for a sum of Rs. 8/ for three years from the beginning of 1239 Fasli till the end of 1241 Fasli and has received the amount in full. Declares that after the expiry of the period he would refund the money and would get the land back into his possession. Further says that if he failed to pay the aforesaid amount, the mortgagee would be liable to get yield from the land unless and until he pays the amount.

The brittle document in Persian *shikasta* executed on 2 *anna* punch marked stamp paper bears signature of the executant with seal and signature of witnesses.

(ACC. NO. 2609/ 10; Original; f1).

20 *Safar* 1247 AH (31 July 1831)	11.	*Parwana* under the seal of Mirza Abu Talib to Hakim Wajid Ali Khan *chaklladar* of Sandila. Refers to a report from Lala Umaid Rai regarding non-payment of Rs. 100/- by the addressee as *nankar* to Debi Den, *qanungo* of *pargana* Sandila. Directs him for immediate disbursement of the same to the *qanungo* and obtain an authentative receipt thereof. The document is written in Persian *shikasta*. **(ACC. NO. 1556; Copy; f1).**
2 Rabi to1287 AH (10 September 1831)	12.	*Hukmnama* of Mahdi Ali Khan to the *tahsildar* and army personnel of *ilaqa* Sandila and the staff of the *Akhbar* (intelligence) of present and future of the aforesaid *ilaqa*. Expresses anxiety on the report received about their atrocities and oppression on the noblemen of the said *ilaqa* which has left them perturbed. Conveys that the *Zill-i Subhani* (the Nawwab Wazir) is quite interested in the welfare and security and dignity of all his inhabitants. Warns them of stern action by the Nawwab Wazir and even dismissal from services if any one found guilty of committing atrocities upon even a single inhabitant of the *ilaqa*. Directs them to cooperate and help Qazi Wajih al-Din and Aslih al-Din who are gentlemen of the area. Also warns that Sita Ram *gumashta* and Chait Ram *harkara* who have been dismissed from service due to their misconduct should not be employed again by any *ahlkar* nor allowed their entry into the fort. Admonishes that if anyone found giving them asylum or protection would

commit a grave mistake and would be punished severely.

The document bears *sarnama Alif* and seal of Mahdi Ali Khan and also official endorsement on the reverse of the document.

(ACC. NO. 1539; Copy; f1).

16 September 1831 13. Petition of Dhari son of Harkaran Machela son of Garibu and other *zamindars* of Chathari, Referring the grant of *patta* of village Chathari *pargana* Sonipat, a *jagir* village of Kunwar Aman Singh to them for three years w.e.f. 1239 *Fasli* (1831 AD) till the end 1241 *Fasli* (1833 AD) against a sum of Rs. 5250/- including the *muqaddami* @ Rs. 5% which excludes the property of gardens etc. in normal condition declare that the *theka* is acceptable to them.

The document bears orders giving acceptance to the petitioner's request and issues *parwana* to the *tahsildar* in this regard.

The document in Persian *shikasta* executed on a punch marked stamp paper of Rs. 12/- bears signatures of the executants.

(ACC. NO. 2656/ 34; Original; f1).

11 *Rabi* II 1247 AH (19 September 1831) 14. *Wasiatnama / Bakhshishnama* executed by *Mst.* Har Kunwar alias Phul Kunwar wife of late Rai Kumari Lal who is 75 years old. Describes her agony being left without heir as her grand-son too left this world at the early age of 26 years and she had to sell all her jwellery and other household items to perform the rites of her grandson. Besides, the hereditary house of Rai Kumari Lal situated in *Balda* Farkhundabunyad Hyderabad in *muhalla* Chunia Mahal was

mortgaged for Rs. 4000/- with Jagat Singh for paying the debt taken from Nawwab Himmat Yar Jang. Declares that she has adopted her two grandsons i.e. Narain Prasad and Kanhia Prasad as her heirs who will inherit all her property left by her and that they would take care of her till she is alive.

The document in Persian *shikasta* contains 28 seals including the seal of the executant and signatures of several witnesses.

(ACC. NO. 2617/ 30; Original; f1).

15 October 1831 — 15. *Parwana* of Colonel Gardiner to Bhim Singh *chakladar* of Salon. Refers to the grant of 25 *bighas* of measured land situated in *qasba* Jais in favour of Saiyid Haibat Allah son of Maulawi Ali Akbar as proven from the *sanads* of Padshah Begum and former *amils*. Instructs him to relinquish the same in his favour.

The document in Persian *shikasta* bears *sarnama Alif* and the attestation seal of Qazi Saiyid Adil Husain.

(ACC. NO. 2098; Copy; f1).

10 *Jumada* I 1247 AH/ 26 *Asin* 1239 *Fasli* (17 October 1831) — 16. *Bainama* executed by Chand Khan son of Jamiat Khan in the *Dar al Qaza, pargana* Okri District Bihar regarding the sale of his one *biswa zamin-i malikana* from Khagri Bagh and 2½ *annas* out of 5 *annas* from *dar-o-bast* of 16 *annas* of *huquq-i milkiyat-i aimma* from *chak* Lanchina situated in *mauza* Makhdumpur Mukanwan *pargana* Okri with all his rights to the *aimmadars* i. e. Shaikh Safdar Ali, Shaikh Mahbub Ali, Shaikh Tufail Ali and Shaikh Zulfiqar Ali sons of Shaikh Muhammad Anwar of *chak*

Lanchina for Rs. 4/-. States that he has received the amount in full and has no claim over that land.

The document in Persian *shikasta* bears *sarnama Alif* and the seal of Qazi Asad Ali and symbol of signature of the executant besides signatures of the witnesses.

(ACC. NO. 2531/ 5; Original; f1).

9 January 1832/ 21 *Pos* 1239 *Fasli*

17. *Ishtiharnama* issued by *Kachehri, zila* Bihar. Notifies that Saiyid Hatim Zaman *mukhtarkar* of *Mst.* Bibi Bhikan, wife of late Shaikh Muhammad Anwar owner and *malguzar* of six *annas* 3 *pie* of *mauza* Nurpur *mutaallqa pargana* Okri has given a petition on 29 December 1831 requesting to delete the name of late Shaikh Muhammad Anwar from the mutation papers of the aforesaid *mauza* comprising *arazi, khiraji* and *lakhiraji* (details given in the text of document) and to enter the name of *Mst.* Bibi Bhikan in his place.

The court notifies that if anyone has any objection on the mutation of the aforesaid request he may do so within specific period of 20 days, as after the expiry of that period, mutation would be executed as per the request.

The bilingual document in Persian *shikasta* and *Devnagri* bears the seal of Collectorate of *zila* Bihar.

(ACC. NO. 2534/ 2; Original; f1).

5 *Phagun* 1888 *Samvat* (7 March 1832)

18. *Parwana* addressed to the *amils* of present and future of *taalluqa* Dhuria. Informs that 25½ *maund* foodgrain has been in assignment of Ganeshgar on account of *dharmarth* from *qasba* Dhika. Directs for the release of food grains to him every year crop after crop without any alteration.

The document in Persian *shikasta* bears *sarnama Alif* and a dim seal.

(ACC. NO. 2580/ 31; Original; f1).

14 *Zilqada* 1247 AH (15 April 1832) (Illus.)

19. *Bainama* executed by Saiyid Farhat Ali son of Saiyid Hadi Ali *wakil* on behalf of *Mst.* Rakkhi and *Mst.* Gauhar daughters of Saiyid Muhammadi, residents of *qasba* Amroha, *sarkar* Sambhal *suba* Shahjahanabad in respect of sale of 8 *biswas* of *muafi* land in village Rasulpur, *pargana* Amroha, *nazranadar sarkar* inherited from Saiyid Muhammadi with its boundaries. States that he has sold his land to Saiyid Waris Ali for Rs. 1356/- w.e.f. *Rabi* crop of 1220 *Fasli* (1821 AD) who has taken possession of the land and he (the seller) has got the money in full.

The document in Persian *shikasta* executed on punch marked stamp paper of Rs. 12/- bears *sarnama Alif* and several seals, along with the signatures of the executants and witnesses, besides the department endorsement on the reverse.

(ACC. NO. 2533/ 42; Original; f1).

17 *May* 1832/3 *Jeth* 1239 *Fasli*

20. Judgment of the Court of *Diwani* District Agra under the session of Mr. Rason Heart Bodhan, Acting Judge on a case filed by Achhanand, resident of Bindraban against Chintan Das and Baldev in respect of a petition dated 26 August 1828 claiming over the property of heritance of late Siva Das worth Rs. 16/- filed in the court of *sadr-amin* and the said *sadr-amin* had dismissed the case on 16 March 1829 which was a matter of disgust to him. The court in its judgment dated 17 May again upheld the decision taken by Mufti *sadr-amin* and dismissed the case and the court also ordered to pay the expenses of the court by the appellant.

The bilingual document on a court paper of Re 1/-in Persian/ Urdu *shikasta* bears a dim seal of the court.

(ACC. NO. 2712/ 9;Copy; ff3).

18 *Zilhijja* 1247 AH (19 May 1832) 21. *Tamliknama* under the seal of Qazi Saiyid Adil Husain, Saiyid Qadir Husain and others executed by *Mst.* Bibi Barkat wife of Saiyid Qudrat Ali of *qasba* Jais in respect of the sale of her entire 1/3rd property inherited from her husband which includes the agricultural and residential land, gardens in *pura* situated in *qasba* Jais village Miranpur, Qasimpur and Tahirpur etc. for Rs. 1000/- in favour of her daughter from the parental side.

The document is written in Persian *shikasta.*

(ACC. NO. 2079; Copy; f1).

7 July 1832/ 7 *Safar* 1248 AH 22. *Ittilanama* issued by Major John Lieu, Resident at Lucknow to *tankhwahdars* of the *wasiqa* of late General Martin. Informs them that their salaries from February to May 1832 would be paid from the Company's treasury. Directs them that every one should submit their *qabz al-wasul* under their seal as their salaries would be issued only after the scrutiny of their *Qabz al wasul.*

The document in Persian *nastaliq* bears *sarnama Alif* and the seal of Major John Lieu and his signature in English.

(ACC. NO. 2391; Original; f1).

1 *Jumada* II 1248 AH (26 23. *Parwana* of Maharaja Chandu Lal (servant of Asaf Jah, Nizam al-Mulk) to the

October 1832) *deshmukhs, qanungos, sardeshpandeyas, muqaddams, Kulkarnis, riaya* and *muzaris* of *pargana* Lohgaon *sarkar* Nander. Informs them that *mauza* Dangi in the aforesaid *pargana* has been assigned to Rai Lachmi Narain as *jagir-i zat* amounting to the total *jama* of Rs. 5250/- from the year 1251 *Fasli* with exemption of *chauth*. Directs them for the payment of *mal-i wajib* to the deputy of the aforesaid grantee in time.

The document in Persian *shikasta* bears *sarnama Alif* and the seal of Maharaja Chandu Lal Bahadur.

(ACC. NO. 2535/ VI; Original; f1).

19 *Rajab* 1248 AH (12 December 1832) 24. *Nikahnama* executed in the presence of the *wakils* of the bride and bride-groom (Muhammad Salih Hasani) against the sum of *mahr-muajjal* of Rs. 400/- and Rs. 1200/- as *mahr-muwajjal* including *than nikah* as an equivalent to 20 *Ashrafi* which too is *muajjal*.

The damaged document is written in Persian *shikasta* bears *sarnama Bi Ism Allah al-Rahman al-Rahim* and a seal of the Qazi along with several seals of witnesses.

(ACC. NO. 2720/ 57; Original; f1).

28 March 1833/ 7 *Chait Shudi*, 1890 *Samvat* 25. *Iqrarnama* executed by Kalal Singh son of Rao Aisri Singh. States that he has no claim *upon* Kunwar Aman Singh and Umrao Singh as after Raja Umed Singh's death the whole territory had been confiscated by the Government. However Chathari and Asoi, the two villages which are granted to Kunwar Aman Singh without any co-sharer as *wagushat*, the said Kunwar would relinquish an income of Rs. 70/- from the aforesaid villages in his (the executant)

favour every year for his livelihood till his death and that in the event of natural calamity in any year he would not claim anything from him.

The document in Persian *shikasta* executed on punch marked paper of 8 *anna* bears *sarnama Alif* with the signature of the executant besides seals and signatures of the witnesses.

(ACC. NO. 2656/ 36; Original; f1).

28 March 1833/ 7 *Chait Shudi* 1890 *Samvat*	26.	*Yaddasht* by Kalal Singh. To the same effect as the foregoing document no. 2556/ 36. The document in Persian *shikasta* executed on punch marked paper of 8 *anna* bears *sarnama Alif* and seals and signatures of the witnesses. **(ACC. NO. 2656/ 37; Original; f1).**
22 *Chait* 1890 *Samvat* (11 April 1833)	27.	*Parwana* to Lala Nawin Shah. States that the *rasad* of 3 men on account of *dharmarth* has been in assignment of Gosain Shivgar and Ganeshgar, residents of Dankian. Directs to make payment of the said *rasad* to them as per the established practice. The document in Persian *shikasta* bears *sarnama Alif* and a seal in Gurmukhi **(ACC. NO. 2580/ 6; Original; f1).**
22 *Zilqada* 1248 AH/1240 *Fasli* 14 April 1833/10 *Baisakh Budi* 1890 *Samvat*	28.	*Qararnama* executed by Mazhar Ali son of Inayat Allah and Itiqad Ali son of Mazhar Ali resident of *qasba* Jalali. State that they have mortgaged their four plots of land and yield of Rs. 3/- out of the revenue of village Dhorrah, Jamalpur (details of the plot and village are given in the body of the text) to Niyaz Ali son of Ihsan Ali and Farman Ali son of Niyaz Ali resident of the fort, old Kol for Rs. 88/- *kaldar* only and has received the amount in full. Add that

Aitamad Ali and Yunus Ali, son of Mazhar Ali who are in job at Gwalior, if any time come to this place and force them to accord their will, it will be their duty to pacify them and pay the amount of *rahn* to them.

The document in Persian *shikasta* bears *sarnama Alif* along with three seals and signatures of the executants and the witnesses, having endorsement of the court on its reverse.

(ACC. NO. 1037; Original; f1).

3 May 1833 29. *Hukmnama* addressed to all the *pujaris* and *kamdars* of Gobind Dev Temple. Directs them to submit their reply in connection to the questions regarding facts and figures of the aforesaid temple within ten days. Those questions are as how and when the *parkhat* of present *thakur* did appear, in whose reign and who constructed the temple and installed the *thakur* and who owned it. How and what were the sources of income of the said temple and who hold them, the type of land, garden etc. attached to the temple and the realization of the whole year, number of *kamdars, pujaris* of the temple and their salary, income received from the pilgrims as *nazr* and *bhaint* etc. paid by the *chelas*, savings of the temple after the expenditure of the whole year and who is the receipient of the amount of the temple and dues of temple, if any and mode of payment.

The document in Persian *shikasta* bears the seal of *kachahri-i nizamat wa faujdari, zila* Mathura.

(ACC. NO. 2691/ 31; Original; ff2).

25 May 1833 30. Court order addressed to Mohan Das

adhikari of Madan Mohanji temple, Gokal Das *adhikari* of Gopinath temple and Bal Mukand *kamdar* of Gobindji temple. Acknowledges receipt of their petition dated 22 May 1833 in response to the *hukmnama* issued to them directing to put forward the facts and figures in connection to the aforesaid temples. The Court expresses resentment on their reply expressing their ignorance about the facts and figures of the temples inspite of their being the kamdars and pujaris of the temples. Directs them to submit a detailed report on the income and expenditure and custody as some questions about *parkhat* and *isthapan* of *thakur* mainly depends upon the owners of the temples.

The document in Persian *shikasta* bears a seal of the *kachehri-i nizamat wa faujdari, zila* Mathura.

(ACC. NO. 2691/ 32; Original; f1).

4 June 1833 31. *Rubakar* of *adalat-i faujdari* of Mathura on the enquiry made by Pandit Birbal, *Sadr Amin* at Bindraban from Govind Charan Das, Ram Das and Balmukand *kamdars* of Shri Thakur Gobind Devji temple to the dispute of the temple of Shri Govind Devji. It records their statement on several questions pertaining to the factual position of the income realized from land, garden, market, rent of the shops, expenditure fixed for *thakurji* or *sewak* etc. of the said temple. The foremost being that when the *parkhat* of Shri Thakur Gobind Devji was installed and their reply that the *parkhat* was installed in the reign of Emperor Akbar about three hundred years ago and the earliest *pujari* was Roop Gosain and the

temple of Thakur was built by Raja Man Singh and idol of Thakurji took shape in the reign of Aurangzeb Alamgir.

The document in Persian *shikasta* executed on punch marked stamp paper of 8 *anna* bears *sarnama Alif* and a dim seal of the *kachahri-i nizamat wa faujdari, zila* Mathura with signatures of the *kamdars* and *Sadr Amin*.

(ACC. NO. 2671/ 35; Copy; f1).

26 *Muharram* 1249 AH (15 June 1833) 32. *Qaul-o-qarar-i patta* executed by Farkhunda Husain in favour of Dena *Muqaddam* and Mangal Khan *karinda* of Qazi Adil Husain alowing cultivation of *muhalla* Saiyidana Khurd against a *jama* of Rs. 401/- for the whole year for 1241 *Fasli* (1834) Instructs them to adhare to the *qaul-o-qarar-i patta* and not to demand more than the fixed amount.

The document in Persian *shikasta* bears *sarnama Alif* and the seal of Farkhunda Husain.

(ACC. NO. 2106; Original; f1).

15 *Rabi* I 1249 (2 August 1833) 33. *Ibranama/ Farighkhati* executed by Muhsina Jiu and Anwar Jiu sons of Munawwar Jiu of *muhalla* Pandan. Declares that the household articles and items of daily use as per the details given in the document owned by wife of Ahmad Jiu which were given in the trust of her brother Nizam Jiu have been taken back from him. Hence they have no claim whatsoever on him.

The document in Persian *shikasta* bears four seals and signatures of informer / witnesses.

(ACC. NO. 2720/ 58; Original; f1).

25 *Sawan* 1890 34. *Parwana* to the *kardaran* of Guzar Jhelam

Samvat (10 August 1833)

(?). Informs them about the assignment in favour of Baba Devgar Jiu on account of *dharmarth* since olden times. Orders for the continuance of the aforesaid assignment without any variation in it.

The document in Persian *shikasta* bears *sarnama Alif* and the seal of Kishan Chand Mehta.

(ACC. NO. 2580/ 5; Original; f1).

25 *Rabi* I 1249 AH (12 August 1833)

35. *Qabuliyatnama* executed by Daraz Khan son of Akbar Khan resident of Badayun *muhalla* Sarai Nau. States that he has taken on lease the farm land measuring 13 *bigha 19 biswas in lieu of annual jama* of Rs. 5/ 10 for biannual *jama* of two years i.e. 1240-41 *Fasli* from Muhammad Roshan and Aman Allah the *kamangaran, muafidar* of *mauza* Atapur. Promises to pay the aforesaid *jama* yearly, crop after crop to the *muafidaran.*

The document in Persian *shikasta* bears *sarnama Alif* and signature of the executants and the witnesses.

(ACC. NO. 2287; Original; f1).

25 September 1833

36. *Yaddasht / Iqrarnama* executed in between Kunwar Aman Singh and Kunwar Totaram. State that he (Kunwar Aman Singh) has come to an agreement with Kunwar Totaram under the seal of the Qazi of Delhi following which a sum of Rs. 260/ - annually is payable by him to Kunwar Totaram from the income of Chathari and Asoi villages w.e.f. 1235 *Fasli.* The agreement also concludes that he (Kunwar Aman Singh) would not pay *salyana* to him (Kunwar Totaram) in case of natural calamity if occurs in any year nor would he demand *salyana* of that year. Clarifies

that in the year 1240 *Fasli* the Company Government had realized half of the *jama* from village Chathari and in 1241 *Fasli* there was draught in the region. Adds that however Totaram has made a request and keeping in mind his hardship he has agreed to conlude further to give Kunwar Totaram 10% of the income received from the Government for 1240 *Fasli*. Clarifies that he would give Rs. 260/- every year w.e.f. 1235 *Fasli* to 1239 *Fasli* and would pay the same amount in the coming years if no calamity natural or otherwise occurs.

The document in Persian *shikasta* executed on 4 *anna* stamp paper bears *sarnama Alif* and the seals and signatures of the executant and the witnesses.

(ACC. NO. 2656/ 38; Original; f1).

7*Makar Shudi* (*Asvina*) 1890 (?) *Samvat* (19 October 1833)

37. Letter addressed to Lala Durga Datt Dilawar Sahai *darogha*. Informs him that 5 *bighas* of grassy land has been granted to Jaggu Pal as *muafi* and directs to distribute the remaining land.

The document in Persian *shikasta* bears *sarnama Alif* and the seal of Fath Singh Sahai.

(ACC. NO. 2768/ 7; Original; f1).

11 *Jumada* II 1249 AH (26 October 1833)

38. *Tamassuk* under the seal of Qazi Muhammad Husain executed in the court at Ahmadabad by Mali Das son of Narain on his behalf and as *wakil* on behalf of his brother Somnath in the presence of Dhamangar son of Shambhu and Hira son of Jutia about a piece of land measuring 63 yard situated under the above walled city in *chakla* Moin Khan (as per the details of the boundaries given in the text) which

is under their possession, has sold to Mansukh son of Mulji in totality for Rs. 25/ (Akbar Shahi coin). Declares that the two parties have made the sale-deed in all its perfections.

The document in Persian *shikasta* on cloth bears the seal of the above Qazi and the symbol of hand impression as well as signature of the witnesses in Persian and Devanagri.

(ACC. NO. 2441/ 4; Copy; f1).

1241 *Fasli* (date in the text) (1249 AH) (1833-34)	39.	Letter of Abdul Ali to Lala Motilal. States that a sum of Rs. 10/-for the year 1241 *fasli* of Muhammad Roshan and other kamangran is due upon him (the writer) which may be realized from the yearly income of Shaikh Ramazani, the cultivator of *mauza* Londasiri on account of *mahsul-i milk*. Desires that if the yield received from the land of Ramazani is less than Rs. 10/- the estimated amount may be acquired from other sources of Ramazani which however, should not exceed more than the due amount. The document in Persian *Shikasta* bears *sarnama alif*. **(ACC. NO. 2255; Original; f1).**
1 *Ramazan* 1249 AH (12 January 1834) (Illus.)	40.	*Parwana* issued under the seal of Hayat Husain Khan, *Nazim* of *ilaqa* Biswarah and Salon to Shaikh Sahib. States that the *pura* of Musharrafnagar, attached to *qasba* Jais has been in the *zamindari* of Mir Ausaf Ali and none ever dared to harass them on the pretext of tax of *nahri* or *begar*. Expresses anxiety that, meanwhile, some sepoys accompanying the addressee are extracting *begar* etc. from the said *pura* and are

indulged in extracting Rs. 8/- from the inhabitants there. Instructs that the sepoys should be restrained from committing any atrocity upon the inhabitants and the extracted money should be returned.

The document in Persian *shikasta* bears the seal of Qazi Saiyid Adil Husain.

(ACC. NO. 2403/ 20; Copy; f1).

1*Ramazan*/18 *Pos* 1241 *Fasli* (1249 AH) (12 January 1834)

41. *Qabuliyatnama* executed by Uttam Mahtun resident of Inayat Chak aimma belonging to the village Gopalpur Dhankhera pargana Bhailawar District Bihar. states that he has taken on lease 2 *anna,* 5½ *dam* from *darobast* of *aimma* of the aforesaid village and 5 *bighas malikana* and 2½ *bighas* of *jagir* land purchased and possessed by *Mst.* Idan, Bahadur Ali and *Mst.* Bichan *aimmadars* comprising a *jama* of Rs. 32/ per annum for five years from 1241 to 1245 *Fasli* (1833 to 1837 AD) and has paid Rs. 100/- as advance through Mirza Muhammad Shaban Beg to the *aimmadars.* Promises for the payment of stipulated *malguzari* to the *aimmadars* annually as per instalments. Declares that in case, he fails to pay the land revenue, the *aimmadars* are free to appoint *sazawal,* the expenses of which would be borne out by him. Also hopes that the *aimmadars* would return the advance money by the end of *Jeth* 1236 and if they failed to return the advance money the *theka* would continue on the same terms and conditions.

The document in Persian *shikasta* bears *sarnama innahu* and signatures of the witnesses.

(ACC. NO. 2531/ 7; Original; f1).

10 *Zilqada* 1249 AH (21 March 1834)

42. *Parwana* issued to Mirza Hasan Ali Beg. Informing that Qazi Wajih al-Din of *qasba* Sandila who is holding the post of Qazi of the said *pargana* from olden times, the people of the region however ignoring him settle their disputes at their own and even *poldar* takes decision and tries to compel the Qazi to affix the seal of *Dar-al -qaza* on it which might be against religion. Directs him to insure that the Qazi holds the post of *qazi* at his own liberty who may take decision at his own and may be able to execute his orders fearlessly. Further directs to keep the *poldar* away from interfering in the affairs of the *qaza* instead he should help and cooperate with the Qazi in implementing the order.

The document is written in Persian *shikasta*.

(ACC. NO. 1630 ; Original ; f1).

15 *Phagun* 1890 *Samvat* (25 March 1834)

43. *Parwana* issued to Sankhan *Jagirdar* of village Goyal (sic). States that the land granted on account of *dharmarth* has been in assignment of Gosain, resident of Vatala (Batala) as *muaf* and *waguzar* since olden times. Directs him that the said land may be treated as ceded and exempted from taxes as per the old practice.

The document in Persian *shikasta* bears *sarnama Alif* and a dim seal.

(ACC. NO. 2580/ 4; Original; f1).

11 May 1834

44. Letter to Izzat Ali Khan, Bande Ali Khan, Jiwan Singh Dubey, Sewa Ram Jai (?) Hira Lal Chaudhari son of Sewa Ram Panchan (?) of *muhalla* Shah Ganj. Informs them about the duties assigned to them for management and arrangement of the

amount of *rasad-bandi* received from the shopkeepers and residents of *muhalla* Shah Ganj for payment of the salary of the *chaukidar* who are appointed for the safety of the residents of that *muhalla*. Also directs them to obseve the following terms and conditions for the appointment of the *chaukidars*. Tells that the realization of the amount should not be more than Re. 1/- and less than 1 *anna* per month on each resident of that *mohalla*. However, the amount realized should not exceed to Rs. 6/4 per month. Even then the poverty ridden persons should be totally exempted from payment of *rasadbandi*. Also directs them to prepare a comprehensive list of the total amount of *rasadbandi* received from each shopkeeper or resident duly prepared and signed by the addressees for its submission to the Magistrate, Furthermore, submit the names of all *chaukidars* appointed under the rule 13 of 1813 to the Magistrate and a report to the *darogha-i police* or Magistrate about the negligence shown by any *chaukidar* at the time of the duty.

The document in Persian *shikasta* bears *sarnama Innahu* and a dim seal of the court.

(ACC. NO. 1040; Original; f1).

11 August 1834

45. *Rubakar-i kachehri,* District Aligarh under the session of Mr. James Davidson Officiating Collector. Communicates the orders of the Commissioner of Agra dated 9 August 1832 for issuance of a *parwana* to the *peshkar* of *huzur-i tahsil* to restore 198 *bighas* 14 *biswas* and 9 *biswansi* of *muafi* land in *mauza* Jamalpur *pargana* Kol previously included in the cantonment of that District

in favour of Amanat Ali Khan, Izzat Ali Khan, Ghulam Mahdi and Murad Ali the *muafidars* of *pargana* Kol, Aligarh.

The document in Persian *shikasta* executed on punch marked stamp paper of 8 *anna* bears the dim seal of the court.

(ACC. NO. 1036; Copy; f1).

25 *Rabi* II 1250 AH (31 August 1834) (Illus.)

46. *Parwana* under the seal of Nawwab Muhtashim Khan Bahadur to the *mutasaddis* of present and future of *pargana* Nasirabad *sarkar* Manikpur *suba* Allahabad. Informs that as per the *sanads* of previous *hakims*, village Gora Sogha (?) in the said *pargana* has been assigned as *inam* to Saiyid Ghulam Muhi al-Din and others. Records that Mulla Muhammad Thatthi, *sadr-i juz* resumed the said village and subsequently released who however imposed a tax of Rs. 53/- on the rest 35 *bighas* of land which too was however waived off by late Daud Khan. Adds that the same practice was followed by late Husain Ali Khan Bahadur, Himmat Khan and Saif Khan. Instructs them to follow the same practice with regard to the exemption of taxes as long as he is alive and is in the possession of the same. Directs to pay the said amount year by year and crop after crop.

The document in Persian *shikasta* bears attestation seal of Qazi Adil Husain and an endorsement on the back for the issuance of *parwana.*

(ACC. NO. 2403/ 22; Copy; f1).

1242 *Fasli* (1250) (1834-35)

47. *Yaddasht* in respect of receipt (*wasulyafti*) of Rs1746 from village Chathari and Asoi, *pargana* Sonipat Khadar, *jagir* of Kunwar

Aman Singh for the year 1242 *Fasli*.

The document is in Persian *shikasta*.

(ACC. NO. 2656/ 35; Copy; f1).

26 March 1835 48. *Ishtiharnama* issued from the Court of Deputy Collector District Bihar to the effect that today on 24 February the solicitation *Mukhtarnama* of Tolaram *mukhtar-i kar* was heard on behalf of *Mst*. Khairun, resident of village Daulatpur *pargana* Okri for entering the names of Jamal al-Haque and Fazl al-Haque sons of late Shaikh Zulfiqar Ali in place of their late father against 14 shares out of 48 shares of the deceased from village Daulatpur, *pargana* Okri. Accordingly a short notice for duration of 20 days is hereby issued enabling the claimant if any, to represent their claims either personally or through his plenipotentiary failing which no excuse shall be made in the name of the aforesaid heirs.

The bilingual document in Persian and Devnagri bears *sarnama Alif* and the seal of the office of Deputy Collector District Bihar.

(ACC. NO. 2561/ 1; Original; f1).

26 March 1835 49. *Ishtiharnama* issued from the court of Deputy Collector (special) District Bihar to the effect that today on 24 February the solicitation of Mohib Ali was heard in the above court on behalf of Jamal al-Haque and Fazl al-Haque (his real nephews) sons of late Zulfiqar Ali for entering their name in place of their father for 6 *annas* and 3 *pais* as *milkiyat* and *malguzari* of village Nurpur, a *deh* of *nizamat-i milkiyat* of the shares of the villages of Daulatpur,

Mianwan, *pargana* Okri District Bihar etc. Accordingly short notice for duration of 20 days is hereby issued so that anyone who has any objection should submit in the court either personally or through plenipotentiary within the stipulated period failing which it would be entered in the name of the aforesaid claimants.

The bilingual document in Persian and Devnagri bears *sarnama Alif and* the seal of the office of the Deputy Collector, District Bihar.

(ACC. NO. 2561/2; Original; f1).

10 *Zilhijja* 1250 AH (9 April 1835)

50. *Qabala-i bai* executed in the Civil Court, Lucknow by Inayat Husain son of Mir Ghulam Husain resident of Masjid Tahsin Ali Khan, Lucknow, *wakil* on behalf of Manuji son of Lalji of Sabzi Mandavi of Lucknow in respect of sale of his *amla* and *arazi* comprising one storeyed *haveli* at Sabzi Mandavi (the details of the property along with the delineation of the boundaries are given in the body of the text) to Dilawar Ali Beg son of Qadir Beg, resident of Sabzi Mandavi *wakil* on behalf of Bindraban and Kishan Lal sons of Samadhan for Rs. 2925/. Confirms that he has received the amount in full.

The document in Persian *nastaliq* bears the seal of Mufti of *Adalat-i Aliya Diwani* Lucknow and that of *Adalat-i Aliya Diwani* Lucknow with the royal emblem of Awadh at the top and departmental endorsement on the reverse.

(ACC. NO. 162; Original; f1).

12 *Chait* 1892 *Samvat*

51. *Parwana* issued to Mian Nadir Singh. Refers the *Parwana-i takid* issued to him

(10 April 1835) appertaining payment of *rasad* on account of *dharmarth* to Baba Ganeshgar which he has not yet received. Directs to make payment of the *rasad* to the said Baba without any excuse and delay.

The document in Persian *shikasta* bears *sarnama Alif* (?) and the seal of Mangal Singh Akal Sahai.

(ACC. NO. 2580/ 19; Original f1).

14 *Chait* 1892 *Samvat* (12 April 1835) 52. *Parwana* issued to Mian Nadir Singh. Refers his previous *parwana* about the grant of *rasad* to Baba Ganeshgar on account of *dharmarth*. Expresses his anguish that the said grant has not yet been confirmed and has made lame excuses. Directs for the immediate payment of the said grant.

The document in Persian *shikasta* bears *sarnama Alif* and two seals in Gurmukhi.

(ACC. NO. 2580/ 3; Original; f1).

20 *Chait* 1892 *Samvat* (17 April 1835) 53. Letter from Devgar addressed to Baba Sahib. Reports of his visit to Lal Singhji. Tells that he has so far collected Rs. 72/- from *qasba* Gujranwala and other places. Also informs about his proposed visit of other places i.e. Vatala now Batala and the visit of Bhai Lal Singh to the prince.

The document is written in Persian *shikasta*.

(ACC. NO. 2580/ 23; Original; f1).

21 *Chait* 1892 *Samvat* (18 April 1835) 54. Letter addressed to Mehta Kishan Chand. Informs that *rasad* of two men has been granted to Baba Ganeshgar from Chabutra Jhelam on account of *dharmarth* since olden times. Adds that the same is recorded in accordance to the receipt about which the *nishan* and *farman* has been issued as per

the *sarrishta* of the sublime office. Directs that as per practice the said grant may be paid to him daily from the beginning of *Aswaj* 1891(*samvat*).

The document in Persian *shikasta* bears *sarnama Alif/ Ba-Fazl -e Sri Akal Purakhji* and two dim seals.

(ACC. NO. 2580/ 7; Original; f1).

26 Muharram 1251 AH (24 May 1835)

55. *Parwana* issued under the seal of Tahawwur Khan Bahadur, *Nazim* of Salon etc. to Lala Teji Lal *naib tahsildar* of *qasba* Jais. Tells that *pura* Musharrafnagar, attached with *qasba* Jais which has been in the *zamindari* of Mir Ausaf Ali has never witnessed any kind of forced labour from blacksmith and others. Directs therefore that none should ever enter in the village for extracting forced labour from the inhabitants there. Further tells that the inhabitants of *mauza* Qasimpur who are presently living at Tee and Sarai have stopped paying taxes. Directs that *sazawals* should be appointed to realize the outstanding amount from them.

The document in Persian *shikasta* bears *sarnama Alif* and the attestation seal of Qazi Saiyid Adil Husain.

(ACC. NO. 2403/ 21; Copy; f1).

1 *Safar* 1251 *AH/1242 Fasli* (29 May 1835)

56. *Bainama* executed by Mangal Chand son of Gulab Chand on behalf of his sister Sarsi Bai wife of Jiv Raj in the court of *Balda Dar al-Fath* Ujjain in respect of her two storeyed house inheriting from her in-laws' property situated in the aforesaid *Balda* in *muhalla* Sarrafa, Kucha Mohan Lal Seth (details of the boundaries are delineated in the text of the document). States that he

has sold the said property in favour of Rajshri Kesh Vitthal son of Vitthal Seth for a sum of Rs. 900/- and has received the amount in full.

The documents in Persian *shikasta* bears *sarnama Huwa al-Ghani* with some description in Devnagri.

(ACC. NO. 2703/ 56; copy; f1).

2 *Safar* 1251 AH (30 May 1835) 57. *Parwana* issued under the seal of Khadim Husain Khan to Mirza Ghulam Raza *tahsildar* of Jais and Rokha etc. Forwards the *fard* furnishing details of 240 *bighas* of *muafi* land of the *muafidars* comprising *sadaat* and *mashaikh* of *qasba* Jais. Instructs him to follow the same practice in year 1242 *Fasli* as was the practice in the previous years till 1241 *Fasli* (1833 AD). Directs him not to create any hindrance in delivering the said grant to the *muafidars.*

The document in Persian *shikasta* bears *sarnama Alif* and an attestation seal of Qazi Saiyid Adil Husain.

(ACC. NO. 2403/ 107; Copy; f1).

5 *Safar* 1251 AH (2 June 1835) 58. *Bainama* executed by Girdhar son of Ganga *wakil* on behalf of Raiji son of Raghunath with regard to the sale of his one storeyed house situated in *muhalla* Haryan Pol towards Paniari inside the surroundings of Bandar Khambayat together with boundaries delineated in the body of the text. States that he has sold the said house for a sum of Rs. 600/- to Babu son of Har Jiwan and has received the amount in full.

The document in Persian *shikasta* executed on cloth bears two seals; one of the *Qazi* and the other of *Muqim-i Adalat-i Muhammadi* Makki al Moosvi and symbol of signature of the executant and the informer.

(ACC. NO. 2695/ 39; Original; f1).

12 *Rabi* 1 1251 AH (8 July 1835)

59. *Bainama* executed by Saiyid Karim Bakhsh son of Saiyid Imam Bakhsh of *qasba* Amroha *sarkar* Sambhal *suba* Shahjahanabad in respect of a piece of land measuring 52 *kham bighas* of *lakhiraji-milk* out of 200 *Kham bighas* of *lakhiraj* land sold to Saiyid Mardan Ali, Saiyid Gulzar Ali sons of Saiyid Nauroz Ali and Saiyid Akbar Ali son of Saiyid Niyaz Ali for a sum of Rs. 250/ and has received the amount in full and the vendees have also brought the land under their control.

The document in Persian *shikasta* executed on punch marked stamp paper of Rs. 4/- bears *sarnama Alif* with the seal of the executant besides several seals and signatures of the witnesses

(ACC. NO. 2533/ 11; Original; f1).

12 *Rabi* II 1251 AH (7 August 1835)

60. *Qabz al-wasul* under the seal of Qazi Saiyid Wilayat Bakhsh executed by Tahawwur Ali son of Saiyid Mir Ali Shah of *sarkar* Sambhal *suba* Shahjahanabad. States that as per the *tamassuk* dated 7 *Rabi II* 1251 AH he has mortgaged his land measuring I *biswa* and 10 *biswasi muafi* land situated in *mauza* Jabbarpur in the *amla* of the aforesaid *pargana* to Saiyid Ghulam Husain, Zulfiqar Ali and Husain Ali for a sum of Rs. 100/. Adds that he has also borrowed another sum of Rs. 11-8/- from the mortgagee on the aforesaid *tamassuk*. Promises to pay all the amount totaling Rs. 111-8/- at the time of redemption of the mortgaged property.

The document in Persian *shikasta* executed on punch marked stamp paper bears *sarnama Alif* with the seal of the executant, besides several seals and signatures of the witnesses.

(ACC. NO. 2533/ 26; Original; f1).

12 *Rabi* II 1251 AH (7 August 1835) 61. *Qubuliyatnama* executed by Madda son of Qaim resident of Kara. States that he has taken for cultivation 20 *bighas* from the land inherited by Muhammad Roshan and Karim Allah situated in *mauza* Atapur. Promises to pay one third of the produce to the owners of the land.

The document in Persian *shikasta* bears *sarnama Alif* and the signature of the witnesses.

(ACC. NO. 2277; Original; f1).

6 *Rajab* 1251 AH (28 October 1835) 62. *Tamassuk* under the seal of Qazi Muhammad Husain executed in the Court at Ahmadabad by Ganesh son of Bhawani. States that one storey house comprising room and courtyard with other paraphernalia situated under the walled city *balda* Ahmadabad, *chakla* Muin Khan (the details of the boundaries are given in the text of the document) which he has inherited from his father and which is under his possession, has sold to Amba Ram son of Bhagwan in totality with all his rights and privileges for Rs. 70/- (Akbar Shahi coin). Further states that Amba Ram has taken the aforesaid house in his possession. Also mentions the names of four persons who appeared in the court as witness to certify the above facts.

The document in Persian *shikasta* on cloth bears the dim seal of the above Qazi and signatures as well as symbol of hand impression of the witnesses and informer.

(ACC. NO. 2441/ 5; Original; f1).

11 *Aghan* 1892 *Samvat* (30 November 1835)

63. *Parwana* of Ajit Singh Sahai to Chaudhari Ghulam Ali Khan. Directs him to keep pending for one month the grant of *dharmarth* assigned to Baba Ganeshgar. Adds that if he (the addressee) does not receive the renewal order from the Maharaja the said grant may be confiscated.

The document in Persian *shikasta* bears *sarnama Alif* and a seal of Ajit Singh Sahai.

(ACC. NO. 2580/ 11; Original; f1).

1251 AH (?) (date in seal) (1835-36)

64. Letter of Saiyid Muhammad Salim to his son. Informs him to receive the goods of Lala Bishambhar Das loaded on a cart. Also directs to provide all the necessary items required by him to facilitate his stay there. Further intimates about the instruction of Raja Sahib to provide all possible help to Lala sahib. Expresses hope that Saiyid Sadiq Hussain would join the army very soon.

The document in Persian *shikasta* bears a dim seal of the writer.

(ACC. NO. 1976; Original; f1).

1251 AH (in seal) (1835-36)

65. Letter of Bhawani Din to Chaudhari Sahib Muhammad.... Conveys his arrival at his home. Intimates that as per his instructions he met Mir Sahib and delivered the letter of Qasim Ali Khan to him. Tells that the *wasilbaqi* of the revenue which is pending with Lala Pawan Lal shall be obtained in writing.

The brittle document in Persian *shikasta* bears *sarnama Alif* and the seal of the writer.

(ACC. NO. 1974; Original; f1).

1251 AH (1835-36)

66. *Bainama* executed by Muhammad Abd al-Rab son of Abd al-Ali Muhammad resident of Lucknow. States that one storeyed haveli along with the land and shop situated in Zaraditola, Lucknow which is in his possession as per the description of its boundaries given in the body of the tax. Further states that in 1250 AH he divided the said property into two parts and one part of the property comprising 131 yard was given to his younger son Abd al-Karim while the other part of the property which was 170 yard along with the shop was given to his wife Mst. Sakina as gift. Also states that he who is in the possession of the property and being guardian of his son and as wakil of the other part of the property which belongs to his wife, has sold to his elder son Abd al-Hakim for Rs. 355/. Declares that he has received the amount in full and the property has been handed over to the vendee.

The document in Persian *shikasta* bears the seal of the executant and several other seals of the witnesses.

(ACC. NO. 2614/ 11; Photocopy; f1).

1251 AH (date in seal) (1835-36 AD)

67. Petition of Sher Ali Khan Bahadur to Maharaja Sahib. Informs of his arrival at Delhi on 29 *kartik* and as soon as he would be a bit free from the affairs there he would do his best to accomplish the wishes of the addressee. Also requests for the payment of Rs. 2375/- as the cost of leopards, dogs, pigeons etc. supplied as per orders. Further requests for the grant of *Athola jagir*.

The document is in Persian *shikasta* bears the seal of the petitioner.

(ACC. NO. 120; Original; f1).

14 *Muharam* 1252 AH (1 May 1836)

68. *Qaul-o-qarar-i Patta* executed under the seal of Saiyid Muhammad Abdullah Naqvi in favour of Imam Bakhsh a resident of Sharafnagar. States that village Qasimpur has been given to him on *patta* for cultivation w.e.f. 1252 AH to 1256 AH. corresponding to 1244 to 1248 *Fasli* ((1840-1844 AD) against a *jama* of Rs. 1382/. Instructs him not to realize more than the stipulated amount as per fixed installments for the payment of revenue to the Government and to inhabitate the village with people excluding Rajputs, Brahmins, and Kayasth.

The document in Persian *shikasta* bears the seal of the executant and the endorsement contains agreement by the assignee for the payment of amount.

(ACC. NO. 2043; Copy; f1).

13 June 1836

69. Letter to Kunwar Totaram. States that following the promulgation of the *lakhiraj*, his request for the grant of *mauza* Bahalgarh as *altamgha* grant was submitted to the Office of the Commissioner under Rule 14 of 1825, clause 12 of Rule 3 of 1828 and thus according to the *sanads* produced by him confirmation order of the said village has been issued in the name of the *tahsildar* for the issuance of *parwana* confirming its continuance from the Government in his favour.

The document in Persian *shikasta* bears the seal of the District Court Shahjahanabad.

(ACC. NO. 2656/ 39; Original; f1).

18 August 1836

70. Letter of Ram Narain Pandit *kotwal* Sadar Bazaar to Pandit Gulab Rai. Expresses

anxiety for not receiving any communication about Shankar Sen Omkar. Requests to communicate him about his well being. Also dispatches letters received from Bholanath from Shahsor and Lala Nand Lal Jiu in his name.

The document is written in Persian *shikasta*.

(ACC. NO. 2733/ 50; Original; f1).

13 *Jumada* I 1252 AH (26 August 1836)

71. Letter of Mir Khalil Ahmad *chakladar* of *pargana* Sandila and Malihabad to Muhammad Wajih al-Din Ahmad Qazi of *pargana* Sandila. Forwards the case of Afzal Ali against Mir Alam *wakil* of Mst. Buba wife of late Alam Ali resident of *qasba* Sandila regarding claim over the property of inheritance left by Kifayat Allah and Farhat Allah comprising a haveli, a piece of garden, jewellery and books etc. Complains against Mst. Buba that she has occupied the property of inheritence without right. Requests to take back all the property from her possession and give him possession over the said property.

The document is written in Persian *shikasta*.

(ACC. NO. 1655; Original; f1).

10 October 1836/ 2 *Makar Shudi (Asvin)* 1893 *Samvat*

72. *Tamassuk* executed by Moti son of Raj Karan resident of *mauza* Anbajosias (?) *qasba* Sonipat in respect of the sum of Rs. 40/- borrowed by him as *dastgardan* from Lala Umrao Singh son of Kunwar Aman Singh. Undertakes to return the said amount along with the interest as per the *sarrishta* of the government.

The document in Persian *shikasta* executed on a punched marked paper bears *sarnama Alif* with signatures of the witnesses and symbol of signature of the executant.

(ACC. NO. 2656/ 47; Original; f1).

22 *Aswaj (Sawan) 1893 Samvat* (31 October 1836)

73. *Tamassuk* executed by Ahmad Didar (?) and Murad Bakhsh residents of Sondha. State that from their villages 30 *bighas* of land has been assigned in *jagir* of Baba Ganeshgar. Promise to pay the revenue of the assigned land to him yearly.

The document in Persian *shikasta* bears *sarnama alif* and the signature of the executants.

(ACC. NO. 2580/ 83; Original; f1).

11 November 1836/ 5 *Kartik Sudi* 1244 *Fasli*

74. *Tamassuk* executed by Tehnan son of Hari Singh resident of Saiyidwara mauza Sirsathir pargana Badayun. States that a sum of Rs. 50/- in kaldar coin from Qasba Badayun in the vicinity of the fort belonging to Maulawi Muhammad Ihsan Allah son of Maulwi Muhmmad Qutb al-Din of Maulawi Tola is due upon him. Assures that out of the said amount he would pay Rs. 25/- by the end of Baisakh 1244 Fasli and another Rs. 25/- in the month of kartik 1245 Fasli.

The document in Persian *Shikasta* bears *sarnama Innahu* and two seals and signatures of the witnesses with symbol of the signature of the executant.

(ACC. NO. 2319; Original; f1).

10 *Shaban* 1252 AH (20 November 1836)

75. *Bainama/ Qabz al-wasul* executed by Saiyid Husain Ali son of Saiyid Meharban Ali resident of *qasba* Amroha *sarkar* Sambhal in respect of sale of one storeyed shop with courtyard and water reservoir *(abchak)* with its boundaries situated in the market

of Saiyid Muhammad Shafaat in the aforesaid *qasba* for a sum of Rs. 50/- to Saiyid Mahfuz Ali and Saiyid Fazl Husain sons of Saiyid Dildar Ali residents of *qasba* Amroha who have brought the said shop under their control.

The document in Persian *shikasta* bears *sarnama Innahu* with the seal and signature of the executant besides the seals of the witnesses.

(ACC. NO. 2533/ 38; Original; f1).

17 *Ramazan* 1252 AH (26 December 1836)

76. *Parwana* issued under the seal of Maharaja Chandulal to the *amils* of present and future *deshmukhs, deshpandeys, muqaddams* and *patwaris* of *pargana* Haveli Muhammad Nagar of the aforesaid *sarkar, suba* Farkhundabunyad Hyderabad. Informs them that *maqta* (a piece of land) belonging to Sandalan Kudah (?) in *mauza* Korimal, the produce/ forest as well as the grass of the aforesaid *pargana* has been in assignment of Haidar Ali as per the old *sanads* against the payment of Rs. 125/-. Directs them to get released the stipulated amount year by year and should not interfere in the process of cultivation and inhabitation.

The document in Persian *nastaliq* bears *sarnama Alif* and seal of Maharaja Chandu Lal.

(ACC. NO. 2536/ 9; Original; f1).

1252 AH (date in seal) (1836-37)

77. Petition of Ram Dayal addressed to Mir Sahib. Refers his orders to him for payment to Lala Hira Lal wakil of Colonel Barlow besides payment of the nankar of 1262 Fasli (1854 AD). Explains that he (the writer) never hesitated in the payment of

Rs. 350/- due to the said Lala and even he has instructed Tulsi Ram Jiu in the matter. Also refers about a payment of Rs. 200/- in the previous year to Lala Reoti Ram for the marriage of his sons who is his nankar. Requests for the payment of Rs. 350/- besides the salary and nankar to Captain Seuks (Sykes?)

The document written in Persian *shikasta* bears the seal of Ram Dayal.

(ACC. NO. 2403/ 89; Original; f1).

1252 AH (date in seal) (1836-37) 78. *Dastawiz* executed by Ifham Allah son of Shaikh Himayat Allah resident of *qasba* Sandila from Ashraf Tola, Lucknow. States that at the time of his *nikah* with Mst. Lihazan daughter of Shaikh Hafiz Mubarak he had accepted to pay her 50,000/- *ashrafi* as *mehr-i muajjal*. Declares that the said amount payable to her by him is obligatory upon him.

The document in Persian *nastaliq* bears *sarnama Alif* and the attestation seal of Qazi Muhammad Wajih al-Din and the seal of the executant.

(ACC. NO. 2738/ 35; Original; f1).

1 January 1837 79. *Yaddasht* of the receipt of the amount of Rs. 966/ 6/ 10 *ganda* against the income of 1245 *Fasli* from *taalluqa* Sonwani *Ilaqa* Jagir Mahal *pargana* Ballia deposited by Shaikh Murtaza Bakhsh *Sarbrahkar* through Maha Upadhya, Manak Misr and Shaikh Ramazan in the District Court of Ghazipur on 1 January. 1838 (?). (Perhaps the year has mistakenly been written as1838 instead of 1837)

The document in Urdu *shikasta* bears the seal of *tahsildar pargana* Ballia.

(ACC. NO. 2764/ 2; Original; f1).

11 January 1837

80. *Parwana* to Har Sahai *muhafiz-i daftar-i kachehri nizamat zila* Meerut. Refers to the appointment of his father as *muhafiz-i daftar-i kachehri* on 14 October 1805 who remained on the said post till his death on 24 January 1829 and thereafter he (the addressee) succeeded him on 10 February 1829. Appreciating his good services rendered by him during the last 3 years and even performing duties of *sarrishtadar* in absentia communicates that he is being confirmed on the said post.

The document in Urdu *shikasta* bears the seal of the District Court Meerut.

(ACC. NO. 2754/ 2; Original; f1).

26 *Magh* 1893 *Samvat* (3 March 1837)

81. *Parwana* addressed to Bakhshi Hari Singh. States that 13 *bighas* of land from village Balut has been in assignment of Baba Ganeshgar of Dangawala on account of *dharmarth* since olden times. Directs him to relinquish it in his favour as *muafi* so that he may remain busy in praying for abundance of wealth and prosperity of the Kingdom and the Raja.

The document in Persian *shikasta* bears *sarnama Sri Ramji* and a seal of Jawala Sahai.

(ACC. NO. 2580/ 50; Original; f1).

4 *Phagun* 1893 *Samvat* (10 March 1837)

82. *Parwana* issued to Baikunth. Informs that Chabutra Dangi has been in assignment of Baba Ganeshgar on account of *dharmarth* since olden times. Directs further to relinquish Math Nurshirah in his favour as well being religious in nature and to pay 3 *annas* 3 *pais* to him every month from this grant.

The document in Persian *shikasta* bears *sarnama Alif* and a dim seal in Devnagri.

(ACC. NO. 2580/ 17; Original; f1).

23 *Phagun* 1893 *(Samvat)* (date in text) (29 March 1837)

83. Letter from Khalsa Darbar to (the Resident). Acknowledges receipt of his letter (sent through Chait Singh) and expresses pleasure on the visit of General Azam (Commander-in-Chief) Sir Henry Fane. Informs that the required items have been sent to the *dera* (destination) of Lord Sahib (Resident) at Panjakada Topkhana. Referring to the marriage of Prince (Naunihal Singh) to be held on 25 *Phagun* invites him (the Resident) to attend the marriage and to visit the state one day in advance to have a discussion on bilateral issues which will further strengthen the friendly relations between the two states.

The illuminated document written in Persian *nastaliq* bears *sarnama Bafazl-i Sri Akal Purakhji.*

(ACC. NO. 229; Original; f1).

14 *Rabi* I 1253 AH/ 1244 *Fasli* (18 June 1837)

84. *Wasiqa* executed by *Mst.* Bibi Tolan daughter of Maulawi Yemen Allah, wife of Shaikh Ahmad Karim resident of *qasba* Sandila from Ashraf Tola. Recalls her husband's will to accept Ali Raza and Muhammad Raza, his nephews as his heirs to inherit all his property of inheritance and thus gives her assent to this effect.

The document in Persian *nastaliq* bears *sarnama Alif* and the attestation seal of Qazi Muhammad Wajih al-Din and signature of the executant besides the seals and signatures of several witnesses.

(ACC. NO. 2738/ 34; Original; f1).

29 *Har (Hadh)* 1894 *Samvat* (31 July 1837)

85. *Tamassuk* executed by Murad Bakhsh, Allah Din and Muhkam Din *namdar* residents of village Sudhna Dangan. State that about one *man* and 15 *paimana* of food

grain has to be given by them to Baba Ganeshgar. Promise to give 15 *paimana* in *Kharif* crop and one *man* in *Rabi* crop to him.

The document in Persian *shikasta* bears signatures of the executants and witnesses.

(ACC. NO. 2580/ 84; Original; f1).

11 *Sawan* 1894 *Samvat* (12 August 1837)

86. *Parwana* issued to *kardars* of *taalluqa* Karyali. Informs about the confirmation of the *muafi* grant in respect of the land assigned to Baba Ganeshgar on account of *dharmarth* from village Konian and Chak Kanyan and Dudsang. Directs them not to interfere in the said grant.

The document in Persian *shikasta* bears *sarnama Alif* and a dim seal.

(ACC. NO. 2580/ 49; Original; f1).

5 *Rajab* 1253 AH (5 October 1837) (Illus.)

87. *Iqrarnama/ Bainama* executed by Bhaiji son of Banmali, in respect of sale of a piece of residential land situated in *muhalla* Bahrampol inside the walled city of Bandar Khambayat with its boundaries (details as given in the text) purchased by his father and now it is in his possession. States that he has sold it for a sum of Rs. 48/- to Bejar son of Waja and has received the amount in full.

The document in Persian *shikasta* on cloth bears *sarnama Alif* having a seal of *Qazi* and that of the *Muqim-i Adalat-i Muhammadi* Makki Al Moosvi with the symbol and signature of the witnesses in Persian and Devnagri.

(ACC. NO. 2695/ 40; Original; f1).

5 *Rajab* 1253 AH (5 October 1837)

88. *Iqrarnama/ Bainama* executed by Bhagwan son of Juhar. States that he has sold his one storeyed ancestral house situated in

muhalla Ilapara near Parbhat Harsad inside the walled city of Bandar Khambayat with its boundaries (details as given in the text) to Shukl Chand son of Din Chand for Rs. 121/-.

The document in Persian shikasta written on a piece of cloth bears *sarnama Alif* along with the seals of the *Qazi* and that of Muhammad Ali al-Moosvi and the symbol of signatures of the executant and the informer in *Persian* and *Devnagri*.

(ACC. NO. 2702/ 14; Original; f1).

17 *Asoj (Asu)* 1894 *Samvat* (15 October 1837)

89. *Sanad/Dastawiz* issued in favour of Raja Hira Singh regarding the grant of *jagirs* as per the detailes given besides *rasum* and nazrs as described in a separate *farman* in perpetuity generation after generation provided he will remain loyal to the Government.

The document in Persian *nastaliq* has been attested by the Assistant Resident at Kashmir. It bears *sarnama Bafazl-i Sri Akal purakhji* and two symbols of seals.

(ACC. NO. 2385/ 6; Copy; ff2).

4 November 1837

90. Census report containing statistical data of houses and persons of Amina (?) Bazar, the property of Govind Devji *qasba* Bindraban under the charge of Saiyid Dildar Ali, *Sadr-i Bakhshi* of *chaukidars* of Agra city on 1 September 1837.

The document in Persian *shikasta* executed on punch marked paper of eight *anna* bears a seal of Saiyid Dildar Ali

(ACC. NO. 2712/ 8; Copy; f1).

24 November 1837

91. *Yaddasht* of the receipt of a sum of Rs. 2661/- against the income of the year 1245 *Fasli* (1837 AD) from *taalluqa* Sonwani *ilaqa*

Jagir Mahal, *pargana* Ballia deposited by Shaikh Murtaza Bakhsh *sarbrahkar* through Shaikh Bandhu, Gulab Khan, Mohan Rai in the District Court of Ghazipur on 24 November 1837.

The document in Urdu *shikasta* bears the seal of *tahsildari, pargana* Ballia.

(ACC. NO. 2764/ 3; Original; f1).

1 *Ramazan* 1253 AH (29 November 1837)

92. *Iqrarnama* executed by Saiyid Saadat Ali and Saiyid Ali Gauhar sons of Saiyid Nawazish Ali of Amroha on their behalf and on behalf of their mother and younger brother Saiyid Ali Husain. State that they have agreed to appoint Maulawi Muhammad Saadat and Haji Ashraf Ali as arbitrators for the division of the property among them hitherto undivided left by their father. They have also agreed to accept their decisions.

The document in Persian *shikasta* executed on an eight *anna* punch marked stamp paper bears *sarnama Alif* with the seal and signature of Saadat Ali (the executant) and several seals and signatures of the executants and witnesses. +

(ACC. NO. 2533/ 10; Original; f1).

1 December 1837

93. *Yaddasht* of the receipt of the amount of Rs. 894/- against the income of the year 1245 *Fasli* (1837 AD) from *taalluqa* Sonwani *ilaqa* Jagir Mahal, *pargana* Ballia deposited by Shaikh Murtaza Bakhsh *sarbrahkar* through Maha Upadhya and Manak Misr in the District Court of *pargana* Ghazipur on 1 December 1837.

The document in Urdù *shikasta* bears the seal of the *tahsildari pargana* Ballia.

(ACC. NO. 2764/ 4; Original; f1).

4 *Ramazan* 1253 AH (2 December 1837) 94. *Razinama* executed by Saadat Ali son of late Saiyid Nawazish Ali resident of *qasba* Amroha. States that he (the writer) with the concurrence of Saiyid Ali Gauhar son of late Saiyid Nawazish Ali and on behalf of his mother *Mst.* Sharf al-Nisa and younger brother Saiyid Ali Husain have appointed Maulawi Saiyid Muhammad Siyadat and Haji Ashraf Ali as arbitrators for the division of their property of inheritance. Elaborates that as Saiyid Ali Gauhar has claimed for more than his actual share and he has agreed to give him equal share and as such the division of the property should be 2/ 3 for Saiyid Ali Gauhar, Saiyid Ali Husain and their mother and only 1/ 3 would remain for him.

The document in Persian *shikasta* bears *sarnama Alif* with the seal and signature of the executant besides several seals and signatures of the witnesses.

(ACC. NO. 2533/ 18; Original; f1).

6 December 1837 95. *Yaddasht* of the receipt of Rs. 1126/1/15 *ganda* against the income of 1245 *Fasli* (1837 AD) from *taalluqa* Sonwani *ilaqa* Jagir Mahal *pargana* Ballia deposited by Shaikh Murtaza Bakhsh *sarbrahkar* in the District Court of Ghazipur.

The document in Urdu *shikasta* bears dim seal of *tahsildari pargana* Ballia.

(ACC. NO. 2764/ 5; Original; f1).

21 Ramazan 1253 AH (19 December 1837) 96. *Parwana* under the seal of Babu Salik Ram *chakladar* of *pargana* Sandila to Masnad Ali Chaudhari. Informs him that a perusal of the past *sanads* presented by Saiyid Aslah Allah resident of Sandila reveals that the *arazi, chak* situated in village Majholi and

Kakun has been granted by Nawwab Wazir as *muaf* to the said Saiyid and the same has been relinquished in his favour further from 1245 *Fasli*. Directs to exempt the same from revenue and not to interfere in its realization and the said Saiyid may use its realization for his own purpose and may remain busy in praying for the everlasting of the Government.

The document in Persian *shikasta* bears *sarnama Huwa*

(ACC. NO. 1632; Copy; f1).

21 December 1837 — 97. *Yaddasht* of the receipt of the amount of Rs. 2780/ against the income of 1245 *Fasli* (1837 AD) of *taalluqa* Sonwani *ilaqa* Jagir Mahal *pargana* Ballia deposited by Shaikh Murtaza Bakhsh *sarbrahkar* through Adhayam Upadhya, Maha Upadhya and others on various dates in the District Court of Ghazipur.

The document in Urdu *shikasta* bears the seal of the *tahsildari, pargana* Ballia.

(ACC. NO. 2764/ 6; Original; f1).

1253 AH (date in seal) (1837-38) — 98. Letter of Mir Ghulam Husain to Chaudhari Murtaza Khan. States that it is learnt through Shah Ahmadji *zamindar* of *pura* Shah Kamgar that he (the addressee) has perhaps inadvertently derived a sum of Rs. 23/-. Requests him to tally the account from the *tamassuk* available with the treasurer and if the payment is deemed necessary he shall make accordingly otherwise whatever is ordered shall be complied with. Brings to notice some more details of the case.

The document in Persian *shikasta* bears *Sarnama Innahu* and the seal of the writer.

(ACC. NO. 1966; Original; f1).

1253 AH (in seal) (1837-38)	99.	To the same effect as the SL. No. 292, document No. 2403/ 116, which, however, contains full date and hence placed in its chronological sequence. The document is written in Persian *shikasta*. **(ACC. NO. 2403/ 85; Copy; f1).**
14 January 1838	100.	*Yaddasht* of the receipt of the amount of Rs. 1215/- against the income of 1245 *Fasli* (1837 AD) from *taalluqa* Sonwani *ilaqa* Jagir Mahal *pargana* Ballia deposited by Shaikh Murtaza Bakhsh through Manak Misr and Mir Tasadduq Husain in the District Court of Ghazipur on 14 January 1837. The document in Urdu *shikasta* bears the seal of the *tahsildari pargana* Ballia. **(ACC. NO. 2764/ 7; Original; f1).**
17 January 1838	101.	*Yaddasht* of the receipt of the amount of Rs. 1689/-agaisnt the income of 1245 *Fasli* (1837 AD) of *taalluqa* Sonwani *ilaqa* Jagir Mahal *pargana* Ballia deposited by Shaikh Murtaza Bakhsh *sarbrahkar* through Maha Upadhya, Adhayam Upadhya and Shaikh Bandhu in the District Court of Ghazipur. The document in Urdu *shikasta* bears the seal of *tahsildari, pargana* Ballia. **(ACC. NO. 2764/ 8; Original; f1).**
22 January 1838	102.	*Yaddasht* of the receipt of the amount of Rs. 1002/- against the income of the year 1245 *Fasli* (1837 AD) from *taalluqa* Sonwani *ilaqa* Jagir Mahal *pargana* Ballia deposited by Shaikh Murtaza Bakhsh *sarbarahkar* through Mir Tasadduq Husain and Zalim Singh in the District Court of Ghazipur on 22 January 1838. The document in Urdu *shikasta* bears the seal of *tahsildari pargana* Ballia. **(ACC. NO. 2764/ 9; Original; f1).**

1 February 1838 — 103. *Yaddasht* of the receipt of the amount of Rs. 713/ 9/-against the land revenue assessment of 1245 *Fasli* (1837 AD) from *taalluqa* Sonwani *ilaqa* Jagir Mahal *pargana* Ballia deposited by Shaikh Murtaza Bakhsh *sarbrahkar* through Mir Tasadduq Husain and Ajit Rai in the District Court of Ghazipur on 1 February 1838.

The document in Urdu *shikasta* bears *sarnama Alif* and the seal of *tahsildari pargana* Ballia.

(ACC. NO. 2764/ 10; Original; f1).

6 *Zilqada* 1253 AH/ 1 February 1838 — 104. *Qabala-i bai* executed by Chhetu son of Yar Muhammad resident of Char Bagh Lucknow. States that he has sold his one storeyed *haveli* situated in Astabal Char Bagh (the details of the boundary are given in the document) to Murad Khan son of Habib Allah Khan, resident of Ismail Ganj *wakil* on behalf of Saiyid Muhammad for a sum of Rs. 8/- . Acknowledges the receipt of the amount in full.

The document in Persian *nastaliq* bears the seal of the *Mufti* and that of *Adalat-i Alia Diwani, Bait al-Saltanat,* Lucknow. It also bears departmental endorsements on the reverse.

(ACC. NO. 2395/ 1; Original; f1).

11 February 1838 — 105. *Yaddasht* of receipt of the amount of Rs. 947/- against the income of 1245 *Fasli* from *taalluqa* Sonwani *ilaqa* Jagir Mahal *pargana* Ballia deposited by Shaikh Murtaza Bakhsh *sarbarhkar* through Tasadduq Husain and Zalim Singh in the District Court of Ghazipur on 11 February 1838.

The document in Urdu *shikasta* bears the seal of *tahsildari pargana* Ballia.

(ACC. NO. 2764/ 11; Original; f1).

25 Zilqada 1253 AH (20 February 1838)	106.	*Parwana* issued under the seal of Maharaja Chandu Lal to the *deshmukhs* and *muzaris* and others of *pargana* Nizam, *sarkar* Madkal, *suba* Dar al-Zafar Bijapur. Informs them that *mauza* Sangmir etc. besides villages towards Bholki in the aforesaid *pargana* having total *jama* of Rs. 8245/-(the revenue free grant of *sarkar*) has been assigned as *madad-i maash* in favour of Banya Patti Raj Dev Maharai Dalwai Pirthi Sousihan Appa Kondhi, in lieu of his 16 *Khandi* land situated in *mauza* Jangal Buzurg etc. and in the villages of *taalluqa* Gangawali from the beginning of the second half year of 1247 *Fasli*. Instructs the Sousihan to contact the *mutasaddi* to make payment to him in time and regularly. The document in Persian *shikasta* bears *sarnama Alif* and the seal of Maharaja Chandu Lal Bahadur with departmental endorsements on the reverse. **(ACC. NO. 2536/ 7; Original; f1).**
21 February 1838	107.	*Yaddasht* of the amount of Rs. 2380/- against the income of 1245 *Fasli* (1837 AD) from *taalluqa* Sonwani *ilaqa* Jagir Mahal *pargana* Ballia deposited by Shaikh Murtaza Bakhsh *sarbarahkar* through Mir Tasadduq Husain and Amrit Singh in the District Court of Ghazipur. The document in Urdu *shikasta* bears the seal of *tahsildari pargana* Ballia. **(ACC. NO. 2764/ 12; Original; f1).**
2 *Zilhijja* 1253 AH (in text) (27 February 1838)	108.	*Arzi* of Wajih al-Din of Sandila to Nawwab of Awadh. Refers his previous representation on 2 *Zilhijja* 1253 AH with regard to the *taahud* of village Mehsona *pargana* Sandila and to revoke *zamindari* rights

usurped by Chotey Lal *mustajir* to Salik Ram *chakladar* of Sandila to this effect which was also endorsed by the Badshah (of Awadh) that in the event of establishment of his right and *malwajib* the petitioner would be allowed possession of his *zamindari* and his usurped rights would be restored to him. Complains that the said *chakladar* inspite of giving *malzamin, mutamid* and also accepting to pay Rs. 55/ - not withstanding availability of all documentary evidences signed by the *sighadars*, did not accomplish the orders of the Sultan (of Awadh) nor even got him returned his *zamindari* rights from the said *mustajir*. Requests for strict injuctions and strong warning to accept his rights and to revoke the rights occupied by the *mustajir* and submit a *razinama* to this office. Accordingly solicits strict injunction in the matter for which appointment of an enforcement officer is a must without which it would not be translated into action.

The document in Persian *nastaliq* bears seal of the writer.

(ACC. NO. 1447; Original; f1).

3 March 1838 109. *Yaddasht* of the receipt of the amount of Rs. 737/5/ 15 *ganda* against the income of 1245 *Fasli* (1837 AD) from *taalluqa* Sonwani *ilaqa* Jagir Mahal *pargana* Ballia deposited by Shaikh Murtaza Bakhsh *sarbrahkar* through Mir Tasadduq Husain and Udhayam Upadhya in the District Court of Ghazipur on 3 March 1838.

The document in Urdu *shikasta* bears the seal of *tahsildari, pargana* Ballia.

(ACC. NO. 2764/ 13; Original; f1).

12 March 1838

110. *Iqrarnama / sulahnama* executed by Bhukan Lal and Darshan Lal owners of 17 *bighas* and 20 *dhur* of land, besides *Mst.* Latifan, Faqiran, Shabratan, Shaikh Safdar Ali and Mahbub Ali and many other *aimmadars* of *pargana* Okri District Bihar declaring that they would continue to pay the *aimmadars* in regular and installments.

The document furnishes detailed information about the terms and conditions of the revenue contractor in respect of the *aimmadars*.

The document in Persian *shikasta* executed on punch marked stamp paper of eight *annas* bears signatures of the executant and witnesses.

(ACC. NO. 2531/ 12; Original; f1).

16 March 1838

111. *Yaddasht* of the receipt of the amount of Rs. 589/ against the income of 1245 *Fasli* (1837) from *taalluqa* Sonwani *ilaqa* Jagir Mahal *pargana* Ballia deposited by Shaikh Murtaza Bakhsh *sarbrahkar* through Shaikh Bandhu and Maha Upadhya in the District Court of Ghazipur on 16 March 1838.

The document in Urdu *shikasta* bears the seal of *tahsildari pargana* Ballia.

(ACC. NO. 2764/ 14; Original; f1).

21 March 1838

112. *Yaddasht* of the receipt of the amount of Rs. 1511/- against the income of 1245 *Fasli* (1837 AD) from *taalluqa* Sonwani *ilaqa* Jagir Mahal *pargana* Ballia deposited by Shaikh Murtaza Bakhsh *sarbrahkar* through Maha Upadhya, Adhayam Upadhya in the District Court of Ghazipur on 21 March 1838.

The document in Urdu *shikasta* bears *sarnama Alif* and the seal of *tahsildari, pargana* Ballia.

(ACC. NO. 2764/ 15; Original; f1).

13 April 1838 113. *Yaddasht* of the receipt of the amount of Rs. 2294/- against the income of 1245 *Fasli* (1837 AD) from *taalluqa* Sonwani *ilaqa* Jagir Mahal *pargana* Ballia deposited by Shaikh Murtaza Bakhsh *sarbrahkar* through Mir Tasadduq Husain, Manak Misr and Maha-upadhya in the District Court of Ghazipur on 13 April 1838.

The document in Urdu *shikasta* bears the seal of *tahsildari, pargana* Ballia.

(ACC. NO. 2764/ 16; Original; f1).

27 *Muharram* 1254 AH (22 April 1838) 114. Letter to Qazi Wajih al-Din. Referring to a dispute between Raunaq Ali Chaudhari, the plaintiff and Muhammad Husain the defendant directs him to settle the matter according to the *shariat* and send a copy of the judgement under his seal.

The document in Persian *shikasta* bears *sarnama Alif* and a dim seal.

(ACC. NO. 1453; Original; f1).

24 April 1838 115. *Yaddasht* of the receipt of the amount of Rs. 1864/- against the income of 1245 *Fasli* (1837 AD) from *taalluqa* Sonwani *ilaqa* Jagir Mahal *pargana* Ballia deposited by Shaikh Murtaza Bakhsh *sarbrahkar* through Shuhar Rai Adhayam Upadhya, Zalim Singh and Shaikh Bandhu in the District Court of Ghazipur.

The document in Urdu *shikasta* bears *sarnama Innahu* and the seal of *tahsildari, pargana* Ballia.

(ACC. NO. 2764/ 17; Original; f1).

14 *Safar* 1254 AH (9 May 1838) 116. Letter under the seal of Rai Jamiat Rai father of Babu Salik Ram *chakladar* of Sandila issued to Lala Jiv Lal *naib tahsil Kachehri* Sandila. Intimates that Ghulam Makhdum Chaudhari of *pargana* Sandila

has come with the petition explaining that after getting his (writer) letter regarding getting issued *nankar* of his uncles Qayam al-Din and Ghulam Shah, the descendants of Chaudhari Muhammad Daim and Rai Salik Ram who also got it verified from Masnad Ali and in spite being Rs. 400/- less he accepted the grant of villages on the condition that he would get assigned *nankar*. Directs him to convey the conversation that had held between Rai Salik Ram and Chaudhari Masnad Ali the time he had accepted the offer in his presence to get issued *nankar* to Ghulam Makhdum Chaudhari and how it was implemented besides the verification of facts about the amount of *nankar* meant for Ghulam Makhdum Chaudhari was made by Masnad Ali or not. Also informs that the amount due upon him is as much as the amount of *nankar* or more. Ditects him to settle the matter of *nankar* and issue *dastak* accordingly. Also directs him to suspend the *dastakat* given to the petitioner till the time of settlement of *nankar*.

The document written in Persian *shikasta* bears *sarnama Alif.*

(ACC. NO. 1635; copy; f1).

19 May 1838 117. *Yaddasht* of the receipt of the amount of Rs. 2806/5/ *ganda* against the income of 1245 *Fasli* (1837) from *taalluqa* Sonwani *ilaqa* Jagir Mahal *pargana* Ballia deposited by Shaikh Murtaza Bakhsh *sarbrahkar* through Maha Upadhya, Manak Misr and Adhayam Upadhya in the District Court of Ghazipur.

The document in Urdu *shikasta* bears the seal of *tahsildari, pargana* Ballia.

(ACC. NO. 2764/ 18; Original; f1).

1 *Jaith* 1895 Samvat *(24 May 1838)* 118. *Parwana* to Chaudhari Ghulam Ali. Refers the previous *parwana* to the effect that whatever assignment on account of *dharmarth* and *rasad* has been assigned to Baba Ganeshgar from *ilaqa* Karyali since olden times shall be given to him. Directs him to follow the same practice with Hiragar who is a disciple of Baba Ganeshgar and should also notice the offerings made to Baba Ganeshgar. Also directs that Hiragar should pay *chauth* to Ganeshgar and whatever he gives him should accept it. Also clarifies that if Hiragar likes anything from the *dharmarth* granted to Baba Ganeshgar, should take only with his permission and whatever *dharmarth* assigned to Hiragar should be recognized separately.

The document in Persian *shikasta* bears *sarnama Alif* and the seal of Mangal Singh Sahai.

(ACC. NO. 2580/ 53; Original; f1).

1 *Rabi* I 1254 AH (date in text) (25 May 1838) 119. *Parwana* of Rai Jamiat Rai (father of Baba Salik Ram), *Nazim* of *pargana* Sandila and Malihabad etc. to Lala Jiwan Lal *tahsildar* of *qila* Sandila. Refers to a complaint made by Shaikh Aslah al-Din brother of Qazi Wajih al-Din against him (addressee) as he has imposed an amount of Rs. 900/- as due for the year1245 Fasli from *mauza* Mahsona as a sum of *dastak-i hazirdar* @ 1-1/4 per diem inspite of the fact he has paid Rs. 200/ -to him. This is also strange that he (the addressee) has already collected more than Rs. 500/-from the *kharif* crop of the said *mauza* even then how could be asum of Rs. 900/- still due which clearly leads one to believe his favouritism for Chotey Lal.

Directs him to impose *dastak* upon Chotey Lal for the payment of revenue realization from the said *mauza* and only the actual amount due upon the Qazi should be realized from him. Further directs to go to realize revenue quickly as only the month of *Jeth* has left There should not be further delay as it would hamper the realization of the Government amount.

The document in Persian *shikasta* bears the attestation seal of Qazi Wahid Bakhsh.

(ACC. NO. 1510; Copy; f1).

24 *Rabi* I 1254 AH (17 June 1838) 120. *Hazir* (*Zamini*) executed by Chotey son of Siya Ram Shukl of *mauza* Mahsona. Stands surety to Ram Kishan of the aforesaid village for his release who is imprisoned in the *sarkar* of Qazi. Promises to produce him before the *karinda* of Qazi as and when demanded and if he fails to produce him he will be held responsible.

The document in Persian *shikasta* bears *sarnama Innahu* and signarure of the executant.

(ACC. NO. 1531; Original; f1).

24 *Rabi* I 1254 AH (17 June 1838) 121. *Hazir* (*Zamini*) executed by Chotey Shukl resident of village Mahsona. Stands surety to Bakhturi resident of Mahsona who is required to appear before the Qazi. Promises to produce him before the *ahalkars* of the Qazi as and when demanded failing which he will be held responsible.

The document is in Persian *shikasta* bears signatures of the executant.

(ACC. NO. 1598; Original; f1).

17 June 1838 122. *Yaddasht* of the receipt of the amount of Rs. 1781/ 10 *ganda* as the income of 1245 *Fasli*

(1837 AD) from *taalluqa* Sonwani *Ilaqa* Jagir Mahal *pargana* Ballia deposited by Shaikh Murtaza Bakhsh through Manak Misr, Tasadduq Husain, Adhayam Upadhya, Maha Upadhya in the District Court of Ghazipur.

The document in Urdu *shikasta* bears the seal of *tahsildari pargana* Ballia

(ACC. NO. 2764/ 19; Original; f1).

3 *Har* (*Asarh*) 1895 *Samvat* (25 June 1838)

123. *Tamassuk* executed by Mir Murad Bakhsh and Allah Din residents of village Sudhna. State that they have to give 3 *maund* wheat to Gosain Gobindgar on account of *dharmarth*. Promise to give one and half *maund* wheat from this year's crop without any excuse.

The document in Persian *shikasta* bears *sarnama Alif*.

(ACC. NO. 2580/ 81; Original; f1).

22 July 1838

124. *Yaddasht* of receipt of the amount of Rs. 1907/-13/ 15 *ganda* against the income of 1245 *Fasli* (1837 AD) from *taalluqa* Sonwani *ilaqa* Jagir Mahal *pargana* Ballia deposited by Shaikh Murtaza Bakhsh through Mir Tassaduq Husain, Maha Upadhiya, Adhayam Upadhiya and Shaikh Ramazan in the District Court of Ghazipur.

The document in Urdu *shikasta* bears *sarnama innahu* and the seal of *tahsildari pargana* Ballia.

(ACC. NO. 2764/ 20; Original; f1).

23 *Jumada* I 1254 AH (14 August 1838)

125. *Parwana* of Rai Jamiat Rai to Babu Salik Ram *chakladar* of Sandila and Malihabad. Refers to a report submitted by Shaikh Aslah al-Din brother of Muhammad Wajih al-Din Qazi of *pargana* Sandila informing that Chotey Lal the former *mustajir* has

taken from the collected realization supposed to be realized @1/10, besides a sum of Rs. 24/-on account of salary of the *patwari* has been usurped by Brij Lal *tahsildar*, and paid him not.

Directs him to enquire the matter from the *sighadars* and if it is due to him it may be paid to him by the addressee. Otherwise, actual position duly verified by the *sighadars* should be submitted. Also directs that the realization from the Qazi's old garden situated at Mahsona besides *Polagah* etc. (place of grass meant for detachment) as a *zamindari* right which too have been usurped by Chotey Lal who has brought them under his control about which the Nawwab Wazir had again issued orders for the restoration to him that should be enquired from the *sighadars* and after a thorough examination whatever the actual realization would be due upon him should be recovered through a *sazawal* and pay the said *Qazi*.

The document is written in Persian *shikasta*.

(ACC. NO. 1287; Copy; f1).

24 *Sawan* 1895 *Samvat* (14 August1838)

126. Letter from Khalsa Darbar (to the Resident). Refers to the friendly relations subsisting between the two governments and hopes that it would be further strengthened in the days to come. Expresses pleasure on his (addressee) proposed visit and on the receipt of the letter of Lord Auckland (the Governor General) in connection to the friendly relation of the two governments as reported by Rai Gobind. Informs about the arrangements of 2 horses for riding and

some camels as beasts of burden (carriage) on his way via *Ghat* Hariki. Also informs that Sardar Dhanna Singhji an intelligent and a confident to him has been deputed today on 24 *Sawan* 1895 *Samvat* with 25 cavalry men to lead the addressee. Requests him to participate in Taran Taranji fair which is a holy fair and not too far from Hariki.

The illuminated document is written in Persian *shikasta*.

(ACC. NO. 231; Original; f1).

20 August 1838

127. *Yaddasht* of receipt of the amount of Rs. 723/ 5½ against income of 1245 *Fasli* (1837) from *taalluqa* Sonwani *ilaqa* Jagir Mahal *pargana* Ballia deposited by Shaikh Murtaza Bakhsh through Ajit Rai and Maha Upadhiya in the District Court of Ghazipur.

The document in Urdu *shikasta* bears the seal of *tahsildari pargana* Ballia.

(ACC. NO. 2764/ 21; Original; f1).

4 *Jumada* II 1254 AH (25 August 1838)

128. Letter to Wajih al-Din Ahmad Qazi of Sandila. Sends a copy of the *arzdasht* received from Abul Hasan resident of Sandila duly signed by His Highness (the Nawwab Wazir). Directs him to enquire into the matter and settle it according to the *shariat* and send the copy of the judgement under his seal.

The document in Persian *shikasta* bears a dim seal.

(ACC. NO. 1464; Original; f1).

12 *Bhadon Budi* 1895 *Samvat* (1 September

129. *Farigh khati/ Ladawa* executed by Bindaban son of Mehar Chand Khatri resident of *qasba* Bindraban. States that he had mortgaged his two shops in favour of

1838) Hardev and Lachhman against a sum of Rs. 500/-borrowed from them @ interest of 14 *anna* per month. Declares that since he is unable to return the amount to them as well as the interest on it even after the expiry of stipulated period of six years, the aforesaid shops may be retained by the mortgagee in lieu of the said amount with all rights over it.

The document in Persian *shikasta* executed on punch marked stamp paper of Rs. 8/- bears *sarnama Alif* and symbol of signature of the executant and signatures of witnesses in Devnagri.

(ACC. NO. 2697/ 20; Original; f1).

18 *Jumada* II 1254 AH (8 September 1838)

130. *Bainama* in respect of sale of a house as per the details of the boundaries given in the text in favour of Narsaon son of Khushhal for *Rs.* 100/.

The incomplete document on cloth in Persian *Shikasta* bears symbol of signatures of the reporters and the witnesses.

(ACC. NO. 2752/ 7; Original; f1)

19 *Jumada* II 1254 AH (9 September 1838)

131. Letter of Mangli Lal to Muradi Beg. Refers to a piece of land in Islamnagar *pargana* Asoha which is in the possession of Qazi Saiyid Hasan Ali since olden times and informs that the land of the said garden was exempted from revenue assessment in accordance to the *parwana* of Maharaja Kundan Lal in the preceeding years. Complains against Chandi Prasad *mustajir* who in collusion with the *Patwari* of the said *mauza* is creating trouble for the Qazi about which the addressee has already been intimated and responding to it he had warned Chandi Prasad not to indulge in

unnecessary interference. Requests him to direct his *gumashta* not to go against the established practice and let leave the said land in the possession of the Qazi.

The document in Persian *shikasta* bears the seal of Mangli Lal.

(ACC. NO. 2618/ 25; Original; f1).

26 September 1838 — 132. *Yaddasht* of the receipt of the amount of Rs. 579/ 3/ 15 *ganda* against the land revenue assessment of 1245 *Fasli* (1837) from *taalluqa*. Sonwani *pargana* Ballia *ilaqa* Jagir Mahal deposited by Shaikh Murtaza Husain through Mir Tasadduq Husain and Zalim Singh in the District Court of Ghazipur.

The document in Urdu *shikasta* bears *sarnama Alif* and the seal of *tahsildari pargana* Ballia.

(ACC. NO. 2764/ 22; Original; f1).

26 *Jeth* 1255 *Fasli*/ 10 *Rajab* 1254 AH (29 September 1838) — 133. *Iqrarnama* executed by Shaikh Najju son of Ghulam Husain and Fath Ali son of Shaikh Muram of mason caste residents of *chak* Mohna *pargana* Okri District Bihar. State that they have received Rs. 16/- from *Mst.* Bibi Amiran wife of Shaikh Tufail Ali *malika* (owner) and *malguzar* (revenue payer) of village Lodhipur Shams etc. for repair and renovation of her house. Promise that if any damage occurs during the period of repair and even after they shall be held responsible for that and would repair without payment.

The document in Persian *shikasta* bears *sarnama Alif* and signature of the executants and the witnesses.

(ACC. NO. 2534/ 12; Copy; f1).

16 October 1838 — 134. *Yaddasht* of the receipt of the amount of Rs. 703/ 12 / 5 *ganda* against the income of 1245 *Fasli* (1837) from *taalluqa* Sonwani *ilaqa* Jagir Mahal *pargana* Ballia etc. deposited by Shaikh Murtaza Bakhsh *sarbrahkar* through Hun Misr and Shaikh Bandhu etc. in the District Court of Ghazipur on 15 October 1838.

The document in Urdu *shikasta* bears seal of *tahsildari pargana* Ballia.

(ACC. NO. 2764/ 23; Original; f1).

22 October 1838 — 135. Proceedings of the Court under the Session of Alexander Reed, Deputy Collector of District Bihar with regard to a case filed by the Government against Ain Allah, Shaikh Inayat Husain, Mir Ghulam Husaini Mst. Bhikan and Mst. Azmat al-Nisa occupying 15 *bighas* of land, besides Maulawi Ghulam Hasan and several other occupants of the land of chak Mustafabad and Muhammadpur from the area of village Har Narayanpur *pargana* Bhailawar, an *aimma* village as per the Rule II of 1819 and III of 1828. The court after a thorough deliberation directs the defendants to explain the reasons of their occupation in accordance to the clause 15 and 16 of 1819 within a week otherwise, after the expiry of the time no explanation would be worth consideration.

The document in Persian *shikasta* bears *sarnama innahu* and the seal of Dy Collector of District Court Bihar.

(ACC. NO. 2531/ 9; Copy; f1).

30 *Kartik* 1895 *(Samvat)* (17 November 1838) — 136. Letter communicating that 8 *anna* on account of *rasad* (provision) has been paid to Baba Hiragar through Baba Ganeshgar as stipend.

The document in Persian *shikasta* bears *sarnama Alif* and the seal of Ghulam Ali.
(ACC. NO. 2580/ 18; Original; f1).

1 *Ramazan* 1254 AH (18 November 1838) 137. *Qabuliyatnama* executed under the seal of Muhammad Raza Khan. Undertakes to pay in installments Rs. 22944/9/3 along with *mal-o-abwab, mujra-i ikhrajat* (on account of *Jama*) after deducting *nankar* of *mauza* Mathipur belonging to District Ulas and Jalapur etc. and *mauza* Mahsona *pargana* Sandila from *kharif* crop of 1246 *Fasli* (1838) till *rabi* crop of 1248 *Fasli* (1840) for a period of 3 years. Promises to treat well the people of that *mauza* and to increase the Government revenue. Assures that even if any natural calamity occurs he would not make any execuse with regard to deposit the Government revenue in the treasury as per the instalments per year. The document is written in Persian *shikasta*.
(ACC. NO. 1479; Copy; f1).

30 November 1838/29 *Aghan Samvat* 1895/11 *Ramazan* 1254 AH/1246 *Fasli* 138. *Qabala-i rahnnama* executed by Ganga Prasad son of Munshi Sundar Lal son of Munshi Naunit Lal of Kol, *mutaallaqa* District Aligarh. States that he has mortgaged his one storeyed shop in Bazar Kalan in Patti Chanauli which is under his possession as per the *qabala Rahnnama* executed by Shiv Ram Brahman to Lala Girdhar Lal Brahman for Rs. 250/- and has received the amount in question. Declares that in lieu of the interest on the amount the mortgagee would be liable to get the profit earned from the shop till he returns the amount to the mortgagee.

The document in Persian *shikasta* executed on a punch marked paper of Rs.

4/- and bears *sarnama Huwa* and signatures of the executant and the witnesses in Persian and Devnagri.

(ACC. NO. 43; Original; f1).

22 December 1838 — 139. Proceedings of the Court under the session of Alexander Reed, Deputy Collector of District Bihar pertaining to a case filed by the Government against Qazi Asad Ali, *Mst*. Faqiran, Latifan and several others with regard to 172 *bighas* of *aimma* land at *chak* Lanchina situated at *pargana* Okri as per the rule II of 1819 and Rule III of 1828. The court after a thorough deliberation directs the defendants to explain their right of their occupation in accordance to the clause 15 and 16 of 1819 within a week otherwise, after the expiry of the period no explanation would be worth consideration.

The document in Persian *shikasta* bears the seal of Deputy Collector of the Court of District Bihar.

(ACC. NO. 2531/10; Copy; ff2).

1246 *Fasli* (date in the text) (1254 AH) (1838-39) — 140. *Arzi* of the *ahalkars* to Nawwab Hakim Ahsan Allah Khan. Refer to the grant of daily allowance granted to them by Khuld Makani Alamgir Badshah from the income of *tappa* Rebupura which they enjoyed till autumn of 1246 *Fasli* (1838) and then stopped. Add that they made continuous efforts from *rabi* harvest of the very year for the restoration of the said grant but were told about the resumption of their said allowance without giving any specific reason. Request to make a thorough investigation into the matter and resolve the matter which have left them in great crisis. Hope for a favourable order for them.

The document in Persian *shikasta* bears *sarnama Huwa*.

(ACC. NO. 62; Original; f1).

19 January 1839

141. Proceedings of the Court under the session of Alexander Reed Deputy Collector of District Bihar pertaining to a case filed by the Government against Qazi Asad Ali, *Mst*. Faqiran, *Mst*. Latifan, *Mst*. Shabratan, Shaikh Safdar Ali, Muhib Ali and several others of *pargana* Okri, District Bihar with regard to 172 *bighas* of *aimma* land at Chak Lanchina situated at *pargana* Okri as per Rule II of 1819 and Rule III of 1828. The court gave judgment in favour of the Government and ordered that as per *dastur al amal* dated 22 February 1837 notification may be issued informing the occupants that after six months these properties would be confiscated and if appeal is not made well in time the *bandobast* of the aforesaid village shall be done accordingly.

The document in Persian *shikasta* bears the seal of Deputy Collector of the Court of District Bihar.

(ACC. NO. 2531/ 11; copy; f1).

2 *Muharram* 1255 AH (18 March 1839)

142. *Bainama* executed by Saiyid Khadim Husain son of Saiyid Zakir Ali, *wakil* on behalf of his mother Mehr al-Nisa of *sarkar* Sambhal *suba* Shahjahanabad in respect of sale of a piece of land measuring one *biswa* and five *biswansis zamindari* of village Rasulpur together with the *milk* of the garden out of 20 *biswa dar-o-bast* in *mauza* Majholi and *zamindari* share in *mauza* Rasulpur with its boundaries. States that

his client has sold his land to Saiyid Wilayat Ali son of Saiyid Fazl Ali w. e. f *Rabi* crop of 1246 *Fasli* (1838) for Rs. 24/-. Adds that he has received the amount in full and has brought it in the control of his client while the said land has been occupied by the vendee.

The document in Persian *shikasta* executed on punch marked stamp paper bears *sarnama Alif* with signatures of the executant and the witnesses.

(ACC. NO. 2533/ 43; Original; f1).

14 *Muharram* 1255 AH (30 March 1839) 143. *Qabala-i bai* executed by Shaikh Manku son of Ramazani, resident of Astabal Char Bagh, Lukcnow in favour of Murad Khan son of Habib Allah Khan resident of Ismail Ganj *wakil* on behalf of Mir Saiyid Muhammad in respect of the sale of one storeyed dilapidated *haveli* situated at Astabal Char Bagh (details of the boundaries are given in the document) for Rs. 15/-. Acknowledges the receipt of the amount in full.

The document in Persian *shikasta* bears the seal of the Mufti and that of the *Adalat-i Alia, Diwani bait al saltanat* Lucknow. It also bears departmental endorsement.

(ACC. NO. 2395/ 2; Original; f1).

28 June 1839 144. Proceedings of the court under the session of Charles H. Lushington, Deputy Collector pertaining to a case filed by the Government against Qazi Asad Ali and *Mst.* Faqiran, Latifan and several others, the occupants of village Daulatpur and Mianwan *aimma* villages situated in *pargana* Okri as per the Rule II of 1819 and Rule III of 1828. The court after a thorough

deliberation directs the defendants to explain their right of occupation in accordance to the clause 15 and 16 of 1819 within a week, otherwise after the expiry of the period no explanation would be worth consideration.

The document in Persian *shikasta* bears *sarnama innahu* and the seal of Deputy Collector, Court of District Bihar.

(ACC. NO. 2531/ 13; Copy; f1).

...*Jumada* I 1255 AH (July-August 1839)

145. *Qabala-i bai* executed in the Civil Court of Lucknow by Shankar Das son of Janki Prasad resident of Katari Tola of Lucknow. States that he has sold his *amla* and *arazi* comprising one storeyed *haveli pukhta* (the details of the property along with the delineation of the boundaries are given in the body of the text) to Shaikh Ahmad Ali son of Mehr Ali resident of Chawk, *wakil* on behalf of Debi Das son of Parmeshari Das of Katari Tola Lucknow for Rs. 1450/ -(?).

The document in Persian *nastaliq* bears a seal of Mufti of *Adalat-i Aliya Diwani* Lucknow and that of the Court of *Adalat – i-Aliya* Lucknow with the royal emblem of Awadh at the top of the document while department endorsements are given on the reverse side.

(ACC. NO. 163; Original; f1).

19 August 1839

146. *Ishtiharnama* issued as per the orders of Lord Auckland, the Governor General. Highlights victory of the British Government in Afghanistan achieved by the Commander of the armed forces posted in Afghanistan as he reported through his letter dated 24 July 1839 which

he captured with the bravery and loyalty of the armed forces without any resistance. Adds that the Commander of the forces also reported that he captured Afghanistan and handed it over to Shah Shja in spite of being surrounded by forts and fortresses and famous Ghaznin fort and walled cities which were built up in a period of thirty years and was guarded by 3500 Afghan troops under the command of Muhammad Haider Khan, one of the sons of Sardar Dost Muhammad Khan. The Commmander of the forces also reported that after capturing Afghanistan he handed it over to Shah Shuja

The incomplete document in Persian *shikasta* bears *sarnama Alif* and the seal of the Governor General.

(ACC. NO. 2762/ 6; Original; f1).

26 August 1839 — 147. *Ishtihar* issued by the orders of Governor General Lord Auckland on the victory of the British forces at Ghaznin.

The incomplete document in Persian *Shikasta* bears the seal of the Governor General Lord Auckland.

(ACC. NO. 2762/ 7; Copy; f1).

2 September 1839 — 148. Letter to Kunwar (Aman) Sahib. Directs him to communicate whether the *bandobast* of Chathari and Asoi, the two villages which are in his *jagir* together with other villages of *pargana* Sonipat Khadar is acceptable to him or not as the *bandobast* of the said *pargana* is to be accomplished and the aforesaid villages also belong to the same *pargana*. .

The document in Persian *shikasta* bears *sarnama Alif.*

(ACC. NO. 2656/ 12; Original; f1).

24 *Jumada* II 1255 AH (4 September 1839)

149. *Qabala-i bai* executed in the Civil Court of Lucknow by Wali Muhammad son of Imam Bakhsh son of Shaikh Nur Muhammad, resident of Takia Shah Fasih, Lucknow. States that he has soled *amla* and *arazi* comprising one storeyed *pukhta* and *kham haveli* along with three shops, situated in Mughalpura (the details of the *haveli* together with the demarcation of boundaries are given in the body of the text) to Shaikh Shabrati son of Dilawar Ali *wakil* on behalf of Kanhi (Kandhi) Lal and Bindraban sons of Samadhan residents of Katari Tola for Rs. 850/- and has received the amount in full.

The document in Persian *nastaliq* bears a seal of *Mufti* of *Adalat-i Aliya Diwani* and that of the Court of *Adalat i-Aliya* with the royal emblem of Awadh at the top, while on the reverse side the departmental endorsements are given.

(ACC. NO. 164; Original; f1).

1255 AH (date in seal) (1839-40)

150. *Fatwa* issued by Shaikh Mahmud, regarding division of the property of inheritance of late *Mst*. Wali al-Nisa Begum among her three heirs; husband Mir Muhammad Ali one share, daughter *Mst*. Muhammadi Begum two shares and her sister *Mst*. Khair al-Nisa Begum one share, of course, after fulfilling 1/ 3rd of the will of the deceased.

The document bears *sarnama yatamana bi zikrihil Ala*, the seal of Shaikh Mahmud and the signature of the *ulama*.

(ACC. NO. 2150; Original; f1).

14 *Zilqada* 1255 AH/2

151. Lease-deed executed by Shaikh Haidar and Shaikh Raham Ali sons of Shaikh

Magh 1247 *Fasli* (19 January 1840) — Daim Ali residents and *maliks* (owners) of village Saiyidpur Mianwan *pargana* Okri, District Bihar. State that they have leased out their 1½ share out of the 11th shares of *Milkiyat-i malguzari* from Chak Ahra and 1½ share out of 11 shares of *Malikana* along with all *zamindari* rights over Chak Shafia comprising one *bigha* to Shaikh Tufail Ali for a period of five years i. e. 1247-1251 *Fasli* (1833-1837 AD) and have received Rs. 50/- as advance money. The document also contains other terms and conditions of the lease.

The document in Persian *shikasta* executed on punch marked paper of eight *anna* bears *sarnama Alif* and the seal of Qazi Asad Ali, *pargana* Okri, District Bihar and signatures of the executants and witnesses.

(ACC. NO. 2531/ 15; Copy; f1).

26 *Poos* 1896 *Samvat*/30 January 1840 — 152. *Dastaviz* executed by Raj Dhari alias Rakhey. States that one *bigha* land has been assigned to Gosain Ganeshgar on account of dharmarth *from village Chahchahra?*

The document in Persian *shikasta* bears signatures of the witnesses and the executants.

(ACC. NO. 2580/ 88; Original; f1).

22 *Zilhijja* 1255 AH/10 *Phagun* 1247 *Fasli* (26 February 1840) — 153. *Ijaranana* executed by Shaikh Amjad Ali and Shaikh Zakir Ali residents and *maliks* of Saiyidpur Mianwan *Pargana* Okri District Bihar. State that they have come to *Dar al qaza pargana* Okri, District Bihar and have leased out their three quarter share out of three shares from total 15 shares of *malikana* situated at village Saiyidpur, Mianwan *pargana* Okri for a

period of five years from 1248 to 1252 *Fasli* (1840-44 AD) to Shaikh Tufail Ali son of Shaikh Muhammad Anwar of *mauza* Saiyidpur Mianwan. Acknowledges the receipt of Rs. 30/- as advance money. The document also contains other terms and conditions

The document in Persian *shikasta* executed on punch marked paper of 8 *anna* bears *sarnama Alif* and the seal of Qazi Asad Ali of *pargana* Okri District Bihar and signatures of executant and witnesses.

(ACC. NO. 2531/ 16; Copy; f1).

25 *Phagun* 1896 *Samvat* (28 March 1840)

154. *Parwana* addressed to Lala Mahbub Rai and Sukhupal. Informs him that Rs. 6/ 4 has been fixed for Baba Ganeshgar on account of *dharmarth* for the whole year (for ten months). Directs him to pay the said Baba ten *annas* every month.

The document in Persian *shikasta* bears *sarnama Alif* and a dim seal.

(ACC. NO. 2580/ 15; Original; f1).

16 *Chait* 1249 *Fasli/1256* AH (March 1840)

155. *Qabuliyat-i theka* executed by Rinku Singh owner and resident of village Ghazipur *pargana* Okri District Bihar. States that he has taken on lease an *aimma* land measuring 3 *anna* out of 4 *anna* situated in *mauza* Saiyidpur Mianwan *pargana* Okri against a total sum of Rs. 186/ 9 for a period of five years from 1250 *Fasli* to 1254 *Fasli* (1842 to 1843) @ 37/5 annually from Shaikh Mahbub Ali, Jamal al Haque and Shaikh Tufail Ali along with *mal-o sair, kaldar, bunker, nahar* and other cesses and has paid Rs. 25/- as advance money. Promises to make payment every year in instalments to the *ahl-i maash* after

deducting a sum of Rs. 3/- as interest on the lease deed. Also hopes that the *ahl-i maash* would return the advance money by the end of *jeth* 1254 *fasli* at once. Subsequently the land would be returned to the *ahl-i mash.* In case they failed to return the advance money the *theka* would continue on the same terms and conditions.

The document in Persian *shikasta* executed on punch marked stamp paper of eight *anna* bears the *sarnama Innahu* and signatures of witnesses in Persian and Devnagri.

(ACC. NO. 2531/ 17; Original; f1).

6 *Rabi* I 1256 AH (8 May 1840)

156. *Qaulnama* issued by Raja Chandu Lal in favour of Raja Kalwah Kolan Lachmi Narsimha Rao, *deshmukh* of *pargana Madhera sarkar Khammamet suba* Farkhundabunyad (Hyderabad). Informs him that considering his request to administer and inhabit the aforesaid *pargana the same has been granted to him besides mal-o-sair, kalali, muhtarfa, baghat, sardarakhti, nazardasti, katai, haqq-i naibana, mahsuldari, dumbala* etc. from the beginning of 1250 *Fasli* (1848 AD) till the end of 1256 *Fasli* (1854 AD) for 7 years against the yearly payment of Rs. 4001/-. Directs him to make his best efforts in the inhabitation of the said *pargana* and deposit the aforesaid amount in instalments per year to the Government treasury.

The document in Persian *shikasta* bears *sarnama Alif* and the seal of Raja Chandu Lal Bahadur (the executant).

(ACC. NO. 2680/ 42; Original; f1).

26 *Rabi* II 1256 AH (27 June 1840)

157. *Bai-Bai'ana* executed by Shaikh Sajjad Ali. States that he has remitted Rs. 2/- as *baiana* (advance money) out of the price value and promises to pay the remaining sum in due course to the seller. Adds that the seller henceforth will not have any ownership right whatsoever except for the price value.

The brittle document is written in Persian *shikasta*.

(ACC. NO. 2534/ 3; Original; f1).

2 *Sawan* 1897 *Samvat* (30 July 1840)

158. Letter addressed to Chaudhari Ghulam Ali. Directs that the sum he has received as a grant for Baba Ganeshgar should be paid to him from the aforesaid *pura* and a *razinama* may also be obtained from the said Baba for submitting further. Also refers the *parwana-i khas* (special *parwana*) issued from Lahore regarding complaint made against the non-receipt of the aforesaid amount. Accordingly instructs to make payment to Baba Ganeshgar to avoid complaints in this regard in future.

The document in Persian *shikasta* bears *sarnama Alif* and the seal of Mangal Singh Akal Sahai.

(ACC. NO. 2580/ 14; Original; f1).

15 *Sawan* 1897 *Samvat* (13 August 1840)

159. *Parwana* addressed to Chaudhari Ghulam Ali. States that 100 *bighas* of land with wells *has* been in assignment of Baba Hiragar in village Raji and Dudsang on account of *dharmarth*. Instructs him not to create obstacles in the assignment. Also refers to the *parwangi-i khas* issued from Lahore directing that whatever *rasads* (provisions) were given should continue as heretofore.

The document in Persian *shikasta* bears *sarnama Alif* and a seal of Mangal Singh while the other is in Gurmukhi.

(ACC. NO. 2580/ 13; Original; f1).

19 *Sawan* 1897 *Samvat* (17 August 1840)	160.	Letter to Faiz Bakhsh. Informs him that 13 *bighas* of land on account of *dharmarth* has been in assignment of Baba Ganeshgar as *muaf.* Directs that in accordance to the *parwana* of Misr Lal Singh Jiu the yields thereof should be given to him since the land has been exempted from revenue assessment. The document in Persian *shikasta* bears *sarnama Alif* and the seal of Misr Lal Singh Jiu. **(ACC. NO. 2580/ 10; Original; f1).**
24 *Jumada* II 1256 AH/23 August 1840/21 *Bhadon Budi* 1897 *Samvat*	161.	*Bainama* executed by Ghulam Muhammad son of Wali Muhammad and Kale Khan son of Jamal Khan resident of *qasba* Rewari adjacent to *Dar al-khilafa* Shahjahanabad. State that they have sold their two pieces of the residential land measuring 590 *ziras,* 16 *tu* (details of boundary have been demarcated in the document) in the aforesaid *qasba, muhalla* Qaziwara to Shivlal, Baldev Sahai and Chatarpal sons of Ganga Dhar for a sum of Rs. 196/ 4/- which they have received in full. The document in Persian *shikasta* executed on two rupees stamp paper bears the seal of Ghulam Muhammad (the executant) and signatures of the witnesses. **(ACC. NO. 2657/ 95; Copy; f1).**
9 September 1840	162.	*Hukmnama* issued to Sada Kunwar and Mangla of Sonipat. Informs that their petitions seeking job has been accepted by Equivant (?) of Agra and as such they are directed to appear in the office for physical verification and that Rs. 85/-8 has been fixed as salary for each one of them The document in Urdu *shikasta* bears

sarnama Alif and the seal of the District Court Shahjahanabad.

(ACC. NO. 2656/ 33; Original; f1).

25 November 1840/ 16 *Aghan* 1248 *Fasli*

163. *Rubakar-i kachehri* of District Bihar under the session of Saiyid Latif Ali Deputy Collector regarding the entry of a piece of hereditary land situated in village Udaipur Shams *pargana* Okri under the *Lakhiraji Shikmi* dispensation.

After going through the papers of *lakhiraj Shikmi* of the said *mauza* as notified under clause II article V dated 1825 the court orders to hand over the copy of the said *rubakar* to the occupant through the *nazir* of the department so that within one week he (the occupant) could prove his claim in the court and submit relevant papers otherwise, after the expiry of the period ex-party decision in respect of *Lakhiraj* land would be made.

The document in Urdu *shikasta* bears *sarnama Innahu* and an illegible seal of the court.

(ACC. NO. 2534/ 4; Copy; f1).

26 December 1840

164. *Rubakar-i kachehri, bandobast zila* Panipat under the session of George Fredrick Edmonstone. Refers to the letter of the Commissioner dated 16 December (1840) for the confiscation of the villages of Chathari and Asoi of *pargana* Sonipat Khadar *jagir* of Kunwar Aman Singh. The Court orders for the inclusion of the said villages into the *khalsa* land and the same may be communicated to the Collector and a *parwana* should be issued in the name of the *tahsildar* directing him to treat the said villages as confiscated and also to see

whether its *khasra, shajra* and *khatoni* has been done in accordance to the measurement. It also contains orders that *wasilbaqi nawis* may include the said villages in the *Khalsa* villages.

The document is in Urdu *shikasta* executed on punch marked stamp paper of eight *annas* and bears the seal of District Court Shahjahanabad.

(ACC. NO. 2656/ 42; Copy; f1).

1256 AH (date in seal) (1840-41) 165. *Parwana* under the seal of Nawwab Ubaid Allah Khan Tarkhan *sadr al-sadur* to Hasan Khan. Informs that Hafiz-Abd al- Ali and others who are holding *mauza Khajari, amla, pargana* Sandila, *sarkar* Lucknow adjoining to *suba* Awadh as heriditary *madad-i mash* grant as per previous *Farman* have reported interference by the Qazi of Sandila claiming as *mashrut-i quza*. Clarifies that as per *sarrishta* land comprising 100 *bighas* in *pargana* Sandila in the aforesaid *sarkar* has been earmarked for the Qazi which ia beyond the land referred above. Directs him to look into th matter and prevent the *Qazi* from interfering in the said *mauza*.

The document in Persian *shikasta* bears a dim seal of Qazi Zahur Wali.

(ACC. NO. 1615; Copy; f1).

1256 AH (?) (in seal) (1840-41) 166. *Parwana* of Imdad Husain Khan to Raja Man Singh *Nazim* of the *mahals* of Daryabad and Sultanpur etc. Refers the petition of Khairat Ali *zamindar* of Muhammadpur and Kanwar Itimadpur who had filed a case in the court of *Sultan–al-Ulama* for the settlement of dispute between the petitioner and Husain Bakhsh the *qanungo* of *pargana* Badusarai over the aforesaid *mauza* and non appearance of the *qanungo* in the Court. Further refers the *Rubakari* and the petitioner's request to give him possession even before the settlement of the case and the directives of the *Muhkama I Sharia* forbidding possession until the final settlement of the case. Directs him to give him formal possession till the case is settled in the *Muhkama I Sharia* (?).

The incomplete document in Persian *shikasta* bears the seal of Imdad Husain Khan.

(ACC. NO. 1669; Original; f1).

1897 *Samvat* (date in text) (1840-41)

167. Letter addressed to Lala Narain Nath and Lala Hindsav Das. Refers the assignment of three *man* food grain on account of *dharmarth* in *taalluqa* Siwala to Shivgar *mahant* of Diwara *taalluqa* Danga crop after crop in equal instalments of 1½ *man* in *kharif* and *rabi* crop. Directs that yield *(faslana)* of *kharif* crop of 1897 *Fasli* may be granted to the aforesaid *mahant* and the same may be adjusted in the royal office and *parwana* shall be issued accordingly.

The document in Persian *shikasta* bears a seal on the back of the document.

(ACC. NO. 2580/ 91; Original; f1).

24 *Zilqada* 1256 AH (17 January 1841)

168. *Parwana* of *Wazir al-daulah* Muhammad Wazir Khan to the *thakurs, patels* and *patwaris* of *ilaqa* Jaipur. Informs that the mischief mongers of his state have entrenched in their territory, and to investigate the matter further a *mutamid* along with a *harkara* and a *naqib* has been sent there. Directs them to help in the

search of the miscreants and hand them over to the said officials.

The bilingual document in Persian and Rajasthani bears *sarnama Alif* and contains the seal of the writer.

(ACC. NO. 2701/ 8; Original; f1)[1]

1*Muharram* 1257 AH (date in text) (23 February 1841)

169. News report of *thana* Khaloni at Fort Hanglakhgarh sent by Rao Lachman qiladar w.e.f. 1st *Muharram* till 8 *Muharram* 1257AH. Reports about Puran Baqqal who complained against Umrao Singh and Ram Chander, soldiers of *qila* Hanglakh who seduced his wife and kept her in the *qila*. The Pandit warned them of stern action for such heinous crime and handed her to Puran Baqqal. Reports about the visit of Sriptat Rao Shiv Ram *ijaradar to Khandu Pandit complaining that Bhimji Patel has absconded from Kothra and has taken asylum in the territory of Raja of Kota. Solicits a parwana for his repatriation to the village. Khandu Pandit issued a parwana* to Rupji Thakur for taking him back along with Shapura to village Kothra and also to receive a fine of Rs. 1/4/- from him together with expenses incurred on him.

Reports that the soldiers of the *qila* met Khandu Pandit and complained that water of Sangram pond in the *qila* had become impure and if feast were arranged for some Brahmins the water would be purified. Accordingly, Khandu Pandit invited some Brahmins on a feast in the fort. Further reports that Khandu Pandit invited all the *baqqals* in the court and informed them

1. ACC. NOs. 2701/ 9 and 2701/ 10 are the copies of the aforesaid document and both documents bear *sarnama Alif* and *Shri Ramji.*

about the movements of thieves and increasing threat of theft in Khaloni town which need precaution. Thakur Bakhtawar Singh explained to Khandu Pandit about illegal imprisonment of Sondarya, the flower seller in Khora which is causing ruin to the garden. Khandu Pandit freed him on the condition he provides him bail.

Tapka Deran complained to the court that Balaji Marhatta and Bhalan residents of Khanti Khetra were committing theft of wheat crop from their field. Khandu Pandit called them and kept them in the custody for four hours, imposed a fine of 12 *annas* on Bhalan while 8 *anna* on Balaji.

Rupji Thakur informed that he persuaded his best to bring Bhimji Patel to Kothra but he refused to live at Kethra. Khandu Pandit did not take any action in the matter

The document in Persian *shikasta* bears *sarnama Alif.*

(ACC. NO. 2668/ 86; Original; f1)

5 *Muharram* 1257 AH (27 February 1841)

170. *Qabz al-wasul* executed by Sada Sukh *qanungo* of *pargana* Sandila. Acknowledges receipt of Rs. 62/- for 1257 *Fasli* on account *of nankar* from Qazi Maslih al-Din in respect of *taalluqa* Mahsuna through Lala Minwah Ram *tahsildar* of Sandila.

The document written in Persian *shikasta* bears a dim seal of Sada Sukh (the executant).

(ACC. NO. 1507; Original; f1).

6 *Muharram/* 23 *Magh* 1249 *Fasli* (1257 AH) (28 February 1841)

171. *Patta* executed in favour of *Mst.* Bhikan and 18 others of Saiyidpur Mianwan, *pargana* Okri District Bihar. Referring to their representation, informs that *Patta* has *been* granted to them in accordance to the

rubakar dated 28 March 1839 AD as per the *chitthi* of *sehbandi* and *jamabandi*. Also lays down the terms and conditions in the matter.

The document is written in Urdu *shikasta* with the symbol of seal of the court.

(ACC. NO. 2534/ 6; Copy; ff2)

7 April 1841/ 26 *Chait* 1247 *Bangla* 172. Judgement of *Adalat-i commissioner* of District Murshidabad under the session of Henry Moure, Special Commissioner under Regulation 3 of March 1828 over the appeal made by Seeb Singh Shukl and Jamuna Dasi, residents of village Purapara against the decision of Deputy Collector of Nadia in respect of imposition of land revenue over 1200 *bighas* of land of *Devatra* situated in village Purapara *chakla* Matyari. The court after hearing the case upheld the decision of the Deputy Collector and also imposed the cost of the case on the appellants or on their *wakil* as they were not present in the court. The court also issued instructions to the Deputy Collector to file a separate case for the *bazyaft* of the *taufir* land.

The document in Urdu *shikasta* bears the seal of the Court of the Commissioner, District Murshidabad.

(ACC. NO. 2693/ 5; Copy; f1).

21 April 1841 173. *Iqrarnama / wasiatnama* executed by Rao Bahadur Singh son of Rao Fath Singh *taalluqadar, jagirdar* of *mauza* Lanchina *pargana* Seyana *zila* Meerut. Refers to the old family relation between his family and the family of Munshi Har Sahai, *muhafiz-i Daftar-i Collectory* from the time of his father late Lala Daulat Rai and Rao Ram

Dhan Singh his grand father on one hand and his father Rao Fath Singh on the other. Futther refers his request for the enhancement in his position as the salary for him was fixed long ago and is not sufficient for his livelihood. Says that although it was proposed to increase his salary but at the moment it is not possible and so the salary of Rs. 5/- would remain intact. Adds that this *iqrarnama/ wasiatnama* has been executed for future reference so long as this government and his family is at the helm of affairs the said amount would be paid to him either annually or monthly and none from his family would object it.

The document in Urdu *shikasta* bears *sarnama Alif* and the seals and signatures of the executants and the witnesses.

(ACC. NO. 2754/ 4; Original; f1).

7 *Baisakh* 1898 *Samvat* (28 April 1841).

174. *Parwana* to Chaudhari Seyanu Bhalwal (?). Directs him to suspend the grant assigned to Gosain Ganeshgar on account of *dharmarth* until he receives another *parwana*.

The document in Persian *shikasta* bears *sarnama Alif* and a seal of Raja Gulab Singh.

(ACC. NO. 2580/ 45; Original; f1).

30 April 1841

175. *Rubakar-i kachehri zila* Mathura in the court of the Collector William Harding Tyler. It contains that the case filed by Thakur Gobindji *Muafidar* for the *bandobast* of 36 *bighas* 11 *biswa* measured land in *mauza* Sonarkha *tahsil* Mathura was perused. The court heard the statement of Balmukand, *karinda* of the aforesaid *thakur* on the assignment of 45 *bigha* land by Raja

Surajmal to Jagannath Gosain as *muafi* for the *bhog* of Thakur Gobindji but the sanad was lost in the mutiny. The court also noticed that the actual land as surveyed now is only 36 *bigha* 11 *biswa* and some land has been earmarked as *khadar* which is available in the record of *patwari* and *qanungo* which certifies that the land belongs to the temple.

The court orders for the continuation of the said land in favour of the *karindas* of the temple and also to submit the report of the case to the office of the Commissioner for perpetual grant of *muafi* of the said land for the maintenance of the temple.

The document in Urdu *shikasta* executed on 8 *anna* punch marked stamp paper bears seal of the court.

(ACC. NO. 2671/ 36; Original; f1).

10 *Rabi* I
1257 AH
(2 May 1841)

176. *Mahzar* recorded by Mir Hasan son of Mir Husain alias Mir Kamil resident of Mahmud Nagar, Lucknow tracing his antecedents to Mir Shah Afzal real brother of Mir Jafar posted as Mir Bakhshi in the reign of King Ali Gauhar (Shah Alam II) and after his death the said post was assigned to his grand father (Mir Shah Afzal). States that he is a trader of *parcha-i wilayati* residing in *muhalla* Mahmud Nagar of Lucknow which is well known to all reputed traders and the well off people of Lucknow.

The document is in Persian *nastaliq*.

(ACC. NO. 2180; Original; f1).

10 *Rabi* II
1257 AH
(1 June 1841)

177. *Yaddasht* of the amount of Rs. 5000/2 the 4th instalment out of the *mahsul* of 1255 *Fasli* from the income of *pargana* Madhera,

sarkar Khammamet has been deposited in the royal treasury through Jati Rai Shivraj *naib* of Raja Lachhman Narsimha Rao *deshmukh* of the aforesaid *pargana*.

The bilingual document in Persian *shikasta* and Devnagri bears *sarnama Alif* and the seal of Qaisar Jang Bahadur.

(ACC. NO. 2680/ 47; Original; f1).

24 *Sarh* 1898 *Samvat* (13 July 1841)

178. *Iqrarnama* executed by Pandit Dabar Chand and other sons of Baba Ram Kalula. State that 25 *bighas* of land on account of *dharmarth* from village Bharut, *qasba* Janak along with the previously assigned *arazi* to Baba Ganeshgar has been granted to Baba Hiragar. Hopes that the said Baba would utilize the produce of the said assignment for himself and be able to pray the Almighty God wholeheartedly.

The documents in Persian *shikasta* bears *sarnama Alif* and the seal of Ghulam Ali Khan with two other dim seals.

(ACC. NO. 2780/ 9; Original; f1).

26 *Jumada* I 1257 AH (16 July 1841)

179. *Parwana* under the signature of Faqir Muhammad Khan Bahadur, *Nazim* of *pargana* Sandila etc. to Gauhar Khan, resident of Sandila. Refers that apparently Chaudhari Ghulam Makhdum who has been exercising his authority for generations over the inhabitants there is however being ousted by the addressee. Directs him to establish his claim, if any. Warns him that unless the matter is settled he should desist from interference in the territory.

The document in Persian *shikasta* bears *sarnama Alif.*

(ACC. NO. 1544; Copy; f1).

29 July 1841 180. *Rubakar-i Kachehri* in respect of the investigation of *lakhiraj* land District Aligarh under the session of William S. Donnithorne, Deputy Collector in charge of the *muafi* Department in the case filed by the Government against Amanat Ali Khan in regard to resumption of 30 *bighas* land situated at Delhi Darwaza. The court found that the defenders were the rightful owners of the aforesaid land and thus the court ordered for its exemption from revenue. The court also directed to send the copy of the *rubakari* together with the paper of the case to the Collector for information and also to the defendants.

The document in Urdu *shikasta* bears a bilingual seal of the court of Special Deputy Collector, District Aligarh.

(ACC. NO. 1038; Copy; ff2).

13 August 1841 181. Letter from Khalsa Darbar (to the Governor General). Expresses pleasure on the friendly relations subsisting between the two Governments. Informs that Mian Din Muhammad who is a confident of the writer has been sent to Pattan instead of General Mohan Lal. Hopes that Mian Din Muhammad would safeguard the interest of the two states and no crisis would arise in future.

The document is written in Persian *shikasta* bears the *sarnama bafazl-i Sri Akal Purakhji*

(ACC. NO. 232; Original; f1).

12 *Rajab* 1257 AH (30 August 1841) 182. *Qabala-i Rahn* executed in the civil court of Lucknow by Raghunath Prasad son of Ram Chand resident of Katari Tola Lucknow. States that he has mortgaged his

amla and *arazi* comprising two storeyed *haveli kham* and *pukhta* situated in Katari Tola (the detail of the haveli along with delineation of boundaries are given in the text) in favour of Shaikh Ahmad Ali son of Mehr Ali resident of Farangi Mahal, *wakil* on behalf of Bindraban son of Samadhan resident of Katari Tola against a sum of Rs. 1000/- borrowed from him. Declares that the mortgagee is at his will to use the mortgaged property either directly or can it give on rent.

The document in Persian *nastaliq* bears seal of the Mufti of *Adalat-i Aliya* Lucknow and that of the court of *Adalat-i Aliya* Lucknow with the royal emblem of Awadh at the top. The reverse side contains departmental endorsements.

(ACC. NO. 165; Original; f1).

13 October 1841

183. *Rubakar-i Kachehri* in respect of the investigation of *Lakhiraj* land of District Aligarh under the session of the Officiating Collector G. Blunt in-charge of *muafi* Department in regard to a case filed by the Government against Amanat Ali Khan for the resumption of 3 *bighas* measured *muafi* land situated at Delhi Darwaza *qasba* and *pargana* Kol. The court orders for the resumption of the said land but it will remain exempted from the revenues realization until the trees are grown. Also directs to send the copy of the *rubakari* together with necessary papers of the case to the Collector of the District for information and also to the defendants.

The document in Urdu *shikasta* bears a bilingual seal of the court of Special Deputy Collector, Aligarh.

(ACC. NO. 1039; Copy; ff2).

1257 AH (date in seal) (1841-42)

184. *Arzdasht* of Aslah al-Din *zamindar* and *malguzar* of village Mahsona *pargana* Sandila to Nawwab of Awadh. States that as per the orders of the *Qaza* after the testimony of the witnesses and *kaifiat* under the signature of *sighadars* of *mauza* Mahsona, *amla, pargana* Sandila was his *zamindari* villages which came into his possession in 1245 *Fasli* (1252 AH) and is still in his possession. Complains against some mischievous Brahmins whom his forefather had engaged as tillers are fomenting trouble among the peasants and creating problem in the administration and government revenue realization causing recession in the income of Government revenue. As a result a sum of Rs. 1400/- incurred as dues till last year and he had to mortgage his territory which is still not been recovered. Requests for orders to Imam al-Din Khan *chakladar* to oust those mischief mongers so that he could promote cultivation and deposit the land revenue thereof.

The document in Persian *nastaliq* bears the seal of Aslah al-Din.

(ACC. NO. 1433; Original; f1).

1257 AH (date in seal) (1841- 42)

185. Physical description and identification of Abd al-Samad son of Muhammad and grand son of Abd Allah of Arab national aged 24 years resident of Yemen having black scars of small pox and injuries etc. The document in Persian *shikasta* bears the seal of Sala Jang.

(ACC. NO. 2536/ 26; Original; f1).

1257 AH (date in seal)

186. Physical description of Daud son of Musa, grandson of Daud resident of Yemen, 36

(1841-42)

years of age having scars of small pox on the face as per the *parwana* of Saiyid Ali.

The document in Persian *shikasta* bears seal of Salar Jang.

(ACC. NO. 2536/ 27; Original; f1).

1257 AH (date in seal) (1841-42)

187. Physical description of Saiyid Ali son of Ahmad grandson of Abbas, Arab national.

The document in Persian *shikasta* bears the seal of Salar Jang.

(ACC. NO. 2536/ 28; Original; f1).

1257 AH (date in seal) (1841-42)

188. Physical description of Muhammad son of Ahmad, grand son of Hasan, Arab national aged 25 years and resident of Yemen having scars of small pox on the face.

The document in Persian *shikasta* bears the seal of Salar Jang.

(ACC. NO. 2536/ 29; Original; f1).

1257 AH (date in seal) (1841- 42) (Illus.)

189. Physical description of Zaid son of Salih, grandson of Ahmad, Arab national, aged 35 years having scar of small pox and a resident of Yemen, as per the *awarja* of Saiyid Ali.

The document in Persian *shikasta* bears the seal of Salar Jang.

(ACC. NO. 2536/ 30; Original; f1).

1257 AH (date in seal) (1841- 42)

190. Physical description of Saeed son of Abbas, grand son of Saeed, Arab national having scars of small pox and 30 years old is the resident of Yemen.

The document in Persian *shikasta* bears the seal of Salar Jang.

(ACC. NO. 2536/ 31; Original; f1).

18 *Zilhijja* 1257 AH (31 January 1842)

191. *Wasil* (receipt) of Rs. 100/- in respect of revenue of village Mahsona of 1249 *Fasli* sent by Qazi Sahib which has been entered in the *siyaha* through Ifham al-Daulah.

The document in Persian *shikasta* bears *sarnama innahu* and the seal of Saiyid Muhammad Baqa.

(ACC. NO. 1590; Original; f1).

9 *Rabi* I 1258 AH (20 April 1842) 192. Letter of Hisam al-Daulah, Faqir Muhammad Khan to Hashmat Ali Chaudhari. Sends the details of the case filed by Alka, resident of Bhagwant Nagar, *pargana* Malanwa against the son of Thekri. Directs him to look into the matter and decide the case as arbitrator.

The document is in Persian *Shikasta*.

(ACC. NO. 1612; Copy; f1).

25 April 1842 193. Notification executed in the name of the *muafidars* of *mauza* Bahalgarh *Pargana* Sonipat. Refers to the letter of the Commissioner dated 20 April (1842) along with the *Rubakari kachehri* dated 9 June 1837 with regard to the relinquishment of *mauza* Aoncha Siwanah etc. (8 nos. of *mauza muafi)* from *mauza* Bahalgarh in their names, perpetually generation after generation. Informs them that the said *mauza* which was earlier settled *(bandobast)* with *pargana* Sonipat Khadar stands cancelled and the same has been relinquished in their favour perpetually, generation after generating.

The document in Urdu *shikasta* bears *sarnama Alif.*

(ACC. NO. 250; Copy; f1).

25 April 1842/ *Baisakh* 1249 *Fasli* 194. *Rubakar-i kachehri-i bandobast* of District Panipat under the session of George Fredrick Edmonstone. Refers to the letters of the Commissioner, dated 3 April (1842) besides the letter of *Sadr Board,* revenue with regard to the relinquishment of *mauza*

Auncha Siwanah *pargana* Panipat Khadar along with the map of relinquishment of 8 villages, which was, however again returned to the Commissioner for some clarification. Adds that today on 25 April 1842 the *rubakari* from Commissioner's office dated 9th June 1836 along with a letter of the Commissioner dated 20 April 1842 in respect of the release of *mauza* Bahalgarh *pargana* Sonipat Khadar perpetually generation after generation has been received. In this perspective the court orders that *mauza* Bahalgar, *pargana* Sonipat khaddar may be relinquished perpetually generation after generation and the *bandobast* (settlement) order issued earlier stands cancelled. The court also directs to collect the papers of the *rubakari* of the said *mauza* from Mirza Shahbaz Beg, the Deputy Collector and inform the *muafidars* accordingly and to issue a *parwana* to the *tahsildars* of that *pargana* in this regard.

The document is written in Urdu *shikasta*.

(ACC. NO. 249; Copy; f1).

14 May 1842 195. *Rubakar-i Kachehri* with regard to the investigation of *lakhiraj* land District Aligarh under the session of Mr. William S. Donithorne, Deputy Collector in charge of *muafi* in a case of Government against Shaikh Amanant Ali Khan claiming for the resumption of 6 *ana* from 166 *bighas* and 10 biswas land and 25 *bighas* and 2 *biswas* measured land in *qasba* Kol, *pargana* Kol. The Court after thorough deliberation found that 2 *bighas* and 18 *biswas* measured land situated at Delhi Darwaza is

comprised of garden and is not total productive and thus the court rectifies the decision of the *Sadr Board* revenue dated 1 July 1836 to keep it exempted from taxes till the trees are grown. Thus the Court orders that the *rubakari* of this case may be sent to the Collector directing him to keep the said land (2 *bigha*, 18 *biswa*) out of 18 *bighas* and 5 *biswas* exempted from the revenue assessment till the trees are grown.

The document in Urdu *shikasta* bears a trilingual seal of the Court of Special Deputy Collector, District Aligarh.

(ACC. NO. 1034; Copy; f1).

23 May 1842 196. *Rubakar-i kachehri* in respect of investigation of *Lakhiraj* land District Aligarh under the session of William Donithorne Deputy Collector in charge of *muafi* Department with regard to a case filed by the Government against Tafazzul Husain and Izzat Ali Khan heirs of Ghulam Rasul claiming resumption of 2 *bighas* and 13 *biswas* measured land out of 175 *bigha* land situated in *qasba* Kol. The Court found that the defenders were the rightful owners of the aforesaid land as it was in their possession without break and thus the Court observed that the aforesaid land was not worth resumption, instead it should be treated as exempted. The Court also directed to send a copy of the *rubakari* to the Collector to treat the land as relinquished.

The document in Urdu *shikasta* bears trilingual seal of the Court of Special Deputy Collector District Aligarh.

(ACC. NO. 1043; Copy; ff2).

11 June 1842 197. Letter of Commissioner E. Ravenshaw of Patna to I. H. Gauri the Collector of Patna. Clarifies that sale of *mauza* Rasulpur (?) was not made in accordance to the prescribed rule and that *Mst.* Maryam the plaintiff has paid her share due upon her of *mauza* Kuchra Chanduri hence she is liable to challenge the validity of the sale in the court.

The document in English executed on eight *anna* court paper bears the seal of the Collectory of District Patna.

(ACC. NO. 2531/ 18; Copy; f1).

13 June 1842 198. *Rubakar-i kachehri* in respect of the investigation of *Lakhiraj* land of District Aligarh under the session of William S. Donnithorne, Deputy Collector in charge of *Muafi* Department with regard to a case filed by the Government against Banda Ali Khan and other sons of Najib Ali Khan, Izzat Ali Khan and *Mst.* Shukr al-nisa claiming resumption of 1 *bigha* and 10 *biswa* of *muafi* land and 27 *bighas* and 17 *biswas* of measured land situated in *qasba* and *pargana* Kol. The court after thorough deliberations, orders for the relinquishment of 27 *bighas* and 3 *biswas* of measured land in *qasba* Kol in perpetuity (in favour of Banda Ali Khan and others) and one *bigha,* 14 *biswas* of land in the said *qasba* in favour of Shukr al-nisa. The Court also orders for the transmission of necessary papers of the case to the Commissioner of Northern part of Doab and District Collector for the implementation of the order.

The document in Urdu *shikasta* bears trilingual seal of the Court of Special Deputy Collector District Aligarh.

(ACC. NO. 1044; Copy; ff5).

19 *Jumada* I 1258 AH (28 June 1842)

199. *Qabala-i bai* executed by *Mst.* Dau, wife of Chhetu resident of Astabal Char Bagh in favour of Murad Khan *wakil* son of Habib Allah on behalf of Saiyid Muhammad in respect of the sale of one storeyed *haveli* situated at Astabal Char Bagh (details of the boundaries are given in the document) in favour of Murad Khan son of Habib Allah resident of Astabal Char Bagh for a sum of Rs. 40/-. Acknowledges the receipt of the amount in full.

The document in Persian *nastaliq* bears the seal of the Mufti and that of *Adalat-i Alia Diwani, Bait al Saltanat* Lucknow. It also bears departmental endorsements on the reverse.

(ACC. NO. 2395/ 3; Original; f1).

21 *Jumada* II 1250 *Fasli* (1258 AH) (30 July 1842)

200. *Tamassuk* executed by Shaikh Chadda, resident of Daryabad. Undertakes to make payment of Rs. 66/-as lump-sum amount against the grant of village Muhammad-pur Mamoon till the end of sawan.

The document in Persian *shikasta* bears the seal of the writer.

(ACC. NO. 1971; Original; f1).

1 *Rajab* 1258 AH/ 5 *Sawan Sudi* 1899 *Samvat* (8 August 1842)

201. *Girvinama* executed by Puran Das son of Siya Charan Jiu resident of *qasba* Rewari adjacent to *suba Dar al-khilafa* Shahjahana-bad in respect of one storeyed shop mortgaged for a sum of Rs. 50/- to Prem Singh son of Girdhari Lal and Umrao Singh son of Prem Singh of the aforesaid *qasba*. Acknowledges the receipt of the amount in full. Declares that the mortgagees would hold the shop unless and until he returns the amount of *rahn* to them. Further clarifies that the interest on

the amount of *rahn* would be equal to the rent of the shop. However the amount spent on the repair of shop would be borne by the mortgager.

The document in Persian *shikasta* executed on punch marked stamp paper of eight *anna* bears *sarnama Innahu* and signatures of the executant and the witnesses in Devnagri.

(ACC. NO. 2657/ 8; Original; f1).

1 *Rajab* 1258 AH (8 August 1842)

202. Letter to Seth Sri Raj Sahu and Mansa Ram Sahu of Badawa? Gives receipt of Rs. 48296/11/3 outstanding against them on account of *dastgardan* which shall be adjusted at the time of reconciliation of accounts.

The document in Persian *shikasta* bears *sarnama Alif* and the seal of Muhammad Wazir Khan.

(ACC. NO. 2701/ 13; Original; f1).

16 *Rajab* 1258 AH (23 August 1842)

203. *Qabala-i bai* executed by Mohan Lal, Sohan Lal sons of Thakur Das of Katari Tola Lucknow and Muhammad Husain *wakil* on behalf of *Mst.* Jubdi, daughter of Dinanath wife of Sunder Das. State that they have sold their amla and arazi comprising one storeyed shop (the details of the shop together with the demarcation of the boundaries are given in the document) to Shaikh Ahmad son of Shaikh Mehr Ali resident of Farangi Mahal *wakil* on behalf of Bindraban son of Samadhan of Katari Tola for Rs. 800/- and have received the amount in full.

The document in Persian *nastaliq* bears seal of the Mufti of *Adalat-i Aliya Diwani* Lucknow and that of *Adalat-i Aliya*

Lucknow with a royal emblem of Awadh at the top. The reverse side contains departmental endorsement.

(ACC. NO. 166; Original; f1).

26 *Sawan* 1899 *Samvat* (1 September 1842)

204. *Parwana* issued to Allah Din and Murad Bakhsh, *zamindars* of Sondha (Sudhna). Informs that a sum of Rs. 30/- granted to Baba Gobindgar on account of *dharmarth* for the whole year has been exempted from *jama* since olden times. Directs for the continuation of the aforesaid grant in his favour on the same condition.

The document in Persian *shikasta* bears the seal of Khwaja Muhammad and on the reverse of Kishan Chand Mehta

(ACC. NO. 2580/ 2; Original; f1).

22 *Shaban* 1258 AH (28 September 1842)

205. Letter of Lala Tika Ram to Shaikh Qadir Ali Mustajir of Sair of *qasba* Sandila. Informs that Shams al-Din Shah has been assigned one *fulus* as daily allowance as *muaf* for a long time and has been receiving regularly. Directs that the same may be continued as usual for his maintenance and may remain busy praying for the well-being of the Nawwab.

The document in Persian *shikasta* bears *sarnama Innahu* and the symbol of seal of Tika Ram.

(ACC. NO. 1610;Copy;f1).

29 *Shaban* 1258 AH/16 *Aas* 1250 *Fasli* / 5 October 1842

206. *Wasiqa* executed by *Mst.* Gulshan alias Puchni resident of village Daulatpur *pargana* Okri District Bihar. Declares that due to poverty and starvation she has come to *Dar-al qaza, Pargana,* District Bihar and has sold herself for Rs. 6/ only on lease of 80 years at the hands of *Mst.* Bibi Amiran daughter of Shaikh Yar Ali and wife of

Shaikh Tufail Ali resident of village Daulatpur and has received the full payment in advance. Also declares that the *mustajir* would hold all the rights over her born child.

The document in Persian *shikasta* bears *sarnama Alif*, besides seal of Qazi Asad Ali, *pargana* Okri, District Bihar and symbol of signature of the executant and signature of the witnesses. It also bears physical description of executant.

(ACC. NO. 2531/ 19; Original; f1).

29 *Shawwal* 1258 AH (3 December 1842)

207. Letter to Ghulam Muhi al-Din. Informs that as per *Parwana* Rs. 30/ annually has been in grant of Baba Ganeshgar on account of *dharmarth* from village Bhunder Chalan since long is exempted from revenue assessment. Directs him to relinquish the same in his favour as per practice followed in the preceding years.

The document in Persian *shikasta* bears *sarnama Huwa* and a seal of Muhammad Sultan.

(ACC. NO. 2580/ 29; Original; f1).

4 *Zilqada* 1258 AH / *Aghan* 1250 *Fasli* (7 December1842)

208. *Dastawiz-i qabuliyat* executed by Hulas and Hemdas of village Ghaibpur Dhankara *pargana* Bhailawar and Lal Chand Das of village Baijupur, District Bihar. State that they have taken on lease 12 shares out of 72 shares from a total of 108 shares together with 200 *bighas* of *qanungoi* land in *mauza* Ghaibpur Dhankara and 1/3 land of *qanungoi* and half land i. e. 100 *bighas* or 1/ 3 share of Mir Ahad Ali from *Mst.* Idan and Chaman, the owners of the said *mauza* for 9 years from 1250 to 1258 Fasli *(1842-50 AD) which includes land tax and other taxes*

like jalkar, bankar, pokhar, *tank, pond, wells, palm and date trees for a sum of Rs. 39/8/-.*

Promise to remit the *malguzari* of the *theka* as per details given in the text to the *ahl-i maash* every year crop afret crop and would not make any excuse on any ground. Declares that if he failed to pay the instalment in any year during the period of *theka* the *ahl-i maash* were free to cancel the *theka* and the *thekadar* would not have any claim for the remaining period of *theka* or the *ahl-i maash* can appoint *sazawal* for the realization of the revenue of the *theka* the salary of the *sazawal*, however would be borne out by him (the *thekadar*).

The document in Persian *shikasta* bears *sarnama Alif.*

(ACC. NO. 2531/20; Original; f1).

10 *Zilqada* 1258 AH (13 December 1842)

209. *Parwana* addressed to the *muqaddams* and *patwaris* of *mauza* Nizam Patta *pargana* Sanjrad. Expresses anxiety as they have not yet made contact with the *naib* of Raja Lachmi Narain. Instructs them to approach the said *naib* immediately and pay the *mal-i wajib* at the time of harvest and restore the village to the *jagirdars.*

The document in Persian *shikasta* bears *sarnama Alif* and the seal of Maharaja Chandulal Bahadur.

(ACC. NO. 2617/ 23; Original; f1).

1258 AH (date in seal) (1842-43)

210. Letter of younger sister of *Amir al-daulah* Muhammad Amir Khan to her brother (Nawwab *Amir al-daulah* Muhammad Amir Khan). Says that the articles of offerings meant for him has been deposited in the *toshaKhana.* Urges that the princess of the

palace may be directed to perform the rituals in proper manner so that the articles may be sent to them. Also says that if the palaces of Azad Begum become vacant it should not be given to her brothers as the houses at Mahesar are lying vacant Further says that if the *qiladar* sells his residential palace (the Haveli) she should be informed about its price so that the repair and renovation work may be done. Further refers her letter to Girdhari Lal *mutasaddi* of Deorhi seeking salary of her father Muhammad Bahadur Khan but received nothing. Requests to receive the distributed amount from the *sahukar* and send her. Also requests for the money assumed to her at the time of her departure.

The document in Persian *shikasta* bears the seal of the writer.

(ACC. NO. 2701/ 11; Original; f1).

1258 AH (date in seal) (1842- 43)

211. Letter of Muhammad Amir Khan's younger sister to her brother (Nawwab Amir al Daulah Muhammad Amir Khan. Refers to the letter of Girdhari Lal *mutassadi* of Deorhi informing that the amount meant for monthly distribution has been taken as loan by Panna Lal Seth and gave nothing to her (the writer). Further elaborates that earlier the said Seth had also embezzled Rs. 3000/- earlier and had fraudulently usurped Rs. 2200/- and obtained forged *tamassuk* under the seal of Muhammad Bahadur Khan. Requests to separate her monthly salary and send her *hindawi* after receiving from Seth Panna Lal. Also complains against Girdhari Lal who she had authorized to issue her, letter of her share of money but he neither reported the

matter to him nor prevented the said Seth from it. Requests to take action against the *mutasaddi* and also take back the authority letter containing amount.

The document in Persian *shikasta* bears the *sarnama Alif* and the seal of the writer.

(ACC. NO. 2701/ 12; Original; f1)

8 May 1843 212. *Rubakar-i Kachehri* of District Aligarh under the session of Mr. George Blunt, Collector of Aligarh. Refers to the letter of the Commissioner dated 3 May 1843 informong about the orders of the Governor General dated 9 April (1843) directing for the exemption of 12 *bighas* of garden land in village Ashrafpur Jalal *Pargana* Kol in favour of Amanat ali Khan the *muafidar* till the time trees are grown and to deduct the sum of Rs. 39/- the annual *jama* from the land of the villages and to return to the *muafidars* the revenue realization deposited in the treasury of the period of confiscation till the time of exemption. The Court gives orders to issue a *parwana* in the name of *tahsildar, pargana* Kol to prepare the revenue realization sheet of the said land from the time of its confiscation till the time of its exemption duly verified by the *qanungo* and *patwari* and submit the same in the court.

The document in Urdu *shikasta* executed on 8 *anna* punch marked stamp paper bears bilingual seal of Aligarh Collectorate in Hindi and Persian.

(ACC. NO. 1042; Copy; f1).

8 May 1843 213. Court order issued to Pandit Pitam Narain officiating *tahsildar* of Kol (Aligarh). Refers to the letter of the Commissioner dated 3

May 1843 informing about the orders of the Governor General dated 9 April (1843) directing for the exemption of 12 *bighas* of garden land in villages Ashrafpur Jalal *pargana* Kol in favour of Amanat Ali Khan the *muafidar* till the time trees are grown and to deduct the sum of Rs. 39/- the annual *jama* from the land of the villages and to return to the *muafidars* the revenue realization deposited in the treasury of the period of confiscation till the time of exemption. Directs him that the said land may be kept exempted and to prepare the revenue realisation sheet of the said land from the time of its confiscation till the time of its exemption deposited in the *kachehri* of *Tahsil* duly verified by the *qanungo* and *patwari* and submit the same in the court.

The document in Urdu *shikasta* executed on 8 *anna* punch marked stamp paper bears a bilingual seal of Aligarh Collector in Hindi and Urdu.

(ACC. NO. 1041; Copy; f1).

1 *Jeth* 1900 *Samvat* (30 May 1843) 214. *Parwana* issued to Khuda Bakhsh. Informs that 4 *bighas* of *aimma* land adjacent to Pindi has been in assignment of Baba Ganesh Dangawala as *dharamarth*. Directs him for confirmation of the aforesaid grant in his favour.

The document in Persian *shikasta* bears *sarnama Alif* and a dim seal.

(ACC. NO. 2580/ 1; Original; f1).

9 June 1843 215. *Rubakar-i Kachehri* in respect of investigation of *Lakhiraj* land of District Aligarh under the session of R. Hutun, Deputy Collector with regard to a case filed by the government against Amanat Ali Khan for

resumption of 6 *anna* out of 166 *bighas* and 10 *biswas* land situated at *qasba* and *pargana* Kol. The Court after a thorough deliberation rectified the decision of the Special Dy. Collector, dated 14 May 1842 keeping exempted 2 *bigha* 18 *biswa* land out of 18 *bigha* 5 *biswa* situated at Delhi Darwaza from the Government revenue assessment till the trees are grown up. In this perspective, the Court orders that the land comprising 11 *bigha* and 4 *biswa* measured land may be taxed by the Government on the basis of 10 *anas* and the defendant may be given 6 *anna* from the treasury of the Government. At the same time a tax reduction of 6 *anas* from the total *jama* of revenue assessment may be executed with the consent of *Sadr* of Revenue Board. The Court further orders to send the copy of the *rubakari* to the Commissioner, Northern Part of Doab as well as the Collector of the District for the implementation of the order.

The document in Urdu *shikasta* bears a trilingual seal of the court of Special Deputy Collector of Aligarh in Urdu, Hindi and English.

(ACC. NO. 1045; Copy;ff4).

16 June 1843 216. *Rubakar-i kachehri* under the session of George Blunt Collector of District Aligarh. Refers to the letter of the Commissioner dated 12 June 1843 informing that the Governor General has sent the map for the disposal of the cases of *lakhiraj* by the Special Commissioner for the perusal of *Sadr* Board Revenue who directed the Collector to place orders with regard to relinquishment of the land. Keeping in

view the directives of the Board of Revenue, the Court issued orders for the issuance of *parwana-i waguzasht* (relinquishment order) to the *tahsildars* of *pargana* Atrauli and Kol to relinquish the *muafi* land on perpetual basis at Kandauli and *Qasba* Kol in favour of Muhammad Bakhsh and Amanat Ali Khan till life as per the *tahqiqat-i qanun* of 19 of 1810. Directs to issue copy of the *rubakar* to the Commissioner for information.

The document in Urdu *shikasta* executed on punch marked stamp paper of 8 *anna* bears a bilingual seal of *kachehri* Aligarh in Urdu and Hindi.

(ACC. NO. 1046;Copy;f1).

29 July 1843 217. *Rubakar-i Muhkama-i* Commissionary of Northern Doab under the session of G. F. Franco in respect of a case by the Government against Amanat Ali for the resumption of 6 *anna* from 166 *bighas* and 10 *biswas* of land situated at *qasba* Kol. Refers to the orders of the Dy. Collector in charge *maafi* District Aligarh dated 9 June for taking away 10 *anna* by the government and paying 6 *anna* from 21 *Bigha,* 4 *biswa* to the defendant from the treasury on perpetual basis. Further refers to the orders of Special Deputy Collector for the exemption of 87 *Bigha* 18 *Biswa* measured land from the revenue till the trees are grown. The Court observes that its opinion is in accordance to the Dy. Collector provided the same is approved by the *Sadr* Board Revenue. The Court therefore orders that the case along with the copy of *rubakar* may be sent to the *Sadr* Board Revenue for the issuance of order and that orders for

the relinquishment may be kept pending till their orders are received. Adds that since the orders of the Secretary *Sadr* Board dated 15 August has been received, this office issues orders for the relinquishment of the said land.

The document in Urdu *shikasta* bears a bilingual seal of the Court of District Aligarh. The document also bears orders for the *tahsildar* in this regard.

(ACC. NO. 1047;Copy;f1).

30 *Rajab* 1259 AH (in text) (26 August 1843)

218. News-report from the *Deorhi* of Mr. Thomas Metcalf, *Nazim* of Delhi w.e.f. 30 *Rajab* 1259 to 6 *Shaban* 1259 AH (26 August 1843 to 1 October).

Reports about the petition of Abdul Haque *thekadar* against Salik Ram *Khazanchi* about *bagh-i nazir* in *dargah* Qutub Sahib which was given on *theka* by Bala Bai *Sahiba* to him (Abdul Haque) and then was sold to Salik Ram for Rs. 280/- even before the end of *theka*. Also reports about a petition to the Collector Martin Kens from an anonymous person in respect of bribe taken by Ghulam Rasul Khan *Kotwal* from Salik Ram *Khazanchi*. Further reports the Nawwab Governor's recommendation for reduction by ¼ the period of imprisonment of all kinds of prisoners and for improvement in the quality of food of life imprisoned prisoners and for a chain only in their legs. The order was issued to be effective from 1 October. Reports the complaints of Nathwa Tilanga and others against atrocities of Hamid Ali Khan and Nawwab Bahadur Jang Khan and issuance of orders against them. Also records the arrival of Taj Muhammad having *shuqqa* of *Huzur* Anwar along with three pieces of newspapers for Lt. Governor of Akbarabad and *Sahib Kalan* (Thomas Metcalf). Also reports the visit of Maulawi Sadr al-Din, *Sadr al-Sudur* reporting about the departure of Session Judge of Saharanpur to England and appointment of Registrar in his place. Also reports General Sir Hugh Gough's entry in Calcutta and salute of 17 guns to him and Nawwab Governor's order for his next visit to Hindustan in the month of October.

Further reports about the charge taken by General Hugh Gough of the army of Hindustan, departure of Maddock towards Ceylon for change of climate. Reports about the death of *Rani* of Raja Balwant Singh. Records the news coming from Qandahar about prince Safdar Jang son of Shah Shuja al-Mulk who is facing atrocities. Also reports that the ruler of Qandahar is arresting those who have served the Company. As a result, many inhabitants of Qandahar have sheltered in Hyderabad and Sindh under Company Government.

Reports about the letter of Mr. Clark, Lieutenant Governor Akbarabad with regard to a request of Yaqub Ali Khan for the grant of his father's title to him in return his offer of his income of one year from the said *jagir* as *nazrana*. Martin Kens the Collector and Magistrate's order to Ghulam Rasul the deposed *Kotwal* for paying the surety of Rs. 4000/- for a missing orphan child aged ten.

The document in Persian *shikasta* bears *sarnama Alif*.

(ACC. NO. 2733/ 52; Original; ff2).

3 *Ramazan* 1259 AH/ 20 *As* (*Asin*) 1251 *Fasli* (27 September 1843)	219.	*Fautinama* and *wirasatnama* asking for the testimony from the general public with regard to the *wirasatnama* of Shaikh Tufail Ali residents and *malguzar* of village Daulatpur Mianwan *pargana* Okri District Bihar of Shaikh Tufail Ali residents and *malguzar* of village Daulatpur Mianwan *pargana* Okri District Bihar who died on 1 *Rajab* 1249 AH/17 *Sawan* 1257 *Fasli* who left behind his two sons, Shaikh Muhammad Hasan, Shaikh Inayat Karim and *Mst.* Kamalan, daughter and *Mst* Amiran wife were the inheritors of al his shares movable and immovable property and *malguzari* of Daulatpur Mianwan besides other *mauzas* such as Muhammadpur, Lodipur, Antiapur, Nurpur etc. etc. besides the properties which *Mst.* Amiran is in possession as her *mahr* have been paying land revenue to the Company Government. The document in Persian *Shikasta* bears *sarnama Alif* and signature and seal of Shaikh Yar Ali as witness besides signatures of other witnesses. **(ACC. NO. 2531/21; Original; f1).**
21 October 1843/13 *Kartik* 1251 *Fasli*/26 *Ramadan* 1259 AH	220.	*Bainama* executed by Tahawwur Khan, son of Jamiat Khan resident of village Makhdumpur, Bukanwan *pargana* Okri District Bihar. States that he has sold the six share out of 2 *biswa zamin-i malikana* from *mauza* Lanchina from the beginning of 1251 *Fasli* to Bibi Amiran wife of late Shaikh Tufail Ali for a sum of Re. 1/- and four *annas* and has received the amount in full. The document in Persian *Shikasta* executed on punch marked stamp paper

of two *anna* bears a seal in Devnagri and signature of the executant and witnesses in Persian and Devnagti.

(ACC. NO. 2531/22; Copy; f1).

29 February 1844/ 20 *Phagun* 1251 *Amli* 221. Judgement of the *Adalat-i Commissioner* under the session of Colonel Cardew, Special Commissioner on the appeal made by the government against Mahant Sudarshan Das *chela* of Mahant Rajgopal Das resident of Kalika Debi Sai in respect of the decision of Deputy Collector, Cuttack for waiving of land tax on 820/ 23 *maan* from *lakhiraj* land situated in *mauza* Arsandhu and Sadiqabad *pargana* Kundes. The Court dismissed the case and rectified the decision of the Deputy Collector, Cuttack, dated 24 december 1839 besides, imposed the expenses of the judgement on the appellant (the Government).

The document in Urdu *shikasta* bears the seal of the Court of Commissioner, District Cuttack.

(ACC. NO. 2693/ 6; Copy; f1).

12 *Chait* 1901 (*Samvat*) (31 March 1844) 222. Letter to Jawahar Singh. Directs him to send following items through Diwan Lodan and Dhakni as soon as he receives the letter (*parwana*) to be presented to the Company Government. The items are as a cash amount of Rs. 5 lakh, jewellery, 4 horses, 2 cannons, 10 bullock carts from Diwan Hari Chand etc.

The document in Persian *shikasta* bears *sarnama Sri Ramjeo Sahai.*

(ACC. NO. 2385/ 7; Photocopy; f1).

18 *Chait* 1901 (*Samvat*) (6 April 1844) 223. Letter to Jawahar Singh. Acknowledges receipt of his letter besides the cash remitted by him (the addressee). Directs

to supply horses also. Forbids to supply the material asked for by Raj Singh. Also directs him to depute two guards of Sahankan at Poni (Pune) for Wazir Baka. Also directs to instruct the said Wazir to take care of the guards.

The document is in Persian *shikasta*.

(ACC. NO. 2385/8; Photocopy; f1)

22 April 1844 224. Letter from Khalsa Darbar addressed (to the Resident). Expressing pleasure on the cordial relations subsisting between the two Governments (Sarkar) hopes that it would get further strengthened. Further refers about the recent happening which has been communicated to him through his *wakil* Rai Kishan Chand from Pattan. Elaborates that Raja Hira Singh who was raised to the throne of *Khalsa* proved unworthy man and his policy was against the tenets of the khalsa. Ultimately the Sarbat Khalsa decided to remove him from the seat but he fled away and was later on captured by Khalsa and then killed. Informs that the state is run quite effectively with complete cooperation of Sarbat Khalsa.

The document in Persian *shikasta* bears *sarnama Alif* and *Ba-Fazl-i Sri Akalpurakhji*.

(ACC. NO. 228; Original; f1).

22 April 1844/12 *Baisakh* 1251 *Amli* 225. Judgement of *Adalat-i Commissioner* under the session of Col. Cardew, Special Commissioner of District Cuttack under Regulation 3 of 1828 AD on the appeal made by Mahant Sudarshan Das *chela* of late Mahant Raj Gopal Das of Kalika Debi Sai against the decision of the Deputy Collector in respect of imposition of *khiraj*

on 937/ 21, 15 *maan* land of Baikunthan Amrit Manohi situated in village Puran with mango garden in *taalluqa* Kachandar *pargana* Chaubis kuki. The Court dismissed the case and upheld the decision of the Deputy Collector dated 26 April 1839 besides imposed the expense of the court on the appellant.

The document in Urdu *shikasta* bears the seal of the Court of Commissioner, District Cuttack.

(ACC. NO. 2693/ 7; Copy; f1).

24 May 1844/ 13 *Jeth* 1251 *Amli*

226. Judgement of *Adalat-i Commissioner* Cuttack under the session of Col. Cardew, Special Commissioner on the appeal made by Mahant Sudarshan Das resident of Buklai *pargana* Panchas against the decision of the Deputy Collector in respect of imposition of *Khiraj* on 12. 5. 9 *maan* of *lakhiraj* land situated in village Girailu and Maharu, *pargana* Purab Duwa (?). The court dismissed the case and rectified the judgement of Deputy Collector dated 15 March 1842 and also imposed the expenses of the court on the appellant. The court also directs that if the appellant has any claim of ownership on the disputed land he should apply in the *Adalat-i Diwani.*

The document in Urdu *shikasta* bears the seal of the court of Commissioner, Distirct Cuttack.

(ACC. NO. 2693/ 8; Copy; f1).

21 *Jumada* I 1260 AH (8 June 1844)

227. *Hukmnama* under the seal of Nawwab Munawwar al-Daulah Ahmad Ali Khan (of Awadh) addressed to Saiyid Ahmad *Tahsildar qasba* Salon etc. Refers the petition submitted by Saiyid Muhammad resident of *qasba* Jais complaing not getting *nankar*

and also execessive demands and *bhaint* by him (the addressee) besides devastation of Qasimpur a zamindari villageof the petitioner by the mischievous elements of the region. Orders him to take necessary steps to restore the *nankar* to him and to desist from execessive demands and to prevent the miscreants forcing them to return the amassed money to the petitioner and send the *razinama* obtaining from the petitioner and also obtain a *muchalka*.

The document in Persian *shikasta* bears the attestation seal of Saiyid Ali Husain.

(ACC. NO. 2042; Copy; f1).

10 July 1844 228. Judgement of the Court of Munsif of Mathura city in respect of the case filed by Brij Nath Gosain (resident of Bindraban) *Mukthar* of Hari Kishan Gosain, *Gaddi-nashin* of Govind Devji temple (resident of Bindraban) against the property of late Anjha Nath Jogi of Bindraban and his heirs Harnya Golnath, Charanji Nath and Khushhali Nath for the payment of 113 *Kaldars* outstanding w.e.f. *Aghan* 1893 *Samvat* till date as the rent of the shops owned by the said temple. The heirs of late Anjha Nath, the defendants accepted before the Judge the claim of the said outstanding amount and promised to pay the amount within one month. In view of this, the Court passed decree of. 113/- *kaldar* along with the expenses of the Court incurred by the claimants upon the defendants with interest.

The slightly damaged document in Urdu executed on 12 *anna* stamp paper bears *sarnama Alif* and two seals of the Court of Agra and Mathura.

(ACC. NO. 2712/ 13; Copy; f1).

4 *Rajab* 1260 AH (20 July 1844)

229. *Qaulnama* issued by Raja Jiwant Ram Bahadur in favour of Raja Kalwah Kolan Lachmi Narsimha Rao Deshmukh of *pargana* Madhera *sarkar* Khammamat *suba* Farkhundabunyad Haiderabad. Informs that considering his request to administer and inhabitate the aforesaid *taalluqa, the* same has been granted to him besides the *mal-o sair, kalali, muhtarfa, sardrakhti, amrai* except *rasum* and *deha* from beginning of 1254 *Fasli* against the payment of Rs. 32501/-. annually. Directs him to make efforts at best in the inhabitation of all the populace of the said villages and deposit the aforesaid amount in installments in the government treasury.

The document in Persian *shikasta* bears *sarnama Alif* and the seal of Raja Jiwant Ram Bahadur.

(ACC. NO. 2680/ 41; Original; f1).

7 *Rajab* 1260 AH (23 July 1844)

230. *Parwana* of Raja Ram Bakhsh to Raja Lachmi Narain. Informs him that it has come to his notice that Jograj Deshpandya of *pargana* Haveli Hyderabad is reluctant in depositing the *rasum-i deshpandiagiri* of *mauza* Malkar Hasangiri *ilaqa* Tarambak since 1253 *Fasli*. Orders him to get deposited the *rusum-i siri etc.* in the *sarkar* without delay and obtain receipt accordingly to avoid further complaints in future

The document in Persian *nastaliq* bears *sarnama Alif* and the seal of Raja Ram Bakhsh (the writer) on the cover with the jist of document.

(ACC. NO. 2535/9; Original; ff2).

2 August 1844/20 *Sawan*

231. Judgement of *Adalat-i Commissioner* District Cuttack under the session of Col.

1251 *Amli* — Cardew, Special Commissioner under Regulation No. 3 of 1828 on the appeal made by Sudarshan Das of Buklai *pargana* Panchas against the decision of Deputy Collector in respect of imposition of *Khiraj* on 3. 14. 15 *maan* of *lakhiraj* land situated in village Sharda *pargana* Panchas. The Court dismissed the case and upheld the decision of Deputy Collector dated 29 September 1841 besides, imposed the expenses of the Court on the appellant.

The document in Urdu *shikasta* bears the seal of the Court of Commissioner, Distirct Cuttack.

(ACC. NO. 2693/ 9; Copy; f1).

9 *Shaban* 1260 AH (24 August 1844) — 232. Receipt executed by Saiyid Muhammad Nazir Ali Khan son of Anwar Ali Khan of *qasba* Amroha. Certifies that he has got back his 20 *biswas dar-o -bast* (in entirety) *muafi* and 20 *biswa dar-o-bast 'Zamindari'* land along with *milk* and garden in village Dhatura *amla* belonging to *pargana* Amroha which was mortgaged to Sahu Balram, son of Jauhar Mal, resident of *qasba* Amroha in the beginning of *Kharif* crop 1252 *Fasli* for a sum of Rs. 3400/-.

The document in Persian *Shikasta* is written on a stamp paper. It bears *sarnama innahu* with the seal of the executant besides several seals and signatures of the witnesses.

(ACC. NO. 2533/ 2; Original; f1).

11 September 1844/ 29 *Bhadon* 1251 *Amli* — 233. Judgement of *Adalat-i Commissioner* under the session of Col. Cardew Special Commissioner District Cuttack vide Regulation 3 of 1828 on the appeal made by Mahant Sudarshan Das *chela* of late

Mahant Raj Gopal Das of Kalika Debi Sai against the decision of Deputy Collector in respect of imposition of *Khiraj* on 268/ 8. 7 *maan lakhiraj* land situated in *mauza* Kasabander *pargana* Kotrabang (?). The court dismissed the case and rectified the decision of Deputy Collector dated 20 April1839. The Court also imposed the court expenses on the appellant.

The document in Urdu *shikasta* bears the seal of the Court of Commissioner, District Cuttack.

(ACC. NO. 2693/ 10;Copy; f1)

21 September 1844 — 234. Letter of Captain Chyrles Aunston Burtan, Officiating Agent at Haroti to Saiyid Aulad Husain. Acknowledges his letter regarding the poverty of Bahlan Badawa and his arrest on the charge of looting property of Muhammad Beg Wilayati and his release subsequently. Refers his earlier *parwana* to him to get him released on bail. Assumes that probably, on the basis of that *parwana* he would have been released.

The document in Persian *shikasta* bears *sarnama* Alif.

(ACC. NO. 2701/ 14; Original; f1).

21 September 1844 (date in text) — 235. Letter of Qalander Ali Khan to Nawwab Wazir. Refers his two letters regarding *malsatta.* States that on 21 September 1844 he was called by Captain Alexander Nixon Louis and asked him whether he had demanded *malsatta* from Nawwab Sahib. He replied that he had made a request to him but got no response. Adds that then he again directed him to make a request for the *malsatta.* Accordingly, requests him (addressee) for the *malsatta* which is very

essential. Also informs about six hundred cattle of *mauza* Kishanpura with *mauza* Satola *ilaqa* Manwar. Requests him to mention in his letter seven more cows of *mauza* Kishanpura with *mauza ilaqa* Raj Manwar as a proven in the *muhkama* of Agent. Hopes that the above mentioned cattle would be obtained from the said *ilaqa*. Requests for early reply to him to proceed further.

The document in Persian *shikasta* bears *sarnama Alif.*

(ACC. NO. 2701/ 15; Original; f1).

25 September 1844/ 12 *Asin* 1252 *Amli*

236. Judgement of *Adalat-i Commissioner* (special) under the session of Col. Cardew, Special Commissioner, District Cuttack (vide Regulation 3 of 1828) on the appeal made by Radhu Adhikari Shivant, resident of Patipadha (?) *pargana* Khudo Kalat in respect of the imposition of *Khiraj* on 21 *maan* of *lakhiraj Devotar* land in Patipadha (?) *taalluqa* Gobind Prasad *pargana* Khudokalat. The Court dismissed the case and upheld the judgement of the Deputy Collector dated 5 November 1841 besides, imposed the court expenses on the appellant.

The document in Urdu *shikasta* bears the seal of the Court of Commissioner, District Cuttack.

(ACC. NO. 2693/ 11; Copy; f1).

7 October 1844/ 24 *Asin* 1252 *Amli*

237. Judgement of *Adalat-i Commissioner* (special) under the session of Col. Cardew, Special Commissioner District Cuttack under Regulation 3 of 1828 on the appeal made by the Government against Mahant Sudarshan Das *chela* Mahant Raj Gopal Das of Kalika Debi in respect of imposition

of *Khiraj* on 140 *maan* land out of 152. 11. 7 *maan lakhiraj* land of Amrit Manohi from 22 villages as mentioned in the text of *pargana* Korpu (?). The appeal was dismissed and the Court upheld the judgment of Deputy Collector dated 8 January 1842. The Court also issued orders to recover the court expenses from the appellant and with regard to the specification of land and the fee of *Mukhtar* a sum of Rs. 3/- will have to be borne by the respondent.

The document in Urdu *Shikasta* bears the seal of the Court of Commissioner District Cuttack.

(ACC. NO. 2693/ 12; Copy; f1).

7 October 1844/24 *Asin* 1252 *Amli*

238. Judgement of *Adalat-i Commissioner* under the session of Col. Cardew of District Cuttack under Regulation 3 of 1828 on the appeal made by the Government against Mahant Sudarshan Das *chela* Mahant Raj Gopal Das of Kalka Debi in respect of imposition of *Khiraj* on 210. 19. 13 *maan* of *lakhiraj* land out of 322/ 14/ 4 *maan* of *lakhiraj* land of Amrit Manohi from 21 villages of *pargana* Panchas. The appeal was dismissed and the Court upheld the judgment of the Deputy Collector dated 6 November 1841. The Court also issued orders to bear the expenses of the court by the appellant. With regard to specification of land and fee of the *mukhtar* a sum of Rs. 4/ would be paid by the respondent.

The document in Urdu *shikasta* bears the seal of the Court of Commissioner District, Cuttack.

(ACC. NO. 2693/ 13; Copy; f1).

8 *Asoj* 1901 *Samvat* (19 October 1844)

239. Letter to Jawahar Singh. Expresses confidence in him. Says that if he comes to Punjab he should go on the pilgrimage of the sacred places and if he desires to stay on reciting *Pothi* that too is acceptable. As a matter of fact in Punjab he would be at his own will to act upon. Assure that there would be no interference by Hira Singh in his affairs as communicated by the agencies.

The document in Persian *shikasta* bears *sarnama* Sri Ramjeo Sahai.

(ACC. NO. 2385/ 9; Photocopy; f1).

22 October 1844

240. Letter from Khalsa Darbar to (the Resident). Acknowledges receipt of his letter. Expresses pleasure on the friendly relations established between the two Governments. Referring to the treasury of late Raja Suchit Singh which is in the possession of Company Government hopes that it is fully safe and will surely reach to the rightful owner. Elaborates that since Raja Suchit Singh had been a subservient of khalsa and thus whatever property he had earned with the grace of Khalsaji and his entire property including his house should reach to the Khalsa darbar in the first instance and from there as per the rule and tenets of the khalsaji should reach in the hands of the rightful owner. Adds that none even the *Rani* (wife of late Raja) should be allowed to obtain anything from the said property as it would be against the interest of the *Khalsa*.

The illuminated document in Persian *Shikasta* bears *sarnama Alif* and *Bafazl-i Sri Akal Purakhji.*

(ACC. NO. 233; Original; f1).

21 *Shawwal* 1260 AH (3 November 1844)

241. *Parwana* of Raja Ram Bakhsh Bahadur to the *Naiks* etc. of *ilaqa* Manwari Palam *pargana* Sanjrad (?) *sarkar* Muhammad-nagar. Informs that after the dismissal of Qadir Khan, *ilaqa* Manwari Palam has been granted to Lachmi Narain. Instructs them (the twelve *naiks*) to contact him and show their allegiance to the Government.

The document in Persian *Nastaliq* bears *sarnama Alif* and the seal of Raja Ram Bakhsh Bahadur (the writer).

(ACC. NO. 2617/ 20; Original; f1).

6 *Kartik* 1901 (*Samvat*) (15 November 1844)

242. *Iqrarnama* executed between Raja Gulab Singh and Jawahar Singh on behalf of Hira Singh with regard to the settlement of the differences arose between the two (by oaths of Shiv Nathji, Guru Granth Sahabji, Shri Gitaji, Shri Bishan Harnamji, Shri Debiji Tarkataji, Baba Sahib Prem Dasji, Pandit Charan Das, Pandit Ram Kishan). It contains six clauses the foremost (i) is that the dignity, honour and pleasure of Hira Singh would be taken the utmost care. (ii) that all landed property besides cash and kind whatever they have inherited from Raja Suchit Singh which have been distributed between the two, none of the two, would claim more than that. (iii) that whatever is due to the Company Government they would adhere to it. (iv) that the contingent of Chhatar Singh and others besides the troops maintained by Raja Singh, their *jagir* and other necessities would be fulfilled as per the order.

The document in Persian *shikasta* bears *sarnama* Sri Ramjeo Sahai and has been attested by Assistant Resident Kashmir.

(ACC. NO. 2385/ 10; Copy; ff2).

1260 AH (1844) 243. *Parwana* of Raja Ram Bakhsh Bahadur to the employees of the government at Nirkabli, *pargana* Udaimiri, *Sarkar* Bhongir. Informs that following the dismissal of Qadir Khan the *siri* and *rusum* etc. *haqq-i lawazima zabti* of Manwari in *ilaqa* Udaimiri etc. has been assigned to Raja Lachmi Narain. Instructs them to present themselves in the services of the *Naib* of *Sarkar*.

The document in Persian *shikasta* bears *sarnama Alif* and the seal of the writer.

(ACC. NO. 2618/ 26; Original; f1).

14 *Muharam* 1261 AH (23 January 1845) 244. *Parwana* of Raja Ram Bakhsh Bahadur to Raja Lachmi Narain. Informs that a sum of Rs. 5250/- has been fixed for payment of monthly salary of contingent of the platoon etc. of Kangar, Amozgar, Baldevgar, Bholgar and other Gosains out of the *mahsul* of 1254 *Fasli* of *Pargana* Patan Khurd *Sarkar* Muhammadnagar *suba* Farkhundabunyad, Hyderabad in lieu of the Manwari. Directs for the payment of the same in three installments of Rs. 1750 each.

The document in Persian *nastaliq* bears *sarnama Alif* while the cover contains the name of the addressee and an incomplete seal of Raja Ram Bakhsh Bahadur with the jist of the document.

(ACC. NO. 2617/19; Original; ff2).

4 *Safar* 1261 AH (12 February 1845) 245. *Tamassuk-i Hazir Zamini* executed by Mahapal Singh *Malguzar* of village Bahadurpur. Stands surety to produce Muzaffar Khan, *Muqaddam* of village Barkhundarpur (?) before the *ahalkar* of Mir Zakir Husain as and when required and if

he failed to do so he would be held responsible.

The document in Persian shikasta bears sarnama Innahu and signatures of the executant and witnesses.

(ACC. NO. 2100; Original; f1).

19 *Safar* 1261 AH (27 February 1845)

246. Letter to .... Refers to the non - receipt of the *wajh-i rusum* of *despandiagiri* from Yograj Tarang *deshpandia* of *mauza* Malkar Jangiri *pargana* Haveli Muhammadnagar etc. for 1254 *Fasli*. Instructs to send the *rusum* as per the rule and obtain the receipt from the *muqaddam* and *patwari*. Further instructs to obtain the receipts of the *rusum* from 1255 *Fasli* every year, crop after crop and let allow other perqisites and demands, *man* and *pan* and signature etc. and be careful of not giving any chance of any complaint in future.

The document in Persian *nastaliq* bears *sarnama Alif* while the additional page contains the gist and date.

(ACC. NO. 2617/ 18; Original; ff2).

7 April 1845/ 27 *Chait* 1252 *Amli*

247. Judgement of *Adalat-i commissioner* under the session of John William Templer, District Cuttack under Regulation 3 of 1828 on the appeal made by Mahant Sudarshan Das *chela* of late Mahant Raj Gopal Das, resident of Kalika Debi Sai against the Government in respect of imposition of taxes on 108. 18. 12 *maan* of *lakhiraj* land of Amrit Manohi situated in village Alandaharha *taalluqa* Jagannathpur, *pargana* Puri Dudwai (?). The judgement was passed in favour of the appellant cancelling the order of the Deputy Collector and restoring the said *lakhiraj* land to the appellant.

The Court also issued order to restore the land confiscated by the government and to return the amount realized after the order of Deputy Collector to the appellant with interest @ Rs. 6/-% till the final payment.

The document in Urdu *shikasta* bears a seal of the Court of Commissioner, District Cuttack.

(ACC. NO. 2693/ 14; Copy; f1).

1 *Rabi* II 1261 AH (9 April 1845) 248. *Bainama* and *qabz al-wasul* executed by Saiyid Nasir al-Din, Saiyid Nasir Ali, Saiyid Faiz Ali sons of Saiyid Inayat Ali residents of *qasba* Amroha, *Sarkar* Sambhal, *Suba* Shahjahanabad in respect of 2 *biswas*, 10 *biswansi* of *zamindari* together with the garden land and *khera* out of 20 *biswas* in entirety situated in village Majhauli, and 18¾ *biswansi* along with garden land, *mazrua* of Rasulpur belonging to the said *pargana* with all the boundaries and *dakhili* and *khariji* rights has been sold to Saiyid Wilayat Ali for a sum of Rs. 46/10 and received the amount in full from the vendee.

The document in Persian *shikasta* bears *sarnama Alif* and the seals and signatures of the executants as well as the departmental endorsement in Persian and Devnagri on the reverse.

(ACC. NO. 2533/ 17; Original; f1).

6 *Jeth* 1902 *(Samvat)* (13 April 1845) 249. Letter to Jawahar Singh. Informs him that the instalment of the sum of Rupees five lakh sent through Shyam Singh has not been received there. Directs him to send Shyam Singh immediately along with the said amount. Says that he can either remit

the amount to him in gold and cash and if it is not possible he could remit the amount as he could.

The document in Persian *shikasta* bears *sarnama Sri Ramjeo Sahai.*

(ACC. NO. 2385/ 11; Photocopy; f1).

24 April 1845/14 *Baisakh* 1252 *Amli*

250. Judgment of *Aadalat-i Commissioner* (special) District Cuttack under the session of John William Templer vide Regulation 3 of 1828 on the appeal made by Mahant Sudarshan Das against the Government in respect of imposition of taxes on 20. 9 *maan lakhiraj* land of Amrit Manohi in village Khamang Sasan *pargana* Kundesh.

The court issued decree in favour of the appellant cancelling the order of Deputy Collector dated 9 September 1839 and restoring the said *lakhiraj* land in favour of the said Mahant. The court also issued orders to restore the land confiscated by the Government and to return the amount realized from the confiscated land to the appellant with the interest @ Rs. 6/-% till the final payment is made.

The document in Urdu *shikasta* bears a seal of the Court of Commissioner, District Cuttack.

(ACC. NO. 2693/15; Copy; f1).

27 *Rabi* II 1261 AH (5 May 1845)

251. Letter from Radhe Misr, resident of *mauza* Jednapur *ilaqa* Ramnagar. Reports that in accordance to the *rubakari* the testimony of Gopal Dubey resident of Raipur *ilaqa* Ramnagar, Malik Singh and Lal Singh, the witnesses were verified before Mansa Singh *harkara* which did not sustain and the *sazawal* too made inquiry into the statement of the witnesses and now the matter is before him.

The document is in Persian *shikasta* bears the seal of the writer.

(ACC. NO. 2753/ 6; Original; f1).

8 *Jumada* I 1261 AH (15 May 1845)

252. *Arzi* of *Mst.* Najm al-Nisa of *qasba* Rudauli to *zill-i subhani* (Nawwab of Awadh). States that after the death of her husband and father she inherited all their property which is in her possession without any co-sharer and as such *nazr-o-niaz* and property in cash and kind of shrine Hazrat Shah Abd al-Haque belongs to her, being share of her father and husband and she distributes it as she wishes. Complains against Talib Ahmad, Nazir Ahmad, Hasan Ahmad - her husband's brothers - who have occupied the shrine by force and captured all its *nazr-o-niaz* etc. and has ousted her from the shrine and threatens to eliminate her. Requests to send *sazawal* to arrest them along with the *nazr-o-niaz* and seeks justice.

The document in Persian *shikasta* bears *sarnama Innahu* and the seal of the petitioner.

(ACC. NO. 2753/ 7; Original; f1).

23 *Baisakh* 1253 *Fasli* (1261AH) May 1845

253. Letter of Maharaja Amar Singh Deo Bahadur to Chheta Bijuk Nayak Sangari, Sardar Bandla Badlath Parosi Jiu(?). Acknowledges the receipt of his letter through Loknath Misr soliciting the amount of village Khadgaon. Communicates that as per the records a sum of Rs. 5/- for 1252 *Fasli* and Rs. 5/- for 1253 *Fasli* on account of *malguzari* of the aforesaid village is unpaid and being remitted through Loknath Misr and the same may be acknowledged.

The document in Urdu *shikasta* bears *sarnama Innahu* and bilingual seal and signature of the writer;

(ACC. NO. 2767/ 22;Photocopy; f1).

5 July 1845/ 24 *Asar* (?) 1252 *Amli*

254. Judgement of *Adalat-i Commissioner* under the session of John William Templer, District Cuttack vide Regulation 3 of 1828 on the appeal made by Mahant Sudarshan Das, resident of Kalika Debi Sai against the decision of the Deputy Collector in respect of imposition of taxes on 14. 15. 13 *maan* of *lakhiraj* land of Amrit Manohi in village Maharna *pargana* Balkhand (?).

The Court dismissed the case and upheld the judgment of Deputy Collector dated 5 September1840. The Court also issued order to bear the expenses of the Court by the appellant.

The document in Urdu *shikasta* bears the seal of the Court of Commissioner, District Cuttack.

(ACC. NO. 2693/ 16; Copy; f1)

8 *Har (Asarh)* 1902 *Samvat* (12 July 1845)

255. Letter to Muri Chand. Orders for the continuation of 30 *bighas* of land yielding Rs. 30/- per annum in favour of Baba Ganeshgar on account of *dharmarth* for his expenditure, crop after crop and year after year.

The document in Persian *shikasta* bears *sarnama Alif* and a seal of Misr Bhagwan Sahai.

(ACC. NO. 2580/ 80; Original; f1).

13 *Har* (*Asar*) 1902 *Samvat* (17 July 1845)

256. Letter to Bakhshi Hari Singh. Directs him to assign a village yielding an annual income of Rs. 300/- to Bakhshi Gur Narain in lieu of the *jagir* previously assigned to Bakhshi Lachman Narain from the

beginning of *Rabi* crop 1902 on account of *dharmarth* and to obtain its receipt so that the said amount may be adjusted as per the receipt.

The document is in Persian *shikasta*.

(ACC. NO. 2398/ 2; Original; f1).

2 *Shaban* 1261 AH (6 August 1845)

257. Cover of the document with the seal of Raja Kishan Singh Bahadur addressed to Raja Ram Bakhsh Bahadur bearing date 2 *Shaban* 1261 AH (6 August 1845).

(ACC. NO. 2535/ 8; Original; f1).

13 August 1845 (date in text)

258. *Iqrarnama* executed by Saiyid Mardan Ali, Saiyid Niyaz Ali and *Mst*. Azim al-Nisa and others. Referring to the orders of the Collector, District Moradabad with regard to the fixation of a sum of Rs. 20/-as *jama* for 15 *biswansi* land comprising *Mazbuta* as well as *toufir* situated in *mauza* Lalitpur, they, in view of the *Parwana* dated 7 March 1845 have agreed to pay the aforesaid *jama* until the *bandobast* of *khalsa* and until the renewal of *bandobast deh* on the following terms and conditions: -

1 That the executants have promised to deposit the stipulated amount @ Re1/- per hundred in regular instalments in Government treasury through Saiyid Mardan Ali and Saiyid Ali Shah (*lambardars*)without getting fixed the *lambardari* rights.

2 That the revenue realization of the produce from the cultivator shall be done as per the settlement given by the *patwari* and if any additional cultivation is made by the cultivator, the realization of the produce shall be made as per the mutual agreement between the cultivator and them.

3 That the preemption right in respect of purchase shall be recognized etc. etc.

4 That there will be no violation of the settlement, the information of which will be given to the *Kachehri Tahsil* through *Patwari*.

The document in Urdu *shikasta* written on eight *anna* stamp paper bears the signatures of the executants and witnesses.

(ACC. NO. 2533/ 48; Original; f1).

2 *Bhadun* 1902 *Samvat* (3 September 1845)

259. Letter to Bakhshi Gur Narain. Tells that sometimes back he along with 100 *Zambura was* deployed towards Ank (?)from where he has not yet sent any report. Expressing anxiety directs him to send a report from that site immediately.

The document in Persian *shikasta* bears *sarnama Siri Akal Purakhji* and three seals: two in Gurumukhi and one in Persian and a seal on the back of the document.

(ACC. NO. 2398/ 3; Original; f1).

24 September 1845

260. *Qabala-i nilami* in respect of one storeyed *pucca* shop of Prem Singh, the plaintiff situated in Rewari who is liable to pay the amount of degree as per the court order dated 18 January 1845 for the *Zar-i Degree* amounting to Rs. 711/4 passed on 15 December 1843 was auctioned by Kishan Sahai and Gopal Sahai through Sham Lal *Amin* on 8 March 1845 which was purchased by Ram Lal *Mahajan* of Rewari against a sum Rs. 416/- in general auction from the *amin*. Adds that the said buyer after making payment has solicited the *qabala-i nilami* which is given to him.

The document in Urdu *shikasta* on a stamp paper of two rupees bears *sarnama Alif* and the seal of the court.

(ACC. NO. 2657/ 47; Copy; f1).

12 *Shawwal* 1261 AH (14 October 1845)

261. Letter addressed to Nazar Ali *Musta'jir* of Jais. States that it has come to his notice that he is involved/indulged in forced labour as well as oppression over the inhabitants in the *Pura* of Musharrafnagar which is attached to Mir Sadiq Husain where never occurred such incident before. Instructs him to restraint himself from indulging in any unwarranted activities in the said Pura or face the consequences.

The document in Persian *shikasta* bears the seal of Raja Man Singh.

(ACC. NO. 2403/ 81; Original; f1).

25 November 1845/ 12 *Aghan* 1253 *Amli*

262. Judgement of *Adalat-i Commissioner* under the session of John William Templer District Cuttack vide Regulation 3 of 1828 on the appeal made by Mahant Sudarshan Das *chela* of late Mahant Raj Gopal Das, resident of Kalika Debi Sai against the decision of the Deputy Collector in respect of imposition of taxes on 9. 12. 2 *maan* of *lakhiraj* land of Amrit Manohi in village Kothanapur, *pargana* Kondesh. The Court dismissed the case and upheld the decision of the Deputy Collector dated 30 september 1839. The court also issued orders to bear the expenses of the court by the appellant.

The document in Urdu *Shikasta* bears the seal of the Court of Commissioner, District Cuttack.

(ACC. NO. 2693/ 17; Copy; f1).

25 November 1845/ 12 *Aghan* 1253 *Amli*

263. Judgement of *Adalat-i Commissioner* under the session of John William Templer of district Cuttack vide Regulation 3 of 1828 on the appeal made by Sudarshan Das *chela* of late Mahant Raj Gopal, resident of

Kalka Debi Sai against the decision of the Deputy Collector in respect of imposition of taxes on 5. 8. 12 *maan* of *lakhiraj* land of Amrit Manohi in the village Jabalpur Sai *taalluqa* Kot Sai, *pargana* Kunda Bang (?). The court dismissed the case and upheld the decision of the Deputy Collector dated 12 February 1839 and also imposed the court expenses upon the appellant.

The document in Urdu *shikasta* bears a seal of the Court of Commissioner, District Cuttack.

(ACC. NO. 2693/ 18; Copy; f1).

26 November 1845/ 13 *Aghan* 1253 *Amli*

264. Judgement of *Adalat-i Commissioner* under the session of John William Templer, district Cuttack vide Regulation 3 of 1828 on the appeal made by Mahant Sudershan Das *chela* of Raj Gopal Das of Kalika Debi Sai in respect of imposition of taxes on 11. 3. 5 *maan* of *lakhiraj* land situated in *mauza* Puran Bijaibad *taalluqa* Kishan Chandar *pargana* Chaubiskud. The court dismissed the appeal and upheld the decision of the Deputy Collector dated 18 February 1839 and also imposed the court expenses upon the appellant.

The document in Urdu *shikasta* bears a seal of the court of Commissioner, District Cuttack.

(ACC. NO. 2693/ 19; Copy; f1).

1261 AH (date in seal) (1845)

265. *Arzi* of Saiyid Hafeez Ali resident of *qasba* Kalpi to the Nawwab. Commends his kindness and describes his precarious condition and circumstances leading to his starvation. Requests for assistance to earn his livelihood.

The document in Persian *shikasta* bears the seal of the writer

(ACC. NO. 2668/90 ; Original; f1).

20 January 1846/ 9 *Magh* 1253 *Amli*

266. Judgement of *Adalat-i Commissioner* (special) under the session of John William Templer of District Cuttack (vide Regulation 3 of 1828) on the appeal made by the Government against Mahant Sudershan Das *chela* of late Mahant Raj Gopal Das, resident of Kalika Debi Sai against the decision of the Deputy Collector in respect of waiving of taxes on 59. 20. 14 *maan* out of 72. 10. 4 *maan* of *lakhiraj* land of Amrit Manohi in 8 villages in *pargana* Saeedabad. The court dismissed the appeal made by the Government and upheld the decision of the Deputy Collector dated18 May 1843. Further orders that the expenses of the court will be borne out by the Government and that the *mehnatana* of 8 *anna* of *mukhtar* by the respondent.

The document in Urdu *shikasta* bears the seal of the Court of Commissioner, District Cuttack.

(ACC. NO. 2693/ 20; copy; f1).

28 January 1846/ 17 *Magh* 1253 *Amli*

267. Judgement of *Adalat-i Commissioner* (special) under the session of John William Templer District Cuttack (vide Regulation 3 of 1828) on the appeal made by Mahant Sudershan Das *chela* of late Raj Gopal Das, resident of Kalika Debi Sai against the decision of the Deputy Collector in respect of imposition of taxes on 22. 8. 8 *maan* of *lakhiraj* land of Amirt Manohi in village Sada Shambu Gram *pargana* Kondesh. The Court dismissed the case and upheld the decision of the Deputy Collector dated 9 September 1839 and also imposed the court expenses upon the appellant.

The document in Urdu *shikasta* bears a seal of the court of Commissioner, District Cuttack.

(ACC. NO. 2693/ 21; Copy; f1)

7 *Safar* 1262 AH (4 February 1846)

268. *Hukmnama* of *Kachehri* under the seal of Nawwab Wazir-al Mulk to Mir Nawwab Mufti of *ilaqa* Sandila etc. Refers to the petition of Saiyid Hafiz Allah Chaudhari of *pargana* Sandila along with a representation of the *zamindars* of Basona, Attanau and Kakrali etc. complaining the usurpation of their cultivated land and forest etc. situated in village Bharkhana with the request to hand him (addressee) over the case to settle the matter. Directs him to settle the case in the presence of the contending parties and send the details of the judgement along with the *razinama* of the appellant.

The document in Persian *shikasta* bears *sarnama innahu* and the symbol of seal of *Muhr-i Kachehri-i Khas,* Nawwab Wazir al-Mamalik.

(ACC. NO. 1597; Copy; f1).

10 *Safar* 1262 AH (7 February 1846)

269. *Hukmnama* issued to Raja Man Singh, *tahsildar* of Daryabad etc. Refers to the petition of Jiwan Ram complaining against Sukh Lal *ziladar* of village Raghupur adjacent to the territory of Daryabad who has usurped his150 *maund* of fruits and flower trees. Directs to settle the case impartially and obtain a *razinama* from him.

The document in Persian *shikasta* bears the royal emblem (of Awadh) at the top and the seal of *Kachehri-i Khas Sultani Khallad Allahu Mulkahu.*

(ACC. NO. 1700; Original; f1).

7 February 1846 / 27 *Magh* 1253 *Amli*

270. Judgement of *Adalat-i Commissioner* (special) under the session of John William Templer of District Cuttack vide Regulation 3 of 1828 on the appeal made by the Mahant Sudarshan Das, resident of Kalika Debi Sai against the decision of the Deputy Collector in respect of imposition of taxes on 67. 14. 2 *maan* out of 94. 22. 10 *maan* of *lakhiraj* land of Amrit Manohi in seven villages of *pargana* Athais. The Court dismissed the appeal and upheld the decision of the Deputy Collector dated 15 January 1842 and also imposed the court expenses upon the appellant

The document in Urdu *shikasta* bears the seal of the court of Commissioner, district Cuttack.

(ACC. NO. 2693/ 22; Copy; f1).

23 February 1846

271. Letter to Har Sahai *Muhafiz daftar-i Kachehri-i Nizamat zila* Meerut. Says that for sometimes it was felt that there was a need of renovation in the administrative set up of the office of *Kachehri* for its good governance and thus there would be two *muhafiz* and one *naib muhafiz* with one officer upon them and also four *muharrirs* and two copyists for their assistance and the proposal was accepted by the addressee. Further informs that a sum of Rs. 60/- has been fixed as their salary which includes the salary of two *muhafiz* and one *naib muhafiz* besides Rs. 30/- for four *muharrir*. Instructs that the entire responsibility of the administration of the office will now lie upon him with custody of the rooms having records and none should be allowed to enter without the permission of *sarrishtadar*.

The document in Urdu *shikasta* bears *sarnama Alif* and the seal of the District Court Meerut.

(ACC. NO. 2754/ 5; Original; f1).

29 *Magh* 1902 *Samvat* (24 February 1846)

272. *Parwana* issued to Lala Shyam Das Kardar of Mandub Khushab. States that 25 maund besides Mandub Khushab have been in assignment of Baba Hiragar on account of *dharmarth* since olden times. Directs him for the continuation of the aforesaid grant in his favour from the beginning of *Aswaj* (Asar) 1902 enabling him to engage himself in praying for the Kingdom and for the lofty fortune of the king.

The document in Persian *shikasta* bears *sarnama Bafazl-i Sri Akal Purakhji* and a dim seal of Kishan Chand.

(ACC. NO. 2580/ 8; Original; f1).

5 *Rabi* I 1262 AH (3 March 1846)

273. Letter addressed to...... Refers his letter sent through the *harkara*. Informs him about the *parwana-i muhri* of Raja Sahib Bahadur in his (addressee) name in respect of taking possession of *taalluqa* Nandni (?) and expulsion of Sahib Din from there. Directs him to act firmly in expelling the said Sahib Din and issue the *siyaha* and also give possession to Raja Ali Bakhsh Khan. Also directs that each *munshi* should act in accordance to the *parwana*.

The document is in Persian *shikasta*.

(ACC. NO. 2403/ 82; Original; f1).

8 *Rabi* I 1262 AH (6 March 1846)

274. Letter of Muhammad Munim to Mir Sahib (Zakir Husain). Dispatches the *parwana* received from Raja Man Singh, *Nazim* of Sultanpur etc. in his name for a sum of Rs. 4000/- on account of salary of army personnel posted at Faizabad and Awadh

for 1253 *Fasli*. Requests to hand over the aforesaid amount to Kaldar Singh, the *jamadar* and obtain receipt thereof from him Also refers the sum of Rs. 5000/ as mentioned by the Maharaja Sahib in his *Parwana*. Elaborates that an amount of Rs. 1000/- spent upon the army stationed at Shahganj till 1253 *Fasli* were taken from *toshak khana* and Rs. 2000/- were received from Chaudhari Mumtaz Ahmad and the receipt of Rs. 3000 has been handed over to Chaudhari Mumtaz Ahmad. Requests to obtain the remaining amount of Rupees 2000/- from the said Chaudhari before the receipt of the total amount is taken from him.

The document in Persian *shikasta* bears *sarnama Innhu* and seal of the writer.

(ACC. NO. 1969; Original; f1).

3 *Rabi* II 1262 AH (31 March 1846) 275. *Hukmnama* issued to Muhammad and Mir Zakir Husain. Refers to the *shuqqa* of Nawwab Wazir al-Mamalik (Nawwab of Awadh) dated 8 *Rabi* I 1262 AH pertaining to the petition of Saiyid Nur-al Hasan resident of *qasba* Jais Fathpur against Aulad Husain filed in the *Muhkama Sharia* and the court's order giving him possession over his property. But when the petitioner went to look after his *zamindari* falling under British controlled territory, Aulad Husain captured his children subjected them to various oppression, usurped Rs. 100/-, and cut down hundreds of his trees. Directs them to prevail upon Aulad Husain preventing him from oppression and get returned the stipulated amount together with the price of the trees to him and obtain a *muchalka* from him declaring that he

would not go any way against the judgement of the court and also get a *razinama* from the petitioner. At the end, the court issues strict injunction for immediate compliance to this effect.

The document in Persian *shikasta* bears seal of Raja Man Singh.

(ACC. NO. 2403/ 84; Original; f1).

9 *Rabi* II 1262 AH (6 April 1846)

276. Letter of Bishambar Das to Mir Sahib (Zakir Husain). Dispatches the *parwana* of Raja Man Singh pertaining to the verification and disbursement of the salary of Thakur Singh *jamadar*, Ram Den Singh and Husain Bakhsh, owners of the Patti Abbas of Daryabad who have been posted with him (the writer) since long and to help him by sending animal fodder etc. In view of the friendly relations between the two, solicits verification and payment of salary of the above mentioned persons through the Bakhshi. Also says that at the moment 200 bamboos and 25 bullock carts of animal fodder besides *polagah* may be provided before the rainy season falls.

The document in Persian *shikasta* bears *sarnama Alif* and the seal of the writer.

(ACC. NO. 1958; Original; f1).

26 *Rabi* II 1262 AH (23 April 1846)

277. Letter to Mir Sahib (Zakir Hussain). Acknowledges receipt of his letter. Referring to the matter mentioned in the letter suggests that instead of informing him the same may be passed on to Chaudhari Shankar Lal. Adds that his objections in respect of the *sazawal* are true but should not be disappointed as the appointment of *sazawal* has been done as per the royal *parwangi*. Also refers the

payment of Rs. 25000/-which will be sent shortly.

The document in Persian *shikasta* bears *sarnama Alif.*

(ACC. NO. 2403/ 80; Original; f1).

2 *Jumada* I 1262 AH (28 April 1846) 278. *Parwana* under the seal of Nawal Singh to Mir Zakir Husain. Refers to the complaint made by Mir Nabi Muhammad against him (the addressee) about not getting the revenue realized by him for the year 1253 *Fasli* for his 51 *bigha* measured land inspite of the order issued earlier. Orders him to make immediate payment of Rs. 51/- to Mir Nabi Muhammad on account of revenue for 1253 *Fasli* (1846 AD) in respect of his 51 *bighas* of measured land assigned to him as per the previous *parwana*.

The document in Persian *shikasta* bears an illegible seal.

(ACC. NO. 2082; Original; f1).

April 1846 279. *Yaddasht-i qabz al-wasul.* Acknowledging the receipt of the monthly allowance of Rs. 12500/- for the month of March 1846 as fixed by the Company Government.

The document in Persian *shikasta* bears *sarnama Alif* and seal of Muhammad Wazir Khan.

(ACC. NO. 2701/ 16; Original; f1).

8 *Baisakh* (?) 1903 *Samvat* (3 May 1846) 280. Letter to Akhwa Sahib Misr. Referring to the royal *parwana* under the signature of Diwan Dena Nath and his (writer) own letter directing to relinquish three *mauzas* i. e. Patri, Kalahand and Golyal in *taalluqa* Neelkanth on account of *dharmarth* to Bakhshi Gur Narain. Hopes that he would have relinquished the same in his favour as per the previous *parwana* so that he may

remain engaged in the service of the addressee and for the maintenance of his men. Further hopes that he would also over come the loss of the grain stock and the camels plundered by Malik Fath.

The document in Persian *shikasta* bears a seal of Shamji Mal on the back.

(ACC. NO. 2398/ 6; Original; f1).

11 *Jumada* I 1262 AH (7 May 1846)

281. Letter to Mir Sahib (Zakir Husain). Refers to a complaint lodged to the Nawwab Wazir al-Mamalik against the *malguzars,* listed separately who do not come to him and commit dacoity and atrocities in the region and pay to the addressee ¼th share from the looted property which is a matter of great surprise to him. Conveys the anxiety of Nawwab Wazir al-Mamalik upon him and sends the list of alleged *malguzars.* Directs him to take undertaking from the mischievous elements preventing them committing such crimes and atrocities.

The document is in Persian *shikasta.*

(ACC. NO. 2108; Original; f1).

22 *Jumada* I 1262 AH (18 May 1846)

282. Letter of Nawal Singh to Saiyid Zakir Husain. Informs that a sum of Rs. 25/- per annum has been assigned to Isar Das Bhagat from the territory of Rudauli which he received till 1252 *Fasli* but has not received the sum assigned to him for the year 1253 *Fasli.* Directs him to remit the stipulated amount to him through the *harkara* (agent) being sent for the purpose as the said Bhagat is incapacitated to move due to his old age.

The document in Persian *shikasta* bears the seal of the writer.

(ACC. NO. 2093; Original; f1).

27 *Jumada* I 1262 AH (23 May 1846)

283. Letter of Nawal Singh to Mir Sahib (Zakir Husain). Intimates that Karim Bakhsh *khasabardar* of the platoon of Mir Madad Ali, as per the *dastak* dated 13 *Jumada* I 1262 AH. (9 May 1846) has been deputed as *sazawal* to collect the sum exacted forcefully by the *zamindars* from the traders and *mallahs* besides the punitive tax. Directs him to collect the exected sum from the *zamindars* and send him for its deposition in the Government treasury. Also directs that daily allowance of the sazawal may be borne by the *zamindars* beginning from the date of *dastak* till the time of depositing the amount.

The document in Persian *shikasta* bears *sarnama Alif* and the seal of the writer.

(ACC. NO. 1967; Original; f1).

29 *Jumada* I 1262 AH (25 May 1846)

284. Letter of Pir Bakhsh to Mir Sahib (Zakir Husain). Referring to the *hukmnama* under the seal of the Royal Court (of Awadh) in regard to salary of the armed forces of the Collectorate under the command of *Darogha* Ghulam Husain Khan solicits grant of Rs. 15000/-as per the receipt of the *mutasaddi* enabling the army to take military expedition without fearing of their livelihood. The receipt thereof would be submitted immediately. Also requests for orders to the army officer to convey his instructions to all army personnel for compliance officers deputed there.

The document in Persian *shikasta* bears the seal of the writer.

(ACC. NO. 1968; Original; f1).

4 *Jumada* II 1262 AH (30 May 1846 AD)

285. Letter to Mir Sahib (Zakir Husain). Acknowledges receipt of his letter informing about the affairs there. Referring his

recommendations to terminate the *sazawal* communicates that in the absence of full particulars of the case it is not possible to put the matter before the Government. Directs him to present full details of such cases in future for consideration of the Government.

The document is in Persian *shikasta*.

(ACC. NO. 2403/ 87; Original; f1).

May 1846 286. *Yaddasht-i qabz al-wasul* for the months of April 1846. To the same effect as SL. No. 268, document No. 2701/ 16

(ACC. NO. 2701/ 17; Original; f1).

May 1846 287. *Yaddasht-i qabz- al-wasul* for the months of April 1846. To the same effect as document No. 2701/ 16

(ACC. NO. 2701/ 18; Original; f1).

7 *Jumada* II 1262 AH (2 June 1846) 288. Letter of Kanwal Singh to Mir Zakir Husain. Complains against the appointment of Salar Bakhsh as *sazawal* by the *tahsildar* of Daryabad upon the *malguzar* of village Mukanwan *ilaqa* Daryabad in spite of the fact that the said village falls within his (the writer's) jurisdiction. Requests for orders in the name of the *tahsildar* of Daryabad to nullify his appointment and not to interfere in his territory. Adds that if Salar Bakhsh has anything to enquire from the *malguzar* of the said *mauza* he may be sent to him (the writer) for the settlement of the matters between the two.

The document in Persian *shikasta* bears *sarnama Alif* and the seal of the writer.

(ACC. NO. 1981; Original; f1).

27 *Jeth* 1903 *Samvat* (20 June 1846) 289. Letter to Kanha Singh. Informs that the specified territory has been assigned to Assa Singh (?) *thanadar* under Bakhshi Gur

Narain. Instructs that in accordance to the *parwana* the said territory may be handed over to him to facilitate construction of the fort on that territory.

The document in Persian *shikasta* bears *sarnama Sat Sri Akal Purakhji* and three seals; one in Gurumukhi and others in Persian.

(ACC. NO. 2398/ 4; Original; f1).

June 1846 — 290. *yaddasht-i qabz- al-wasul* for the months of May 1846. To the same effect as document No. 2701/ 16

(ACC. NO. 2701/ 19; Original; f1).

14 *Rajab* 1262 AH (8 July 1846) — 291. Letter to Mir Zakir Husain *chakladar* of Daryabad etc. Informs about the grant of village Makhorah and Chakya of Sandila territory to Lachman Prasad by Raja Man Singh. Tells that meanwhile, Babu Daljit Singh *taalluqadar* of Asauni, Chandi Singh and Akoran entered the said villages with a huge crowd, committed atrocities upon the villagers and plundered it which led the cultivators to fly away from the village and many were to escape. Orders him to prevent them from such activities.

The document in Persian *shikasta* bears as dim seal.

(ACC. NO. 2089; Original; f1).

30 *Rajab* 1262 AH (24 July 1846) — 292. Petition of Khairat Ali through his *wakil* Farkhand Ali addressed to *Sultan al-Ulama.* Informs that *mauza* Muhammadpur and Kanwar ltimadpur are in his possession as these are his *zamindari* villages. Complains against Husain Bakhsh resident and *qanunqo* of Badusarai who had filed a case in the Court of *Sadr Amin* claiming his ownership over the aforesaid villages

which could not stand valid in the eyes of justice. Adds that instead, abstaining from unlawful claim he (the petitioner) has filed a case in the *muhkama Shariat* for the redressal of his grievances. Requests him (the addressee) to prevail upon the said person from making unlawful claim as he, with the collusion of the *amil* thereof want to seize the petitioner's *zamindari* without *rubakari* and firm proof. Requests to forward his petition to the *kachehri wazarat* for issuance of a *hukmnama* forbidding him to occupy these villages without having solid proof so that he (petitioner) could be saved from further harassment.

The document is in Persian *shikasta* bears *sarnama Alif.* The document is also to the same effect as document no. 2403/ 85.

(ACC. NO. 2701/ 17; Original; f1).

12 *Shaban* 1262 AH (5 August 1846)

293. Letter addressed to Mir Zakir Husain. Refers to the complaint of Ghulam Nabi Khan *muafidar* who as per the *parwana* has been assigned the land measuring 4 *bighas* situated in the suburb of *qasba* Jais which is to be measured and handed over to him. Expresses displeasure that the same is not done by Ghulam Husain *mustajir* of *muhalla* Subhana Lakhna. Instructs to depute a *sazawal* to help him collecting the revenue from Subhana Lakhna, come to his rescue as and when required and also instruct his agents at *qasba* Jais to assist the assignee in the revenue realization.

The document in Persian *shikasta* bears dim seal of Raja Man Singh.

(ACC. NO. 2403/ 88; Original; f1).

29 *Shawwal* 1262 AH

294. Statement of expenditure account of elephant keeper spent on fodder of

(20 October 1846)

elephants from 1 *Zilqada* to 29 *Safar* 1262 AH and from 1 *Rabi* 1 to 29 *Shawwal* 1262 AH.

The document is in Persian *shikasta*.

(ACC. NO. 2403/ 90; Original; f1).

3 *Zilqada* 1262 AH (23 October 1846)

295. *Hukmnana* under the seal of *Kachehri-i Wazarat* to Wazir Mirza, Wilayat Husain *Salars* and other Army Officers posted at Sandila. Refers to the petition of Haji Muzaffar Ali informing about the non-compliance of his order by Murlidhar *chakladar* of Sandila directing him to demolish the shivala etc. built by Govardhan Lal on the land owned by the appellant favouring Goverdhan Lal. Directs them to demolish the shivala in question in accordance to the decision of *Sultan al-Ulama Mujtahid al-Asr wa al-Zaman* and give possession of the land to the petitioner and send a *razinama* by obtaining from him.

The document in Persian *shikasta* bears *sarnama innahu*.

(ACC. NO. 1613; Copy; f1).

3 *Zilqada* 1262 AH (23 October 1846)

296. *Hukmnama* issued under the seal of *Kachehri-i Wazarat* to Murli Dhar *chakladar* of the *mahals* of Sandila etc. Refers to the application of Haji Muzaffar Ali informing that in spite the orders of the court, the *shivala* built by Govardhan Lal on the land of the petitioner has not yet been demolished. Orders to demolish the *shivala* forthwith and to restore the land to the rightful owner. Also directs to send a *razinama* obtaining from the complainant.

The document in Persian *shikasta* bears *sarnama innahu*.

(ACC. NO. 1851; Copy; f1).

20 *Kartik* 1903 *Samvat* (12 November 1846)

297. Letter to Bakhshi Gur Narain. Informs him that Mr. Elliot and Diwan Ajodhaya Prasad who have crossed over river Ravi would soon come to settle and demarcate the boundaries of mountainous region and plain territory. Referring to a communiqué received from Diwan Ajodhaya Prasad directs him to render wholehearted support to Mr. Elliot and Diwan Ajodhaya Prasad and also produce the *Zamindars* and other aged persons of the region from the villages of Kalhata, Markheri Kharyali and Manawar etc. to furnish facts and figures honestly so that they could decide the matter effectively.

The document in Persian *shikasta* bears *sarnama Ba Fazl-i Sri Akal purakhji.*

(ACC. NO. 2398/ 5; Original; f1).

2 *Makar* *(Magh)* 1903 *Samvat* (20 November 1846)

298. *Parwana* to Lala Shyamji Mal. Communicates confirmation of the grant of one maund wheat to Gosain Ganesh Dangiwala on account of *dharmarth* for the whole year from the region of Dhuria that he gets accordingly. Directs him to issue a fresh *parwana* as he has lost the previous one.

The document in Persian *shikasta* bears *sarnama Alif* and the seal of Amir Chand Jeo Sahai.

(ACC. NO. 2580/ 72; Original; f1).

2 *Zilhijja* 1262 AH (21 November 1846)

299. *Ruqqa* issued by Maulawi Mir Muhammad Husain Mufti of Salon. Refers to the petition of Ghulam Raza and Ghulam Imam along with the *shuqqa* of the Government dated 17 *Zilqada.* States that according to the request of Mir Nauroz (?) Ali grand-son of Mir Ghulam Raza, the

case is referred to him. Orders him to investigate the case and send the report to this department so that decision may be taken in this matter accordingly.

The document in Persian *nastaliq* bears *sarnama Bi- ismihi Subhanahu* and seal of *Muhkama Sadr al-Shariah*.

(ACC. NO. 2189; Original; f1).

5 *Zilhijjia* 1262 AH (24 November 1846)

300. *Parwana* of Maharaja Murli Dhar *Nazim* of Sandila etc. to Lala Raman Lal *tahsildar* of *ilaqa* Kukrali etc. Informs him that as per the *sanad* produced by Saiyid Faiyaz Ali, it is evident that 100 *bighas* measured land situated in the vicinity of *mauza* Aldoon has been in his assignment as *muafi* since long and has been realizing its revenue till last year. Expresses anxiety that during the current year a *shahna* is deputed there who is reported is withholding the produce of the said land (and not allowing the assignee to collect the revenue). Orders him to make an enquiry into the matter, remove the *shahna* and should not be interfered in the said land enabling the said Saiyid to realize its revenue.

The document in Persian *shikasta* bears the seal of Maharaja Murli Dhar.

(ACC. NO. 1594; Copy; f1).

14 *Zilhijja* 1262 AH (3 December 1846)

301. *Yaddasht* of the income of *qasba* Jais received through Mir Zakir Husain *mustajir* of *qasba* Jais amounting to Rs. 359/ 13½ *anna* for the year 1253 *Fasli* corresponding to 14 *Zulhijja* 1262 AH (as per the details given in the body of the text) and have been entered in the *Siyaha-1 Sarkar* as per the receipts and *parwanas* possessed by Gulab Rai *potadar*.

The document in Persian *shikasta* bears a note in *modi* script.

(ACC. NO. 1978; Original; f1).

1262 AH (date in seal) (1846)

302. Letter of Imdad Husain to Mir Sahib (Mir Zakir Husain). Refers his letter asking about the cultivation of village Chaudharipur towards Kamlaha which has also been directed by Chaudhari Murtaza Husain. Informs about his inspection of the *mauza* and that the cultivation is well in all his satisfaction and that he would not be untouched about its revenue realization. Adds that Patti Teja Singh could not be cultivated untill his brother is released who is aware of the region. Solicits for necessary instructions to Sadhan Singh for making utmost endeavour to promote cultivation of Shankar Patti. Informs about the deposition of Rs. 575/- through Lala Daulat Rai to Lala Raghu Nath Prasad which should be entertained as per the schedule. Requests to send Janki Prasad and Bundi Singh for computation and record of account as in their absence Shiv Ghulam Singh has objection in making the payment. With regard his previous request for *dastak-i barkhast* in favour of Hirday Singh *havaldar* and his order to wait till the payment of the whole year. Adds that an amount of Rs. 150/- is now pending against him (Hirday Singh) who promises to pay within eight days. Hence *dastak* may be issued. Also sends Rs. 325/- as well and hopes that its entry will be made as per *sarrishta*.

The document in Persian *shikasta* bears the seal of the writer.

(ACC. NO. 1970; Original; f1).

1262 AH (date in seal) (1846)

303. *Arzdasht* of Jiwan Ram *Zamindar*. Referring the *wujuhat-i zamindari* grant to him complains against Sukh Lal *ziladar* of *mauza* Raghupur who has forcibly confiscated 150 *maund* bushes of the trees from his *zamindari* villages attached to Daryabad. Adds that he (the petitioner) reported the matter to Saiyid Zakir Husain *Tahsildar* Daryabad appointed by Raja Man Singh but he did not take action in the matter. Requests for the issuance of a Royal *hukmnama* to Raja Man Singh so that he could instruct the *tahsildar* Daryabad to force the *ziladar* to return him the cost of the trees.

The document in Persian *shikasta* bears the seal of *Kachehri-i Insha-i Sultani*.

(ACC. NO. 2403/ 145; Copy; f1).

1903 *Samvat* (in the text) (1846-47)

304. Letter to Misr Rup Lal. Communicates confirmation of the grant of land as *muaf*, from village Munian to Ganeshgar and Shyamgir. Directs to relinquish the aforesaid land from the beginning of *Kharif* crop of 1903(*samvat*) in their favour and not to harass him in any way.

The document in Persian *shikasta* bears *sarnama Alif*.

(ACC. NO. 2580/ 74; Original; f1).

1 *Safar* 1263 AH (19 January 1847)

305. *Parwana* of Raja Man Singh to Mir Zakir Husain. States that renovation of the buildings at Shahganj Mubarak is urgently required. Directs him to dispatch mesons as much as possible to Shahganj Mubarak for the purpose.

The document in Persian *shikasta* bears *sarnama innahu* and the seal of *Muhr-i Kachahri taaluqa Khas* of Raja Man Singh Bahadur Qaim Jang.

(ACC. NO. 1663; Original; f1).

7 *Safar* 1263 AH (25 January 1847AD) 306. *Hukmnama-i Kachehri* under the seal of Nawwab Wazir al-Mulk to Mir Nawwab, Mufti of Sandila. Refers to the petition of Saiyid Hafiz Allah Chaudhari of *pargana* Sandila complaining against the *zamindars* of Bistuna, Atamu and Kakrali for the usurpation of his agricultural and forest land situated in village Bharkhana falling in the territory (*deh*) of the petitioner requesting for orders to him (the addressee) for a suitable settlement. Directs him for the settlement of the dispute amicably in the presence of the contending parties and send a copy of the settlement along with the concurrence of the petitioner.

The document in Persian *shikasta* bears *sarnama innahu* and symbol of seal of the Court of Nawwab Wazir al- Mulk

(ACC. NO. 1405; Copy; f1).

29 January 1847 307. *Mukhtarnama* executed by Saiyid Amanat Ali on his behalf and that of his sons Saiyid Mazhar Ali, Saiyid Israr Ali and Saiyid Abrar Ali, residents of Amroha. State that they have sold their 2 *biswas* and 10 *biswansi muafi, nazrana* land out of 20 *biswa muafi* land in village Sidhar, belonging to *pargana* Amroha as per the *Qabala - i-Bainama* dated 15 *Muharram* 1263 AH for a sum of Rs. 1650 to Maulawi Muhammad Askari and Saiyid Muhammad Hasan, sons of Maulawi Saiyid Muhammad Siyadat. State that as per the rule the *dakhil kharij* of the said land is required in the *Nizamat* office, District Muradabad and thus Shaikh Muhammad Azim is hereby appointed as *mukhtar-i kar* for mutation of the land in the *Nizamat* office.

The document in Urdu *nastaliq* executed on punch marked stamp paper of eight *anna* and a seal and signature of executant besides signatures of witnesses. It also bears departmental endorsements in Devnagri.

(ACC. NO. 2533/ 32; Original; f1).

15 *Magh* 1903 *Samvat* (31 January 1847)

308. Letter to Akku Khan etc. *zamindars* of *mauza* Kurpa. Informs them that *mauza* Kurpa has been granted in the *jagir* of Bakhshi Gur Narain from the beginning of *kharif* crop 1905 *Samvat* to meet the expenses of his *sawars* and *piadas* which excludes the *jagir* assigned to him as *inam* and *dharmarth*. Orders them to pay the revenue realization of the said *mauza* to him without any excuse.

The document is in Persian *shikasta*.

(ACC. NO. 2398/ 32; Original; f1).

3 *Jumada* I 1263 AH (19 April 1847)

309. *Hukmnama* under the seal of *Kachehri-i Wazarat* to Murli Dhar, *amil* of Sandila. Refers to the petition of Haji Manzar Ali against the atrocities of Ata Allah, Roshan Zaman, Husain Ali, Khuda Bakhsh, Hasan Raza and other brothers of Chaudhari Subhan Ata who robbed the mosque built by the petitioner and injured guards for which a *hukmnama* for their arrest was issued. Further adds that now they have forcibly caught fishes from his pond and it is apprehended that they might kill him. Orders for the arrest of the culprits, make them pay the cost of the fishes to the petitioner and produce them in the court, otherwise, a *sazawal* would be deputed for the matter.

The document is in Persian *shikasta*.

(ACC. NO. 1398; Copy; f1).

19 *Jumada* I 1263 AH (5 May 1847)

310. *Parwana* under the seal of Maharaja, Nazim of *pargana* Sandila and Malihabad etc. to Saiyid Rahat Ali *tahsildar* of Sandila. States that as per the report of Shaikh Jafar Ali he, in accordance to his *hukmnama* issued on the petition of Muzaffar Ali, has arrested Ata Allah, Roshan Zaman and other *chaudharis*. Expresses anxiety that previously order was issued to him to submit true facts in the matter, instead on the contrary has been done which was not expected from him. Clarifies that they are the *sighadars* and are not supposed to go against the Royal orders as they would have explained their position on the petition of Muzaffar Ali. Directs him to release the arrested persons forthwith and submit true facts in his regard.

The document in Persian *shikasta* bears *sarnama innahu* with an endorsement directing to adhere to the true facts and not to deviate from it and a note on the top indicating that the addressee's companions have been extracting five rupees in one day while they should not be paid more than one rupee.

(ACC. NO. 1517; Copy; f1).

26 *Baisakh* 1904 *Samvat* (11 May 1847)

311. *Parwana* addressed to the *kardars* of Sair Chabutra Jhelam. States that Rs. 39/ and 4 *annas* has been in assignment of Ganeshgar as *rasad* (provision) from the aforesaid Chabutra on account of *dharmarth* since old time. Directs that as per practice, the said grant may be released in his favour for the whole year from the beginning of *Rabi* crop of 1903.

The document in Persian *shikasta* bears

sarnama Alif/ Akal Purakhji Sahai and six seals in Persian and Gurmukhi.

(ACC. NO. 2580/ 73; Original; f1).

12 May 1847/ 25 *Jumada* I 1263 AH/ 12 *Jeth* 1254 *Fasli*

312. *Tamassuk* executed by Shaikh Fazl Karim son of Shaikh Tufail Ali resident of *mauza* Daulatpur *pargana* Okri District Bihar as *Mukhtar* on behalf of his mother *Mst.* Amiran daughter of Shaikh Yar Ali co-sharer in *mauza* Bahrampur *pargana* Naubatpur Ballia (?) *Zila* Patna. States that one share out of 5 shares from 2 *anna* share of the entire 16 *anna* share of Shaikh Yar Ali and *Mst.* Fazilat al-Nisa in *mauza* Bahrampur has been given to Din Dayal Bhagat on lease against an annual *jama* of for Rs. 181/ 5 w.e.f. 1251 *Fasli* to 1259 *Fasli* and has received Rs. 290/-as advance. Says that she has borrowed a sum of Rs. 101/- from the said *thekadar* on interest @ one rupee per mensum which he would pay within one year or by the end of *theka* in 1259 *Fasli* and then only he would be liable to get return and to take control over his land. In case, he failed to pay the amount of *theka* as well as the advance money the *theka* would continue on the same terms and conditions as stated.

The document in Persian *shikasta* executed on one rupee stamp paper bears the seal of Qazi Muhammad Wajih al-Din Khan and seal and signature of *Mst.* Amiran and signatures of the witnesses. It also bears physical description of the attorney.

(ACC. NO. 2531/23; Original; f1).

30 *Jumada* I/ 16 *Jaith* 1254

313. *Tamassuk* executed by *Mst.* Amiran daughter of Shaikh Yar Ali wife of late

Fasli (1263 AH) 17 May 1847) Shaikh Tufail Ali *malikan, malguzaran* of *mauza* Daulatpur *pargana* Okri District Bihar and a share holder in village Bahrampur *pargana* Ballia District Patna. States that one *siham* out of 5 *siham* from the two *anna* share of Shaikh Yar Ali and *Mst* Fazilat al-Nisa situated in *mauza* Bahrampur has been given on *theka* to Babu Din Dayal Bhagat of *muhalla* Sadiqpur for Rs. 108/5/2. Says she has borrowed a sum of Rs. 100/- on interest from the said *thekadar* and again Rs. 25/- @ Re 1/-interest per month. Declares that she would return the borrowed money to the *thekadar* within a period of one year. Adds that if she failed to return the borrowed money within the stipulated time of one year she will be bound to return the said amount by the end of *theka* to the *thkadar* along with the advance money, only then she would be liable to take back her land. Further declares that unless and until she pays the entire amount *theka* would continue in favour of the *thekadar* on the same terms and conditions.

The document in Persian *Shikasta* executed on punch marked stamp paper of four *anna* bears the seal of *Mst.* Amiran and signature of witnesses etc. as well as endorsement on the reverse.

(ACC. NO. 2531/24; Original; f1).

26 *Jumada* II 1263 AH (11 June 1847)

314. *Parwana* of Raja Man Singh to Mir Zakir Husain. Informs that Ghansiawan Kurmi resident of village Bhat Kotwan who had purchased an ox from Biju Dalal resident of *Qasba* Jais for Rs. 5/ 2 *anna* which however, was owned by Damar iron-smith

resident of Salon *ilaqa* Aeti and took possession of the ox. Directs him to get return the amount from Biju Dalal to Ghansiawan Kurmi or produce the said Biju in the camp.

The document in Persian *shikasta* bears the seal of Raja Man Singh (the writer).

(ACC. NO. 1933; Original; f1).

5 *Jaith* 1904 *Samvat* (18 June 1847)

315. Letter to Lala Tek Chand. States that village Chander Daragi and 10 villages from Maluwal situated at Shi Kuryalwala has been in assignment of Baba Ganeshgar and Shyamgar *sanyasi* as *waguzasht* and revenue free grant. Directs to relinquish the said grant in their favour for the current year 1904(*samvat*) too as followed in the preceding year 1903(samvat).

The document in Persian *shikasta* bears *sarnama Alif/ Akal Purakhji Sahai* and 6 seals in Persian and Gurmukhi.

(ACC. NO. 2580/ 76; Original; f1).

8 *Rajab* 1263 AH (22 June 1847)

316. *Qabala-i Bai* executed by Ahmad son of Faiz Ali resident of Sarai Maali Khan, Lucknow *wakil* on behalf of *Mst.* Waziran daughter of Meharban Ali wife of Imam al-Din Khan, resident of Bazar Jhaulal in respect of the sale of one storeyed *haveli* situated at Bazaar Jhaulal (details of the boundaries are given in the document) in favour of Saiyid Azam Ali son of Saiyid Ali for a sum of Rs. 101/- and acknowledges the receipt of the amount in full.

The document in Persian *nastaliq* bears the seal of Mufti and that of the *Adalat-i Alia Diwani Bait al saltanat* Lucknow. It also bears departmental endorsements on the reverse.

(ACC. NO. 2395/ 4; Original; f1).

14 *Bhadon* 1904 *Samvat* (date in the text) (23 September 1847)	317.	Letter of Baba Budastagar to Gosain Sahib Taran Taran. Informs that Ilahi Bakhsh has been sent to meet him on 14 *Bhadun* 1904 (*samvat*) along with evidences circumstantial to the murder of Baba Gobindgar and hopes that justice would be done accordingly. Otherwise, the addressee's aide should visit the spot to assess the situation as some one provokes him to put the blame of the murder upon Akku Karnalwala *(zamindar)* and in retutn would get Rs. 100/- for his *marghat*. Seeks his permission to appear before him along with the *marghat*. Adds that the issue of land at *mauza* Ghatwala would remain pending till the aide of the addressee arrives. Also says that search of horses for him is in process. The document is in Persian *shikasta*. **(ACC. NO. 2580/ 79; Original; f1).**
3 *Zilqada* 1263 AH (13 October 1847)	318.	Letter to Lala Sahib. Refers his letter (addressee) to Mathura Prasad informing about Rai Sahib's visit to Shahganj and if desired he may reach Shahganj to see him. Also reminds him of his promise to execute the *patta* of *qasba* Jais in his favour. Tells that although none in the perview of this government has *patta,* however if a new *hakim* takes charge and wants to see the *patta* prevail hence in view of this Mathura Prasad is being sent to him to execute *patta* which would an act of kindness on his part. The document in Persian *shikasta* bears *sarnama innahu.* **(ACC. NO. 2116; Original; f1).**
12 December 1847	319.	*Patta-i theka* executed by Amiran daughter of Shaikh Yar Ali *Ahl-i maash* leasing out

her share of 3 *dams* out of 15 *dams* from *mauza* Lodipur Sartha and Fathpur Sartha and 8 *dam* from Jamalpur Jangi *pargana* Bhailawar for a total annual *malguzari* of Rs. 30/- together with the usual cesses along with advance interest free payment of Rs. 15/- in favour of Sohan Lal and Malik Sahu for a period of 7 years from 1255 to 1261 *Fasli*. The lease-holder should pay the *malguzari* every year crop after crop. In case, the lease holder fails to pay the revenue demand in time, she (the executant) would be free to cancel the *theka* or to make fresh *bandobast*. In case she collects the yield through her *sazawul* the salary of the *sazawul* would be paid by the *thekadar* till the end of *theka* i. e. 1261 *Fasli*. There would be no claim on their part for the remaining period of *theka*. Undertakes to return the advance money to the leaseholder. In case she fails to pay the advance money the lease- deed would continue in favour of *thekadar*.

The document in Persian *shikasta* executed on an eight *anna* stamp paper bears the seal of *Mst*. Bibi Amiran.

(ACC. NO. 2534/ 8; Original; f1).

12 December 1847 320. *Qabuliyat-i theka* executed by Sohan Lal, resident of village Fathpur Sartha and Malik Sahu (?) resident of Jamalpur *pargana* Bhailawar District Bihar. State that they have taken on lease from Bibi Amiran, *ahl-i maash* the said village for a period of 7 years from 1255 to 1261 *Fasli* (1847 to 1853 AD) a share of 3 *dams* out of 15 *dams* from village Lodipur Sartha, Fathpur Sartha and 8 *dams* from village Jamalpur *pargana* Bhailawar totalling the annual amount of *malguzari* to

Rs. 30/- and Rs. 15 as an advance to *ahl*-i *maash* together with land tax and other taxes and cesses like *jalkar, bunkar, ahar, pokhar,* tank, pond, well, garden etc. Add that after the expiry of 7 Years in 1261 *Fasli* the *ahl-i maash* would return the advance money to them and the *theka* would be nullified. In case she is unable to return the money the *theka* would continue.

The document in Persian *shikasta* executed on an eight *anna* stamp paper bears signatures of the executant in Persian and that of the witnesses in Devnagri.

(ACC. NO. 2534/ 7; Original; f1).

1264 AH (in seal) (1847-48)

321. *Nikahnama* executed by Ali Mirza son of Mirza Mughal in respect of his marriage with *Mst.* Mahdi Begum daughter of Mirza Fazl Ali through the *wikalat* of Mir Jafar Ali and two witnesses including Mir Khan Sahib against the *mahr* of Rs. 5000/- besides subsistence allowance to her.

The document in Persian *shikasta* bears *sarnama Alif* and the seals of Ali Mirza (the executant) and Mirza Mughal besides two other seals.

(ACC. NO. 148; Original; f1).

24 *Safar* 1264 AH/ 11 *Magh* 1255 *Fasli* (31 January 1848)

322. *Qabuliyat-i theka* executed by Del Chand, son of Fath Singh resident of *mauza* Chari *Pargana* Bhailawar District Bihar. States that he has taken on lease a total *jama* of 8 *anna* out of 2 *anna* from *pragana* Bhailawar from Bibi Amiran daughter of Shaikh Yar Ali for a period of six years w.e.f. 1255 to 1260 *Fasli* (1847 to 1852 AD) excluding other rights like *mal-o-jihat, sairjihat* and *kulhububat*.

Agrees to pay annual *malguzari* of Rs.

50 /- every year to the leaseholder. Also agrees that in case he fails to pay the said revenue the leaseholder is free to cancel the lease-deed and can also make fresh *bandobast* or appoint *sazawal* to collect the *malguzari* from him of the land in question or from the property owned by him.

The document in Persian *shikasta* on an eight *anna* stamp paper bears endorsement on the reverse in Devnagri.

(ACC. NO. 2534/ 9; Original; f1).

5 *Magh* 1904 *Samvat* (9 February 1848)

323. *Parwana* addressed to Sardar Ram Singh. Refers his previous *parwana* and expresses anxiety on the inaction in respect of the murder of Baba Ganeshgar and his *Kahar* (palanquin bearer) by Akku *Zamindar Karnalwala* and that their jewellery has been snatched. Directs him to do justice with the victim or produce the murderer (Akku *zamindar Karnalwala)* before the Sahib Bahadur for justice to be done in the case.

The document in Persian *shikasta* bears *sarnama Alif.*

(ACC. NO. 2580/ 78; Original; f1).

6 *Rabi* I 1264 AH/1 *Phagun* 1255 *Fasli* (11 February 1848)

324. *Patta-i theka* granted by Mst Amiran, d/o Shaikh Yar Ali to Samru son of Khairu resident of village Daulatpur *pargana* Okri District Bihar with regard to her share of land both *aimma* and *Khalsa* situated in *mauza* Sulaimanpur and Husainpur for a period of 6 years from 1255 to 1260 *Fasli* (1847 to 1851 AD) with all rights like *mal-o-jihat, Sair jihat, Jalkar, bunkar, ahar, pokhar,* tanks, ponds, wells, fruit, gardens etc. excluding *niyaz-i dargah* and other items with the total annual *malguzari* of Rs. 12/

without any concession on account of natural calamities or otherwise. Clarifies that all the expenses as the auxiliary troops (*sehbandi*) and *Khana sazi* and digging of *kachha* wells etc. shall be exclusively borne out by the leaseholder whereas other specified expenses shall be made by the *madad-i maash* grantees. The lease holder should pay the *malguzari* every year crop after crop. In case the leaseholder fails to pay revenue demand in time she would be free to cancel the *theka* or to make fresh *theka*. In case she collects the yields through *sazawul* the salary of the *sazawul* would be paid by the lease holder till the end of the *theka*.

The document in Persian *shikasta* on an eight *anna* stamp paper bears the seal of *Mst* Bibi Amiran. On the reverse there is a note by Samru *Thekadar* declaring that he has returned the said *theka* on 24 *Shaban* / 11 *Sawan* 1256 *Fasli* and has no claim whatsoever on the *theka*.

(ACC. No. 2534/ 10; Original; f1).

15 *Mangh* (*Magh*) 1904 *Samvat* (19 February 1848)

325. Letter to Lala Thakur Das. States that the grant from *taalluqa* Giuhar has been in assignment of Shyamgar Dangawala on account of *dharmarth* since olden times. Directs for the continuance of the aforesaid grant as heretofore without creating any hindrance.

The document in Persian *shikasta* bears *sarnama Alif / Bafazl-i Sri Akal Purakhji* and a seal of Sri Ramji in Gurmukhi.

(ACC. NO. 2580/ 75; Original; f1).

22 *Magh* 1255 *Fasli* (1264 AH)

326. *Iqrarnama* executed by Ram Dayal Jiwan, resident of Kharoch and Dular Jiwan

(February 1848) resident of Ambasa *pargana* Bhailawar District Bihar lease holders of 8 *dams* out of 16 *anna* of the land share of *Mst.* Bibi Amiran the *ahl-i maash.* Refer to a decree granting Rs. 167 / 7½ *zar-i tankhuh* to Saiyid Shah Mubarak Husain against the annual *malguzari* due upon Bibi Amiran who has passed on her share to the leaseholder for a period of three years w.e.f. 1255-7 *Fasli* for the payment of the aforesaid amount and the leaseholder agreeing to pay the amount to the *digreedar*. Promise to deliver the stipulated amount to the degree holder from the revenue amount year by year and in instalments without any excuse. Also agree that in case they fail to make the payment, the *digreedar* has every right to collect the amount from his property.

The document in Persian *shikasta* executed on eight *anna* stamp paper bears *sarnama Alif* and signatures of the executants and witnesses in Persian and Devnagri and departmential endorsements on the back.

(ACC. NO. 2534/ 11; Original; f1).

6 *Rabi* II 1264 AH (12 March 1848) 327. Letter to Mir Sahib. Informs that Anant Misr, the cultivator of village Surmu *ilaqa* Surajpur, Narela is a respectable person and is prompt in making payment of land revenue. Directs him not to harass him on account of excessive demand and not to demand more than the stipulated amount. The document in Persian *shikasta* bears *sarnama Alif* and the seal of Nawal Singh.

(ACC. NO. 2403/ 114; Original; f1).

12 *Rabi* II 1264 AH (18 328. *Bainama* executed by Lakhmi Das son of Gopal Das himself and as *wakil* on behalf

March 1848) of his brother Daji and sister *Mst.* Hari Bai in respect of the sale of one piece of land situated in *muhalla* Unchi Siri inside the walled city of Bandar Khambayat (details delineated in the body of the text) to Kalia, son of Ganga Ram for a total sum of Rs. 16/- only.

The document in Persian *shikasta* written on cloth bears *sarnama Alif* and two seals including a seal of *Qazi* and symbol of signatures of the executant and the informer in Persian and Devnagri.

(ACC. NO. 2746/ 3; Original; f1).

28 *Phagun* 1904 *Samvat* (2 April 1848)

329. Letter (of Raja of Kashmir) to (the Governor General). Expresses his deep sense of gratitude for his kind attention in strengthening and stabilizing his state. Expresses his concern on the departure of Henry Montgomry Colonel Lawrence to England who was the Resident of his State. Conveys that his visit to Lahore is a matter of great pleasure for him.

The document is in Persian *shikasta*.

(ACC. NO. 121; Original; f1).

6 *Jumada* II 1264 AH (10 May 1848)

330. Letter of Nawal Singh to Mir Zakir Husain. Refers to the *hukmnama* of Nawwab Wazir al-Mamalik addressed to the Army Officers posted at Rudauli and Basudhi in the case of reducing the imprisonment period of Ganj Ali Khan, Hasan Raza Khan and others of village Moi attached to the territory of *Huzur, Tahsil* Rudauli and Basudhi has been received through Raghunath peon of *Kachehri-i Huzur*. Directs him for immediate redressal of the order so that the matter should not be referred again to the Government.

The document in Persian *shikasta* bears the seal of Nawal Singh (the writer).

(ACC. NO. 1953; Original; f1).

15 *Jumada* II 1264 AH (19 May 1848)

331. *Ariatnama* executed by Fazl Ali Khan son of Pir Ali Khan, resident of *qasba* Sandila *muhalla* Chunartola. States that he has obtained a stable situated in the west of the residential land from Sarfaraz Ali, Mian Khadim Ali and Shaikh Ahsan Allah on rent of 4 *annas* per annum. Promises not to renovate stable in any form .

The document in Persian *shikasta* bears *sarnama* Alif and the seal of the writer, besides the signature of the witnesses.

(ACC. NO. 2672/ 47; Original; f1).

15 *Jumada* II 1264 AH (19 May 1848)

332. *Ariatnama* executed under the seal of Fazl Ali Khan and witnesses Shaikh Khair Ali and Karamat Khan Balloch with the attestation seal of Qazi Muhammad Wajih al-Din Ahmad. (To the same effect as the foregoing).

(ACC. NO. 2672/ 48; Copy; f1).

19 *Jumada* II 1264 AH (23 May 1848)

333. *Qabala-i Bai* executed in the Civil Court of Lucknow by Khushwaqt Rai son of Kashinath resident of Katra Rani, Lucknow. Informs that he has sold his *amla* and *arazi* comprising one storeyed *pukhta haveli* situated at Katari Tola (the details of the *haveli* along with the demarcation of boundary are given in the document) to Karam Ali, son of Basharat Allah, son of Zia Allah resident of Saiyidwari *muhalla*, *wakil* on behalf of Kandhi (Kanhi) Lal and Bindraban, sons of Samadhan of Katari Tola for a sum of Rs. 1500/ and has received the amount in full.

The document in Persian *nastaliq* bears a seal of the *Mufti Adalat-i Aliya* Lucknow and that of *Adalat-i Aliya* Lucknow with a royal emblem at the top. The reveres side contains departmental endorsements.

(ACC. NO. 167; Original; f1).

4 June 1848 334. *Arzi* of Narayan Das. Submits that he was holding the post of *Munshigiri* of Khalsa Sharifa with a rank of 500 *zat* and Rs. 50/- as cash allowance for the last eight generations. Further state that from 1182 *Fasli* Tappa Rabupura was also granted to the *ahalkars* of Khalsa Sharifa, *Bakhshigiri* and *Daftar-i Tan.* States that from the total annual cash allowance of Rs. 600/- granted to his grand father Naunit Rai used to receive Rs. 171/-7 from the said Tappa while the rest amount was received from other properties of Maharaja Madhav Rao Sindhia which added Rs. 114/-4/- thereby making total sum of Rs. 285/-11. Informs that in the 4th regnal year of Muhammad Akbar Shah II the said Tappa was detached from the (granted) property of the *ahalkars* and attached to the *tuyul-i khas* and a sum of Rs. 14/ 7 was fixed as allowance which Naunit Rai, his grand-father received till his death. After him Hira Lal, his uncle and Thakur Das his elder brother were the recipients of this grant. Expresses his anxiety that from 1246 *Fasli* this meager amount was too withdrawn. Requests the addressee for orders to Hakim Ahsan Allah Khan Bahadur to restore his old *ulufa* grant to him.

The document is in Persian *shikasta*.

(ACC. NO. 66; Original; f1).

(4 June 1848) 335. *Arzi* of Narayan Das and Ganga Prasad grand sons of Naunit Rai. To the same effect as the document O. R no. 66

The document is in Persian *shikasta*.

(ACC. NO. 65; Original; f1)

25 *Shaban* 1264 AH/27 July 1848/11 *Sawan* 1255 *Fasli* 336. *Qabala-i Bai* executed by Bhikan, daughter of Qazi Rajab Allah, widow of Shaikh Muhammad Anwar. States that she had sold her own share owned from the side of her husband in satisfaction of her *mahr* claim and half of her share in *mauza* Makhdumpur and Ibrahimpur inherited from her father consisting of 18 *dams* to Shaikh Jamal al-Haq and Sajjad Ali for a sum of Rs. 1000/- only. Acknowledges the receipt of the amount in full.

The document in Persian *shikasta* executed on an eight Rupee stamp paper bears symbol of signature of the executant and signatures of the witnesses.

(ACC. NO. 2531/25; Original; f1).

5 *Bhadon Budi* 1905 *Samvat* /2 September 1848 337. *Rahnnama (iqrarnama)* executed by Hashmat al-Nisa, daughter of Saiyid Abd Allah Khan, wife of Saiyid Imtiaz Husain Khan, resident of *muhallah* Harharpura of Benaras. Says that she has borrowed Rs. 1 lakh 20 thousand @ 12 *anna* % interest for a period of 22 years from Babu Kishore Das and Babu Madhu Das, sons of Babu Barkha Chand for the payment of the amount of *rahn* taken against *taalluqa* Kanghat *pargana* Zamania *Zila* Ghazipur mortgaged before Harsudh Narain Singh as per the *dastawiz* dated 26 September 1846 besides for the payment of debt taken from other persons against her property at different places. Promises to pay the amount of *rahn* under

the terms and conditions as mentioned by her in the text of the document.

The document in Urdu *shikasta* contains dim seals of the court with symbol of seals of the executant and witnesses.

(ACC. NO. 2764/ 24; Copy; f1).

29 Shawwal 1264 AH (28 September 1848)

338. Petition of Ishari Singh, *hawaldar* of 10th Company Battalion of 43rd Regiment posted at Shahjahanpur Cantonment to *Sultan-i Alam* (Nawwab of Awadh). States that an annual *jama wajibi* of Rs. 5200/- from *taalluqa* Dadarpatti Rawat *pargana* Asoli belonging to his forefather *zamindari* had been in his assignment which he was paying before the *tahsildar*. Adds that against this *jama* he was also getting a nominal *nankar*. Elaborates that during the time of Raja Man Singh, the former *chakladar* and Ahmad Ali Khan Bahadur, the present *chakladar* in the year 1253 & 1254 *Falsi* and during the time of Mir Baqir Ali *tahsildar, mustajir* of the aforesaid *pargana* in 1255 *Fasli* used to receive 4 *annas* share of the *chakladar* and paid nothing to him. Instead forced him and the *raiyat* to sell each and every household item and got benefited. Adds that due to the oppression of the aforesaid *tahsildar*, many more *raiyats* left the place resulting in the said *taalluqa* remained uncultivated (barren) in 1256 *Fasli*. Further complains that the present *chakladar* while obtaining an order of the *Sultan* dated *Ramzan* 1264 AH showing favouritism to the *tahsildar* ignored the payment of 4 *annas* and other cesses and even did not submit the *jama* papers in the office. Requests for his (the Sultan) orders in the name of *Mushir al-daulah* to take

notice of discrepancy committed by the *amin* regarding the calculation of the aforesaid *taalluqa* and to obtain *iqrarnama/ qabuliyatnama* from him (the *amin*) to deposit *zar-i jama* of the *taalluqa* besides *malzamini* of *mahajan* of the year 1256 *Fasli.* Further requests that the said *taalluqa* may be assigned to him so that he could be able to rehabilitate the *raiyats* and deposit the *zar-i jama* of the *taalluqa* as per the installments.

The document in Persian *shikasta* bears *sarnama Alif.*

(ACC. NO. 2514/4; Original; f1).

31 October 1848 — 339. *Rubakar* executed in the Court of Assistant Collector District Jaunpur on 20 October 1848 regarding a case filed by Raja Raghubir Singh, guardian of Raja Ram Nath Singh of *taalluqa* Bazar Raja Barger Gardaha against Jokhu Singh, Zair Singh, Shiv Prasad Singh and Chait Singh cultivators of village Bishara of the aforesaid *taalluqa* for non-payment of Rs. 25/91/2as the land revenue arrear of 1255 *Fasli.* The *rubakar* also contains reference regarding warrants and notification issued for the arrest of respondents when they did not appear in the court on the previous occasion. Similarly it also contains the statement of Sardha Lal Patwari regarding the payment of land revenue and the balance pending against the respondents. It also contains that the descendents of Zair Singh i. e. Lekhu Rai and Bagh Singh, the respondent left cultivation which was given on *theka* @ Rs. 2/- per *bigha.* The court accepting the payment of Rs. 2/- per *bigha* issued orders to pay the amount realized

through *theka* to the claimant. Finally, the court issues decree in favour of the appellant directing the defendants for the payment of outstanding revenue together with expenses of the court to the appellant.

The document in *Urdu shikasta* bears seal of the court.

(ACC. NO. 2764/25; Copy;f1).

15 *Maghar* 1905 *Samvat* (10 December 1848)

340. Letter to the Chiefs of Mulkaran particularly Qaim, Maddo and Biru. Informs them that *mauza* Mulkaran has been granted in *jagir* of Bakhshi Gur Naraian from the beginning of *kharif* crop 1905 *(Samvat)* to meet the expenses of the *sawars* and *piadas* which excludes the land granted as *dharmarth* and *inam*. Orders them to pay the revenue realization to him without any excuse.

The document is in Persian *shikasta*.

(ACC. NO. 2398/ 35; Original; f1).

15 *Maghar* 1905 *Samvat* (10 December 1848)

341. Letter to the Chiefs of Kohra (Kuwarah). Informs them that the territory of Kohra has been assigned in the *jagir* of Bakhshi Gur Narain to meet the expenses of his *sawars* and *piadas* from the beginning of the *Kharif* crop 1905 *(Samvat)* which excludes the land meant for *dharmarth, inam* and other *jagirs*. Directs them to pay the revenue realization of the aforesaid territory to the assignee.

The document is in Persian *shikasta.*

(ACC. NO. 2398/ 25; Original; f1).

15 *Maghar* 1905 *Samvat* (10 December 1848)

342. Letter to Seedu, Saida, Sher Akram and Sher Kalan, Chiefs of *mauza* Malikpur. *Informs* them that *mauza* Malikpur along with other territories including Kohra etc. have been granted in the *jagir* of Bakhshi Gur Narain from the beginning of *Kharif*

crop 1905 *(Samvat)* to meet the expenses etc. of the *sawars* and *piadas* which excludes the land granted as *dharmarth* and *inam*. Directs them to accept him as their *hakim* and pay the revenue realization to the said Bakhshi without any excuse.

The document is in Persian *shikasta*.

(ACC. NO. 2398/ 38; Original; f1).

15 *Maghar* 1905 *Samvat* (10 December 1848)

343. Letter to Pir Bakhsh, Naubat (?), Khan, Akku Khan and other *zamindars* of *mauza Ojhari*. Informs them that *mauza* Ojhari has been granted in the *jagir* of Bakhshi Gur Narain from the beginning of *Kharif* crop 1905 which excludes the land granted as *Inam* and *dharmarth* to him. Orders them to pay the revenue realization to the said Bakhshi without any excuse.

The document is in Persian *shikasta*.

(ACC. NO. 2398/ 37; Original; f1).

15 *Maghar* 1905 *Samvat* (10 December 1848)

344. Letter to the *zamindars* of *mauza* Pind, Mirah of District Baikunth. Informs them that the aforesaid villages have been assigned in the *jagir* of Bakhshi Gur Narain from the beginning of *Kharif* crop 1905 to meet the expenses of the *sawars* and *Piadas* which excludes the lands granted as *Inam* and *dharmarth* and *muafi*. Orders them to pay the land revenue realization to the assignee without any excuse.

The document is in Persian *shikasta*.

(ACC. NO. 2398/ 36; Original; f1).

15 *Maghar* 1905 *Samvat* (10 December 1848)

345. Letter to Muhammad Ali Khan, Muqim Khan *zamindars* of *mauza* Chirah. Informs them that *mauza* Chirah has been granted in the *jagir* of Bakhshi Gur Narain from the beginning of *Kharif* crop 1905 *(Samvat)* to meet the expenses of his *sawars* and *piadas*.

Orders them to pay the land revenue to him regularly without any excuse.

The document is in Persian *shikasta*.

(ACC. NO. 2398/ 34; Original; f1).

15 *Maghar* 1905 *Samvat* (10 December 1848)

346. Letter to the *Chaudharis*, Kaman, Teja, Pir Bakhsh and Bakhshi Akud of Kak, Koral, Adra (?) Arhir etc. Informs them that the *villages* mentioned above have been assigned as *jagir* to Bakhshi Gur Narain from the beginning of *Kharif* 1905 *(Samvat)* which excludes the *jagir* assigned to him as *inam* and *dharmarth*. Orders them to pay the revenue realization to him without any excuse or objection.

The document is in Persian *shikasta*.

(ACC. NO. 2398/ 31; Original; f1).

15 *Maghar* 1905 *Samvat* (10 December 1848)

347. Letter to the *Saiyids* of Shaladatta particularly to Karim Haider Shah, Qurban Husain, etc. Informs them that their villages have been granted in the *jagir* of Bakhshi Gur Narain from the beginning of *Kharif* crop 1905 *Samvat* to meet the expenses of his *sawars* and *piadas* which excludes the *jagir* assigned to him as *dharmarth* and *Inam*. Orders them to pay the revenue realization of those villages to him without any excuse.

The document is in Persian *shikasta*.

(ACC. NO. 2398/ 32; Original; f1).

15 *Maghar* 1905 *Samvat* (10 December 1848)

348. Letter to Jafar Khan, Ali Askar and Sultan Ali Shah chiefs of *mauza* Jehta and Shahur. Informs them that the specified villages in Kohra region have been assigned in the *jagir* of Bakhshi Gur Narain from the beginning of the *Kharif* crop 1905 *Fasli (Samvat)* to meet the expenses of the *sawars* and *piadas*. Orders them to recognize him

as their *hakim* and pay the *mal-i wajib* to him without excuse.

The document is in Persian *shikasta*.

(ACC. NO. 2398/ 26; Original; f1).

15 *Maghar* 1905 *Samvat* (10 December 1848)

349. Letter to Sharaf Shah and Mahtab Shah. Refers to a royal order directing them to come through Gur Narain Singh who would explain about requests before him (the Maharaja) and need not to worry.

The document is written in Persian *shikasta*.

(ACC. NO. 2398/ 27; Original; f1).

15 *Maghar* 1905 *Samvat* (10 December 1848)

350. Letter to Haider Khan and Akku Khan etc. *zamindars* of *mauza* Tamair. Informs them that *mauza* Tamair has been assigned in the *jagir* of Bakhshi Gur Narain from the beginning of *Kharif* crop 1905 *(samvat)* to meet the expenses of his *sawars* and *piadas* which excludes *dharmarth jagir* and *muafi* amount. Orders them to pay him the revenue realization without any excuse.

The document is in Persian *shikasta*.

(ACC. NO. 2398/ 28; Original; f1).

15 *Maghar* 1905 *Samvat* (10 December 1848)

351. Letter to Quli Khan, Sardar Khan, Jang Khan *zamindars* of Moharyan, Ahara and Pokri (?). Informs them that the aforesaid villages have been assigned to Bakhshi Gur Narain from the beginning of *Kharif* crop 1905 *(samvat)* to meet the expenses of his *sawars* and *piadas* which excludes the *Jagir* granted as *dharmarth* and *Inam* to him. Orders them to pay him the revenue realization without any excuse.

The document is in Persian *shikasta*.

(ACC. NO. 2398/ 29; Original; f1).

15 *Maghar*

352. Letter to Fath Ali and Madad Khan, chiefs

1905 Samvat (10 December 1848)		of *mauza* Mahalka. Informs them that mauza Mahalka has been assigned in the *jagir* of Bakhshi Gur Narian from the beginning of *Kharif* crop 1905 *(samvat)* to meet the expenses of *sawars* and *piadas* which excludes the jagir assigned as dharmarth and *inam*. Orders them to pay him the revenue realization without any excuse. The document is in Persian *shikasta*. **(ACC. NO. 2398/ 30; Original; f1).**
6 *Poh* 1905 *Samvat* (31 December 1848)	353.	Letter (of Chhatar Singh Akal Sahai) to Bakhshi Gur Narain. Orders him to produce every *alusa* (tribe people) before him and assures of their forgiveness. Also assures that they will be enrolled as *sawar* and *piada*. The document in Persian *shikasta* bears the seal of Chhatar Singh Akal Sahai. **(ACC. NO. 2398/7; Original; f1).**
6 *Poh* 1905 *Samvat* (31 December 1848)	354.	Letter (of Chhatar Singh Akal Sahai) to the Officials. Informs them about the assignment of certain villages to Bakhshi Gur Narain on account of his loyalty to Maharaja Dalip Singh from the beginning of *Rabi* crop 1905 *Fasli*. Orders them to realize the fixed revenue from these villages and deposit the same to him (Gur Narain). Clarifies that he would be granted *jagir* in the month of *Rabi* for the maintenance of *sawar* and *piada*. The document in Persian *shikasta* bears two seals of Chhatar Singh Akal Sahai. **(ACC. NO. 2398/ 8; Original; f1).**
6 *Poh* 1905 *Samvat* (31 December	355.	Letter (of Chhatar Singh Akal Sahai) to Sardar Nihal Singh. States that Gur Narain Singh has been deputed to manage the

1848)		affairs of the territory situated below and above the hills. Orders him to provide military assistance including *piada* and *sawar* according to his requirement and not to make any excuse. The document in Persian *shikasta* bears the seal of Chhatar Singh. **(ACC. NO. 2398/ 9 Original; f1).**
6 *Poh* 1905 *Samvat* (31 December 1848)	356.	Letter (of Chhatar Singh Akal Sahai) to Bhai Dal Singh. Intimates that the villages of *Zila* Kuwarah, Shaladatta, Malikpur, Aharah, Tumair Chirrah, Kripa Pand Bhikwal, Shivalgran etc. situated below and above the hills have been assigned to Bakhshi Gur Narain by way of *amanat* (gift). Directs him not to interfere in these villages. The document in Persian *shikasta* bears the seal of Chhatar Singh Akal Sahai. **(ACC. NO. 2398/ 10; Original; f1).**
6 *Poh* 1905 *Samvat* (31 December 1848)	357.	Letter (of Chhatar Singh Akal Sahai) to Bhai Dal Singh. Intimates him that Bakhshi Gur Narain has been deputed to manage the affairs of the territories lying at the foot of the hills etc. and for the repair of the forts there. Orders him to provide all the men and material required by him. Also instructs that the sepoys of the forts who are under him may be sent before Bakashi Gur Narain for erecting police post (*thana*) in every fortress. The document in Persian *shikasta* bears the seal of Chhatar Singh. **(ACC. NO. 2398/ 11; Original; f1).**
1265 AH (date in seal) (1848-49)	358.	Letter of Nasir Muhammad Ali to Mirad (?). Informs that the payment of arrears of the revenues had been carried away by two

horsemen to the court of *Kachehri-i Diwan Khana-i Wazarat*. Expresses ignorance about the remittance of the instalment of the territory of Islamabad and says that the arrears will be paid shortly. Requests to inform him about the persons against whom the outstanding arrears are pending.

The damaged document is in Persian *shikasta* bears seal of Nasir Muhammad Ali (the writer).

(ACC. NO. 1947; Original; f1).

5 January 1849/ 9 *Safa* 1265 AH/ 26 *Paus* 1256 *Fasli*.

359. *Sanad-i Rasid Muafi* executed by Shaikh Wajid Husain son of Shaikh Yar Ali alias Ain Allah, resident of *mauza* Mustafabad *pargana* Bhilawar District Bihar. Authorises his sister *Mst*. Amiran of *mauza* Daulatpur *pargana* Okri District Bihar to receive form Safdar Ali an amount of Rs. 170/ 11-3 which includes principal with interest and court expenses as per the decree, dated 20 January 1847 in the case filed by his father (Shaikh Yar Ali) in the Court of Additional Judicial Magistrate at Gaya against Shaikh Safdar Ali claiming upon him his ¼th share amounting to Rs. 130/ 11/2-and declares that he will have no claim whatsoever upon the amount realized.

The document in Persian *shikasta* executed on an eight *anna* stamp paper bears signature of Shaikh Wajid Husain, the executant besides seal and signature of the witnesses including that of *Mst*. Kangu and *Mst* Bhikan wives of Shaikh Wajid Husain.

(ACC. NO. 2531/26; Original; f1).

15 *Poh*

360. Letter (of Chhatar Singh Akal Sahai) to

1905 *Samvat* (8 January 1849)

Bakhshi Gur Narain. States that he has come to know about all his affairs through his letters as well as through verbal communication of Makhan Singh. Advises him that it would be best for him to engage himself in repairing the fort of Saiyidpur and to produce the elites of the region before (Dalip Singh) who is about to visit the region within a week who may consider all his demands on that occasion. Also asks to keep him informed about Ram Raja Ratan Chand's movement.

The document in Persian *shikasta* bears the seal of Chhatar Singh.

(ACC. NO. 2398/ 12; Original; f1).

16 *Poh* 1905 *Samvat* (9 January 1849)

361. Letter (of Chhatar Singh Akal Sahai) to Bakhshi Gur Narain. States that he has come to know about all his affairs through his letter. Orders him to reach Saiyidpur along with a contingent of 500 troops as soon as he receives the *parwana* and repair the fort (of Saidpur) and come all along the other necessities so that the repairing of the fort could be accomplished before the arrival of (Dalip Singh) and that all the hilly people should be present before him (the addressee). Also expresses anguish on the skirmish that occurred amongst the hilly people in the fort of Gori at the time of his arrival in the fort. Instructs him to manage the affairs of Kutch region and above the hills with utmost care. Adds that as far as the fort of Gori is concerned he should not be worried as it will be handed over to him at the right moment.

The document in Persian *shikasta* bears the seal of Chhatar Singh.

(ACC. NO. 2398/ 13; Original; f1).

13 January 1849 — 362. Letter addressed to Lala Shyamanand wakil of the Maharaja of Riwan. Referring to a letter of the Resident at Lahore dated 5 January 1849 informing that Raja Ajit Singh Ladowala of Lahore who was confined at Allahabad has fled away on 28 December 1848 has to be arrested and the arrester will get a reward of Rs. 5000/-. Directs him to issue a notification in the Riwan region and if he receives any information about him he may be arrested and may be produced before him.

The document in Urdu *shikasta* bears a seal of the Agent to the Governor General.

(ACC. NO. 2762/ 8; copy; f1).

28 *Poh*1905 *Samvat* (22 January 1849) — 363. Letter (of Chhatar Singh, Akal Sahai) to Bakhshi Gur Narain. States that he has come to know of all the matters through his *arzi* and also through verbal communication of Gyan Singh and Deva Singh. Referring to a previous plan to despatch a detachment via Shaladatta and Kuwarah to chastise the enemy informs that however, as per his request the troops have now been deployed directly on the spot. Urges him to pacify the people of Kuwarah who render their services to the Maharaja. Directs him to make necessary arrangements for the construction of the fort of Saiyidpur.

The document in Persian *shikasta* bears the seal of the writer.

(ACC. NO. 2398/ 14; Original; f1).

1 *Rabi* I 1265 AH (25 January 1849) — 364. *Parwana* under the seal of Naqi Ali Khan, *Nazim* of Sandila to Hafiz Shaukat Ali Chaudhary. Communicates grant of 50 *bighas* measured revenue free cultivable

land in village Tikra Barar attached to Kakrali situated in *pargana* Sandila for the expenses of the *imambara* and *taziadari* in favour of Inayat Husain resident of Sandila from 1256 *Fasli*. Instructs to measure and relinquish the land in favour of the grantee and his heirs and not to ask for a fresh *sanad* enabling them to spend its proceeds on the *imambara* and *taziadari*.

The document in Persian *shikasta* bears *sarnama Alif*.

(ACC. NO. 1528; Copy; f1).

1 *Magh* 1905 *Samvat* (25 January 1849) 365. Letter (of Chhatar Singh Akal Sahai) to Bakhshi Gur Narain. Orders him to submit a detailed statement about every person of Kutch as to who reported to him as well as those who did not so that the platoon of army could be deployed accordingly, besides arrangements could be made for the payment of every architect .

The document in Persian *shikasta* bears a dim seal of Chhatar Singh.

(ACC. NO. 2398/ 15; Original; f1).

8 *Magh* 1905 *Samvat* (1 February 1849) 366. Letter (of Chhatar Singh Akal Sahai) to Mir Wali Khan. Directs him to appear before Bakhshi Gur Narain as early as he receives the *parwana* and produce mischievous chiefs of Saiyidpur before the said Bakhshi. Assures him of every favour and special attention.

The document in Persian *shikasta* bears *sarnama innahu* and the seal of Chhatar Singh.

(ACC. NO. 2398/ 16; Original; f1).

8 *Magh* 1905 *Samvat* (1 February 1849) 367. Letter (of Chhatar Singh) to Saiyid Pir Kamal al-Din. Directs him to produce himself as well as all the people of hilly region

before Bakhshi Gur Narain. Assures him of his favour and benevolence.

The document in Persian *shikasta* bears *sarnama Alif* and the seal of Chhatar Singh.

(ACC. NO. 2398/ 17; Original; f1).

8 *Magh* 1905 *Samvat* (1 February 1849)

368. Letter (of Chhatar Singh) to Bundu Khan Dattahwala. Directs him to appear before Bakhshi Gur Narain and produce the chiefs of Saiyidpur before the said Bakhshi. Assures that by producing the mischievous chiefs he would get special favour.

The document in Persian *shikasta* bears sarnama *innahu* and the seal of the writer.

(ACC. NO. 2398/ 18; Original; f1).

8 *Magh* 1905 *Samvat* (1 February 1849)

369. Letter (of Chhatar Singh) to Bhai Dal Singh. Orders him to handover all the captives of Baloot (?) to Bakhshi Gur Narain.

The document in Persian *shikasta* bears *sarnama innahu* and the seal of the writer.

(ACC. NO. 2398/ 19; Original; f1).

8 *Magh* 1905 *Samvat* (1 February 1849)

370. Letter (of Chhatar Singh Akal Sahai) to Naurath Purawala and Mahmud Sikriwala. Orders them to present themselves before Gur Narain and also produce the mischievous chiefs of Saiyidpur with their belongings before the said Bakhshi. Assures them of his kindness and benevolence.

The document in Persian *shikasta* bears *sarnama innahu* and the seal of the writer.

(ACC. NO. 2398/ 20; Original; f1).

8 *Magh* 1905 *Samvat* (1 February 1849)

371. Letter (of Chhatar Singh Akal Sahai) to Karam Khan and Purshuttam (?). Orders them to present themselves before Bakhshi G'ur Narain and also produce all the mischievous chiefs of Saiyidpur with their

belongings before the said Bakhshi. Assures them of royal patronage and favour.

The document in Persian *shikasta* bears *sarnama Innahu* and the seal of the writer.

(ACC. NO. 2398/ 21; Original; f1).

8 *Magh* 1905 *Samvat* (1 February 1849) 372. Letter (of Chhatar Singh Akal Sahai) to Peer Mahtab Shah, Sharaf Shah and Saiyid Shah. Orders them to present themselves before Bakhshi Gur Narain and also produce all the mischievous chiefs of Saiydpur before the said Bakhshi. Assures them of royal favour and kindness.

The document in Persian *shikasta* bears seal of the writer.

(ACC. NO. 2398/ 22; Original; f1).

9 *Magh* 1905 *Samvat* (2 February 1849) 373. Letter (of Chhatar Singh Akal Sahai) to Ali Sher Khan and Bakhshi Jamil Singh. Orders them to present themselves before Bakhshi Gur Narain having letter of Bhai Dal Singh. Warns not to go against the wishes of the said Bakhshi.

The document in Persian *shikasta* bears *sarnama innahu* and the seal of the writer.

(ACC. NO. 2398/ 23; Original; f1).

9 *Magh* 1905 *Samvat* (2 February 1849) 374. Letter (of Chhatar Singh) to Bhai Dal Singh. Orders him to help Bakhshi Gur Narain with men and money which, in actual, is the service of the Maharaja.

The document in Persian *shikasta* bears *sarnama innahu* and the seal of the addressee.

(ACC. NO. 2398/ 24; Original; f1).

19 *Magh* 1905 *Samvat* (11 February 1849) 375. Letter (of Chhatar Singh Akal Sahai) to Bakhshi Gur Narain. States that it has been learnt that the mischievous chieftains have

assembled troops in Rawalpindi and owing to this concentration of troops, the entire territory has been devastated. Directs him that as soon as he receives the royal orders he should set the affairs of the region at right immediately. Also informs that necessary instructions have also been issued to Colonel Rattan Singh Man to remain encamped in Rawalpindi with one platoon and two cannons. Further informs that troops will also be sent by Amir Sahib to assist him.

The document in Persian *shikasta* bears the seal of Chhatar Singh.

(ACC. NO. 2398/ 39; Original; f1).

19 *Magh* 1905 *Samvat* (11 February 1849) 376. Letter (of Teja Singh Akal Sahai) to Misr Gur Narain. Acknowledging receipt of his letter informs that day after tomorrow one platoon of troops and four hundred artillery (*piada*) would be sent help him in chastising the rebels.

The document in Persian *shikasta* bears *sarnama Innahu* and the seal of Teja Singh.

(ACC. NO. 2398/40; Original; f1).

20 *Magh* 1905 *Samvat* (12 February 1849) 377. Latter (of Chhatar Singh) to Bakhshi Gur Narain Singh. Says that in accordance to his wishes and as per *parwana* he was vested with the entire responsibility of the whole District ranging from the upper-side of Rawalpindi up to Khandi mountain. Expresses anxiety that in spite of having full authority over the *zila*, the entire Muslim population has risen in revolt and has occupied Saiyidpur resulting in the addressee's expulsion from there. Now the *Ghazis* have also revolted and determined to seize *qasba* Kori while the addressee is

sitting calm and quite. Directs him to reach Kori along with the troops (*piada and sawar*) under him as soon as he received his *parwana* and stand firm against the *Ghazis* without giving any chance to the *Ghazis* to destroy anything or to hurt anyone. Warns that if he is unable to lead the expedition he would be replaced by some more capable person to lead the expedition against the rebels.

The document in Persian *shikasta* bears *sarnama Bafazl-i Akal Purakhji* and the seal of Chhatar Singh.

(ACC. NO. 2398/ 41; Original; f1).

15 March 1849 — 378. Letter to Raja Sahib (Raja of Riwan). Refers to a report of the *Nazir* dated 15 March about a clash between Babu and others on one hand and Jagarnath and others on the other with regard to Isa, the offender of *mauza* Bhawar who has fled to the adjoining area of Megwan which falls under his territory (the addressee). Directs him to arrest the said offender and produce him in the court.

The document in Persian *shikasta* bears *sarnama Alif* and a bilingual seal of *Adalat-i Faujdari suba* Allahabad in Persian and Devanagri.

(ACC. NO. 2762/9; Original; f1).

29 *Jumada II* 1265 AH. (22 May 1849) — 379. Orders of the Court authorizing *Mst.* Basawan to receive 1/ 4th of her share in her mother's property of inheritance including *mahr* from Faqir Muhammad while the shares of the other share- holders are to be kept in the possession of Saiyid Ali Hasan along with the realization as a trust and whoever from the share-holders

approaches him he should be paid with the intimation to this court.

The other part of the document contains a copy of the letter of Saiyid Ali Hasan to Ganga Prasad Mahajan asking him to handover the share of *Mst.* Basawan and to keep with him the remaining shares of other share-holders and if any share-holder presents himself or submits a *wakalatnama* that should be brought to his notice.

The document is written in Persian *shikasta*.

(ACC. NO. 2080; Original; f1).

29 *Jumada* II 1265 AH (22 May 1849)

380. Order issued by *Sadr al-Shariat* under the seal of the *Kachehry* in respect of distribution of the property of inheritance left by late *Mst.* Bibi Munna daughter of Muhammad ...as desired by Saiyid Ali Hasan Khan. It contains that Mst. Basawan would get 1/4th share from her mother's inheritance granted in her *mahr* by Faqir Muhammad which the said occupant (Faqir Muhammad) should relinquish henceforth whereas the shares of the other co-sharers as per their *siham* described in the text including the realization shall be kept with Saiyid Ali Hasan as trust which should be handed over to them as and when they demand under intimation to this office. The document also records a letter of Saiyid Ali Hasan to Ganga Prasad Mahajan instructing him to release the share of *Mst.* Basawan and keep the shares of others in his possession.

The document in written in Persian *shikasta*.

(ACC. NO. 2403/ 86; Original; f1).

25 *Rajab* 1265 AH/ RY 3 of Wajid Ali Shah (16 June 1849)

381. *Farman* of Muhammad Wajid Ali Shah (of Awadh) addressed to the present and future *mutasaddis* of important affairs of *ilaqa* Sandila. Informs them that a sum of Rs. 200/- has been assigned to Mst. Lado on account of *nankar nagdi* from the territory of Sandila w.e.f. 1255 *Fasli* besides 55 *bighas* of measured land situated in village Adoba in the aforesaid *ilaqa* as *muafi*. Directs them to handover the amount of *nankar* to *Mst* Lado and her descendents, generation after generation year after year,crop after crop and not to create any obstruction on account of *mahsul* etc. to her progeny and need not to demand fresh *sanad* every year.

The document in Persian *shikasta* bears the seal of the Qazi.

(ACC. NO. 1416; Copy; f1).

7 *Shawwal* 1265 AH (26 August 1849)

382. *Qabala i-Bai* executed by Shaikh Ahmad son of Faiz Ali resident of Sarai Maali Khan, Lucknow as *wakil* on behalf of Shaikh Mahr Ali son of Muhammad Ali, resident of Farangi Mahal in respect of *amla and arazi* comprising one storeyed shop including the land surrounding the shop situated at Chowk Lucknow in favour of Ikram Allah son of Habib Allah resident of Haider Ganj wakil, on behalf of Bindraban son of Samadhan resident of Kataritola for a sum of Rs. 800/-. (The details of the boundaries are given in the text of the document).

The document in Persian *nastaliq* bears a royal emblem of Awadh with two round seals; one of the Mufti of the *Adalat-i Aliya Diwani Bait al-Saltanat* Lucknow and the other of the *Adalat-i Aliya Bait al-Saltanat*

Lucknow and departmental endorsement on the reverse.

(ACC. NO. 168; Original; f1).

9 September 1849 383. *Ijaranama* executed by Shaikh Inayat Karim alias Sajjad Ali son of Tufail Ali resident and *malik-i malguza*r of the share from *mauza* Daulatpur *pargana* Okri District Bihar. States that he has given on lease his *muqaddami* comprising 7 *dams* out of 8 *anna* to *Mst.* Zahuran and *Mst* Huran wives of Shaikh Mahbub Ali for a period of three years from 1258 to 1260 *Fasli* (1850 to 1852). States that he has received Rs. 50/- as the advance money (*nazr-i peshgi*). Declares that he would return the advance money by the end of *jeth* 1260 *Fasli* and then only he would be liable to get return the land in question. Further declares that if he failed to return the advance money the *ijara* would continue on the same terms and conditions unless he pays the advance money.

The document in Persian *shikasta* executed on a stamp paper of 8 *anna* bears *sarnama innahu* and signatures of the executant and witnesses in Persian and Devnagri.

(ACC. NO. 2531/27; Original; f1)

10 September 1849 /8 *As* (*Asin*)1257 *Fasli* 384. *Parwana* of Nimat Ali *Amin* of *Sadr-i Ala* District Tirhut to Shaikh Muhammad Jamal al-Haq. Referring to the petition of Munshi Mahbub Ali *Siyahnawis* and *rudadnawis* who has been granted leave permission w.e.f. 19 October to 16 November 1849 informs him that he has been appointed on the said post for the aforesaid period. Directs him to perform the Government duties with full care and honesty.

The document in Urdu *shikasta* bears the seal of Nimat Ali *Amin-i Sadr al-Awwal* of District Tirhit (the writer).

(ACC. NO. 2531/29; Original; f1).

25 *Zilqada* 1265 AH/12 *Kartik* 1257 *Fasli* (12 October 1849)

385. *Qabuliyat-i Theka* executed by Shaikh Kaifiat Ali son of Shaikh Imam Ali, resident of *mauza* Sarmawah, *pargana* Bhailawar, District Bihar. States that he has taken on lease land comprising 8 *dam* out of 2 *anna* from the share of *Mst*. Bibi Amiran for a period of 5 years from 1257-1261 *Fasli* (1849 to 1853 AD) for the total *malguzari* of Rs. 11/- along with Rs. 5/- as advance together with all rights like *mal-o-jihat, sairjihat, Jalkar, bunkar, ahar, pokhar,* tanks, ponds, wells etc. excluding *niyaz-i dargah, rozina* etc. Agrees that the expenses of the maintenance of auxiliary troops (*sehbandi*), *Khana-sazi* and digging of muddy wells etc. shall be borne out exclusively by the leaseholder whereas the other specified expenses shall be mated out by the grantee. Agrees to pay the *malguzari* every year in time without fail. Also agrees that in case he fails to pay the *malguzari* in time during the period, the grantee would be free to cancel the *theka* or make a fresh *bandobast* and there will be no claim from him for the remaining period of *theka* or to realize the yield through appointing *sazawal*. The salary of the *sazawal* would be paid by the leaseholder till the end of *theka*.

The document in Persian *shikasta* written on eight *anna* stamp paper bears the signatures of the executant and witnesses in Devnagri.

(ACC. NO. 2534/ 14; Original; f1).

6 *Kartik* 1906 *Samvat* (22 October 1849)

386. *Yaddasht* about a sum of Rs. 2701/11 *annas* 17 *gandas* with regard to the payment from the time of Maharaja Narain Singh till the time of *Maharani* Mokhdai wife of the late Raja as per the *qararnama* dated 6 *kartik* 1906 *Samvat*.

The document is written in Persian *Shikasta*.

(ACC. NO. 1856; Original; f1).

12 *Zilhijja* 1265 AH/ 29 *Kartik* 1257 *Fasli* (29 October1849)

387. *Istipha -i Theka* executed by Kanwal Narain Hun, Panch Narain Hun, Mira Hun and Khub Lal Hun heirs of late Prem Hun, residents of *mauza* Dodupur Badel and *thekadar* of *mauza* Dhodha *pargana* Bhailawar District Bihar. State that 8 *dams* land out of 2 *anna* share of *Mst.* Bibi Amiran *ahl-i maash* was taken by Prem Hun for a period of five years from 1254 to 1258 *Fasli* (1846 to 1850 AD) with total annual *malguzari* of Rs. 11/ 7-3 who has died in *Magh* 1256 *Fasli.* Expressing their inability to pay the *malguzari* for the remaining years of 1257 and 1258 *Fasli* of the aforesaid *theka* they have offered to surrender the said *theka* to the *ahl-i maash* who may occupy the same and they henceforth will not have any claim on the *theka.*

The document in Persian *Shikasta* executed on eight *anna* stamp paper bears the *sarnama innahu* and *a*signatures of the executants and witnesses in Devnagri.

(ACC. NO. 2534/ 15; Original; f1).

24 *Zilhijja* 1265 AH/10 *Aghan* 1257 *Fasli* / 10 November 1849

388. *Fautinama* given by Sarnam Singh son of Asman Singh resident of Bhailawar and Bhatan Singh son of Fath Singh resident of *mauza* Muhammadpur *pargana* Bhailawar in the *Dar al Qaza, Pargana*

Bhailawar. Testify that Shaikh Tufail Ali son of Shaikh Muhammad Anwar son of Shaikh Muhammad Munawwar Allah has died on 1 *Rajab* 1258 AH / *Bhadon* 1249 *Fasli* and his shares of properties in *mauza* Qazipur, Mustafabad, Qita i-Koha(?), Kafurpur, Sulaimanpur, Husainpur, dependencies of *pargana* Bhailawar besides shares in *mauza* Daulatpur, Mianwan, Saiyidpur Mianwan, Muhammadpur, Chak etc. dependencies of *pargana* Okri District Bihar, his ancestral property, was inherited by his wife *Mst.* Amiran daughter of Shaikh Yar Ali in her *mahr* and otherwise who has been in the possession of these properties both immovable and movable in accordance to her right of inheritance and as her *mahr* who pays the land revenue to the government regularly and punctually.

The document in Persian *shikasta* bears the seal of Ghulam Husain and physical description of Sarnam Singh and Bhatan Singh aged 39 and 51 respectively, the reporters besides signatures of the witnesses.

(ACC. NO. 2531/ 28; Original; f1).

9 *Muharram* 1266 AH (25 November 1849)

389. *Parwana* of Muhammad Wazir Khan to Nasir Ali Khan. Acknowledges receipt of his letter dated 7 *Muharram* (1266 AH) informing about the postponement of the visit of the Agent and thus his request for the postponement of the dispatch of troops which could be resumed after receiving request afresh. Informs that since the troops etc. were dispatched to him before the receipt of his letter and in view of the postponement of the proposed visit

besides the grass becoming more costly, staying of the troops there for a longer time would harm them and therefore they may be sent back at the moment which could be dispatched again after receiving a request from him.

The document is written in Persian *shikasta* bears *sarnama Alif* and the seal of the writer.

(ACC. NO. 2701/20; Original; f1).

16 *Muharram* 1266 AH/ 2 December 1849/ 2 *Paus* 1257 *Fasli*. (Illus.)

390. *Qabuliyat-i Theka* executed by Dular, of *mauza* Ambasa *pargana* Bhailawar *zila* Bihar. States that he has taken on lease 8 *dams* out of 2 *anna* share of *Mst* Bibi Amiran *ahl-i maash* which includes all rights like *mal-o-jihat, sair jihat, jalkar bunkar* etc. excluding *rozina, abkari, niaz-i dargah* etc. for a period of 5 years w.e.f. 1257 *Fasli* to 1261 *Fasli* for a total sum of *malguzari* of Rs. 160/-. Agrees to pay the *malguzari* every year in time without fail. Also agrees that the expenses of the maintenance of auxiliary troops (*seh bandi*) *Khanasazi* and digging of muddy wells etc. shall be borne out exclusively by him (the lease holder) whereas the other specified expenses shall be mated out by the grantee. Also agrees that in case he fails to pay *malguzari* in time during the period, the grantee will be free to cancel the *theka* or make fresh *bandobast* - there will be no claim from him for the remaining period of *theka* - or to realize the yield by appointing *sazawal* and *piada* their salary would be paid by the leaseholder till the end of *theka*.

The document in Persian *shikasta* executed on 8 *anna* stamp paper bears signatures of the executant and witnesses in Devnagri.

(ACC. NO. 2534/ 16; Original; f1).

3 December 1849/ 3 *Paus.* 1257 *Fasli.*

391. *Parwana* of Nimat Ali *Amin-i Sadr-i Ala Awwal* of District Tirhut to Shaikh Muhammad Jamal al-Haq of Tirhut. Issues him a certificate of good performance and good conduct for serving as *siyahnawis* and *rudadnawis* in the absence of Munshi Mahbub Ali from 19 October 1849 till date when he resumed his duties after the completion of his leave.

The document in Urdu *shikasta* bears the seal of Nimat Ali, *Amin-i Sadr-i Ala* (the writer).

(ACC. NO. 2531/ 30; Original; f1).

19 *Muharram* 1266 AH (5 December 1849)

392. *Parwana* of Raja Ram Bakhsh to Rafiq Yawar al-Daulah Bahadur. Informs him about the assignment of *taalluqa* Sad-o-Panj Kokan to Rai Lachmi Narain from 1 *Muharram* 1266 AH. Directs that since the *kachehri-i sadr* of the said *taalluqa* is situated at Birh, the *naib* of the said Rai should be given the administrative responsibility of the said *taalluqa* and to be given all the cooperation.

The document in Persian *nastaliq* bears *sarnama Alif* and seal of Raja Ram Bakhsh (the writer) on the cover with the jist of document.

(ACC. NO. 2535/ 10; Original; ff2).

21 *Muharram* 1266 AH (7 December 1849)

393. *Parwana* of Raja Ram Bakhsh to Rai Lachmi Narain regarding fixation of Rs. 3/ 8-as daily allowance on account of *madad-i maash* to Bhawani Dutt and other astrologers in lieu of revenue of Machli Bandar. Directs for the payment of the said

allowance to them from I *Muharram* 1266 AH day by day and obtain authoritative receipt so that the amount could be adjusted in the account in the office of audit and revenue.

The document in Persian *nastaliq* bears *sarnama Alif* and the cover having writer's seal and jist of the document.

(ACC. NO. 2535/ 4; Original; ff2).

23 *Muharram* 1266 AH (9 December 849) 394. *Bainama* and *qabz al-wusul* under the seal of Qazi Saiyid Wilayat Bakhsh executed by Saiyid Shakir Ali and Saiyid Baqir Ali, sons of Saiyid Wilayat Ali and Saiyid Khadim Husain, son of Saiyid Zakir Ali resident of *qasba* Amroha *sarkar* Sambhal, *suba* Shahjahanabad in respect of 8 *biswas* of *muafi* land together with 4 *biswas* and 1¼ *biswansis* of *zamindari* of *pargana* Amroha with its boundaries. State that they have sold the aforesaid land along with gardens out of a total 20 *biswas* in entirety *muafi* and *zamindari* situated in village Rasulpur to Saiyid Qurban Husain son of Saiyid Ahmad Raza from the beginning of *kharif* crop of 1257 *Fasli* (1849 AD) for a sum of Rs. 3000/- and they have received the whole amount from the vendee.

The document in Persian *shikasta* executed on a stamp paper of Rs. 16/- bears *sarnama innahu* with several seals and signatures of the executants and witnesses besides the departmental endorsement on the reverse.

(ACC. NO. 2533/ 13; Original; f1).

13 *Safar* 1266 AH (29 December 395 Court order addressed to Shamsher Khan Jamadar. Informs about the dismissal of a soldier from the troop of Qazi Hasan Ali.

1849) However, some provision and Rs. 1. 50/- may be provided to him.

The bilingual document in Persian *shikasta* and Devanagri bears *sarnama Alif and* the seal of the court of Nizamat *ilaqa* Rasulabad.

(ACC. NO. 2620/ 18; Original; f1).

14 *Safar* 1266 AH (30 December 1849) 396. *Parwana* (addressed to Lachmi Narain). Informs him about the sanction of the monthly salary of Rs. 150/- as per the yield from I *Muharram* 1266 AH to Balmukand *mansabdar*, an employee of the *sarkar*, *sarrishta* of Raja Ram Prasad Lala Bahadur in lieu of the *taalluqa* Sad-o Panj against *mahsul-i namak* (salt tax) from Machli Bandar. Directs for the payment of the salary to him regularly as per the annual yield (*maujudat*) and obtain *qabz al wasul* under the signature of *sarrishtadar* and office of audit and revenue.

The document in Persian *shikasta* bears *sarnama Alif.*

(ACC. NO. 2681/ 29; Original; f1).

14 *Safar* 1266 AH (30 December 1849) 397. This is the cover of the above Document No. 2681/29 which contains that a monthly sum of Rs. 150/- has been granted to Balmukand *Mansabdar*, an employee of *Sakar Sarrishta* Raja Ram Prasad Lala Bahadur w.e.f. 1 *Muharram* 1266 AH in lieu of *taalluqa* Sad o Panj against the *mahsul-i namak* from Machli Bander as per the yields and obtain *qabz al wusul* from him.

(ACC. NO. 2681/ 30; Original; f1).

2 *Rabi* I 1266 AH/10 *Phalgun* 1257 *Fasli* (16 January 398. *Qabuliyat-i theka* executed by Shaikh Amjad Ali and Tilak Dhari Singh, residents of village Seul, *pargana* Okri District Bihar. State that they have taken on lease the land

1850) comprising the share of 2 *annas* out of 8 *annas milkiyat-i malguzari* in *mauza* Ikhtiarpur, Dholi and one *anna* 4 *dam* out of 8 *anna* in *mauza* Ghauspur from *Mst.* Bhikan, *Mst.* Kangu and *Mst.* Amiran for 7 years from 1258 to 1264 *Fasli* (1850 to 1856 AD) against the total annual *malguzari* of Rs. 14/ 8 together with all rights like *jalkar, bunkar, ahar, pokhar,* tanks, ponds excluding *niaz-i dargah* etc. and have paid Rs. 7/ 8 as an advance. Agree to pay the annual *malguzari* of Rs. 14/ 8 to the *ahl-i maashan* year after year without fail. Further state that at the end of *theka* in 1264 *Fasli* they would get return the advance money from the *ahl-i maash* and would return the land to the *ahl-i maash.*

The document in Persian *shikasta* on an eight *anna* stamp paper bears *sarnama Alif* and signatures of the executants and witnesses.

(ACC. NO. 2534/ 13; Original; f1).

14 *Rabi* I 1266 AH (28 January 1850)

399. *Parwana* of Raja Ram Bakhsh Bahadur to Raja Lachmi Narain. States that as per the orders of Siraj al-Mulk Rs. 3/- per diem has been fixed as *madad-i maash* grant in favour of the dependants of late Saiyid Musa Qadri from the *sair Balda Farkhundabunyad* Hyderabad in lieu of *taalluqa* Sad-o-Panch against the *mahsul-i namak* of Machli Bandar which they received till the end of *Zilhijja* 1265 AH. Instructs for the continuation of the grant to them from 1 *Muharram* 1266 AH as usual day after day and obtain the authoritative receipt as per rule which shall be adjusted in the income and expenditure of the said *taalluqqa* in accordance to the receipts.

The document in Persian *nastaliq* bears *sarnama Alif* while the cover curtains the name of addressee Raja Lachmi Narain and seal of Raja Ram Bakhsh Bahadur with the jist of document.

(ACC. NO. 2617/ 26; Original; ff2).

19 *Rabi* I 1266 AH (2 February 1850)

400. *Parwana* of Raja Ram Bakhsh to Rai Lachmi Narain regarding fixation of salary amounting to Rs. 600/- in kind in favour of Kanwal Nain Munshi, an employee of *sarkar, sarrishta* of Raja Ram Prasad Lal Bahadur on the basis of production from 1st month of *Mah-i Ilahi* corresponding to I *Shawwal* 1265 AH till the end of the month of *Shahrivar Mah-i Ilahi* corresponding to 10 *Shawwal* 1266 AH in lieu of *taalluqa* Sad-o-Panj against the *mahsul-inamak* of Machli Bandar from the total *mahsul* of 1259 *Fasli*. Directs for the payment of salary to him according to the yearly yield and obtain receipt under the seal of the *sarrishtadar* and the office of audit and revenue so that the amount could be adjusted in the accounts.

The document in Persian *nastaliq* bears *sarnama Alif* and the writer's seal on the cover with departmental endorsements and jist of document.

(ACC. NO. 2535/ 5; Original; ff2).

3 February 1850

401. *Iqrarnama* executed by Gokul Das *chela* of Ishar Das, resident of village Radha Kund *pargana* Arhak (?) District Mathura. States that the *sewapuja* of Thakur Sri Gobind Devji Maharaj placed in village Radha Kund besides other housing properties of the said temple i. e. houses, ponds and gardens situated in the said *mauza* was

assigned to him by Sri Gosain Ram Chandra Dev, the owner of the temple. States that the expenses of the offerings of Thakurji are met out of the income received as *bhaint, nazr,* from rent of the houses and through ponds and it is his duty to bring to the notice of the owner the account of income and expenditure of the temple. In return he receives Re. 1/- per mensum from the *bhandar* (treasury) of the said Maharaj situated at Bindraban. Declares that as per the practice he would maintain the expenditure of *bhograk* of Thakurji from the income received from the above mentioned sources and would deposit the remaining amount in the *bhandar*. Assures that he would relinquish his duties until he is replaced by some-one and that he would bring all the account of income and expenditure etc. into the notice of owner of the temple except his personal utensils and clothes which shall be deposited in the *bhandar* of the temple after his death. Futther declares that if anyone of his heirs/ *chelas* makes any claim that should be treated as null and void.

The document in Urdu *shikasta* is written on a stamp paper of Rs. 4/. It also bears symbol of signatures of the executant and signatures of the witnesses.

(ACC. NO. 2691/ 34; Original; f1).

7 *Rabi* II 1266 AH (20 February 1850) 402. *Parwana* under the seal of Khwaja Husain Bakhsh, *Naib Nazim* of the *mahals* of Sandila and Malihabad to Qazi Aslih al-Din. Informs that Saiyid Sarfraz Ali would arrive there for purchasing *roghan-i zard* etc. required by the Nawwab. Directs to give him Rs. 100/- from the income of his

territory. Adds that the amount in question shall be adjusted at the time of evaluation. The document in Persian *shikasta* bears *sarnama innahu* and the attestation seal of Mufti Mir Nawwab Ali and the symbol of seal of the writer.

(ACC. NO. 1626; Copy; f1).

22 *Rabi* II 1266 AH (7 March 1850)

403. *Tamassuk* executed by Chhattoo Brahmin resident of village Mukandpur qasba Jais. Undertakes in the presence of Gangaji and Mahadeva to return within three years in instalments a sum of Rs. 197/- borrowed from Mir Zakir Husain. Assures that in case, he fails to pay the amount in the stipulated time he would be liable for the punishment as dictated by Gangaji and Mahadeva.

The document in Persian *shikasta* bears *sarnama innahu* and a seal of Qazi Maslih al-Din as wetness along with the signatures of the executant and witnesses in Devnagri.

(ACC. NO. 1982; Original; f1).

25 *Rabi* 11 1266 AH (10 March 1850)

404. *Arzdasht* of Muhammad Husain resident of *qasba* Jais. Complains against Fazl Husain and Muhammad Husain who have grabbed his one storeyed residential house and the other properties including agricultural land which he had inherited from his grandfather Shaikh Muhammad Ali situated in Jais in Salon despite the evidences and proofs possessed by him (the complainant) which causes much distress to him. Requests to investigate the matter and get him returned his grabbed properties.

The document in Persian *shikasta* with

attestation by the Mufti of Salon to settle the case judiciously.

(ACC. NO. 1985; Copy; f1).

3 *Jumada I* 1266 AH/ 20 *Chait* 1257 *Fasli* (17 March 1850)

405. *Ijararnama* executed by Shaikh Inayat Karim alias Sajjad Ali son of Shaikh Tufail Ali *malik* and *malguzar* of *mauza* Lanchina *pargana* Okri District Bihar. States that he has given on lease his share of 1 *anna,* 5 *dam* and 17 *kauri* in *mauza* Lanchina to Shaikh Waris Ali son of Shaikh Akbar Ali of *mauza* Daulatpur *pargana* Okri District Bihar for a period of 5 years from 1258 to 1262 *Fasli* and has taken Rs. 50/- as advance money. Clarifies that the leaseholder would get control over the produce of the said land and in return would pay him Rs. 4/- annually in instalments as a right of lease deed after deducting all kinds of expenditure such as *sehbandi, kaldari, Khanasazi* etc. Promises to pay the advance money at the end of the lease period in *Jeth* 1262 *Fasli* and would bring the *chak ijara* under his control and if he fails to pay the advance money the lease deed would continue on the same conditions as declared in the deed until he pays the advance money.

The document in Persian *shikasta* executed on an eight *anna* stamp paper bears *sarnama innahu* and seal of Qazi Asad Ali, *Pargana* Okri District Bihar besides signatures of the executant and witnesses. The document also bears a statement of Shaikh Muhammad Waris Husain declaring that he has received back the advance money on 6 *Jumada* 1 1269 AH from Shaikh Inayat Karim.

(ACC. NO. 2531/ 31; Original; f1).

1 April 1850. 406. *Rubakar*-i *Adalat-i Faujdari,* District Mirzapur under the session of William Roberts, Joint Magistrate. Contains statement of Jagrup Singh son of Shiv Raj Singh, resident of *mauza* Bharkhan *ilaqa thana* Ghorawal about the murder of his brother Mohan Singh who as he explained in his statement, was killed by the robbers at Kataighat *ilaqa* Raj Rewan at the time of his return from his in-laws' house in Deora along with other persons. On the question whether he has doubt upon any one, he replied none upon. The Court ordered to produce the petition along with *rubakari*.

The document in Urdu *shikasta* bears a seal of the Agent to the Governor General.

(ACC. NO. 2762/ 10;Copy; f1).

20 April 1850 /9 *Baisakh Shudi* 1257 *Fasli* /1907 *Samvat*. 407. News report about the visit of the Resident on 20 April 1850 to the State of Dhar and instructed the Rajas of Panwar to write about the benevolence and bravery of their forefathers in details for publication. Accordingly, they recalled that their forefather Sabhu Singh originally a Rajput of Hindustan came to Deccan to settle. His son Krishnaji Panwar had three sons namely Butaji Panwar, Ranaji Panwar, Geru Panwar. Later on the three brothers met Chhatrapati Shivaji with their large forces. Shambhaji Maharaj and Raja Ram, the sons of Chhatrapati being appeased by their bravery gave the management of Telangana to the elder son i. e. Butaji Panwar who suppressed the insurgency there and was granted the title of Vishwas Rao at the fort of Jaiji in Karnataka and enhanced his position. Further adds that thereafter Srimant Sahu Maharaj was

appointed from Delhi and was very appeased about the performance of Butaji Panwar in regard to the management of the affairs of the state who granted him *chauth* and further enhanced his position and for his personal expenditure made a grant from the *zila* of Deccan and Khandesh which was divided among the brothers. Says that Rudaji and Anand Rao Panwar fought battles after battles and conquered many places. Consequently, Chhatrapati Maharaj and the Peshwa rewarded them *zila* Gujarat, Malwa, Namar, Kutch, Marwan, BundelKhand, Khandesh etc. yielding lakhs of rupees. Also records about a war between Rudaji Panwar and Baji Rao Peshwa in the year 1654. Lastly an agreement was concluded by Sir John Malcolm with Ram Chander Rao Panwar and in accordance to that *amaldari* of the *parganas* and *mahals* of state Dhar still exists.

The document in Urdu *shikasta* bears *sarnama Alif.*

(ACC. NO. 2733/ 53; Original; f1).

22 *Jumada* II 1266 AH (5 May 1850)

408. *Hiba Bil Muawaza* executed by *Mst*. Zohra Bi, wife of Mir Ghulam Ali. States that her 8th share which she inherited in village Khapra belonging to *Mahalat Balda* Farkhundabunyad, Hyderabad along with wells and trees bearing fruit assigned to Mir Shah Niaz al-Husaini has given (as gift) to Saiyid Shah Wali Allah Husaini for a sum of Rs. 50/- and has received the amount in full.

The document in Persian *shikasta* bears the seals of the executant and witnesses.

(ACC. NO. 2681/ 31; Original; f1).

22 *Jumada* II 1266 AH (5 May 1850)

409. *Parwana* of Raja Ram Bakhsh Bahadur to Rai Lachman Narain. Informs that Lachman Singh, *mansabdar, Sarrishtadar* of Raja Dilsukh Ram has been fixed a salary of Rs. 280/- in kind from the beginning of *Amardad Ilahi* corresponding to 7 *Shaban 1266 AH till the month of Shahrivar Ilahi* corresponding to 21 *Shawwal* 1267 AH in lieu of *taalluqa* Sad-o-Panj and the *mahsul-i namak* (revenue of salt) of Machli Bandar out of total *mahsul* of 1259 *Fasli*. Directs for the payment of salary to him according to yearly yield and obtain authoritative receipt under the signature of the sarrishtadar and the office of the audit and revenue so that it could be adjusted in the account.

The document in Persian *nastaliq* bears *sarnama Alif* and the cover having a seal of the writer and jist of document.

(ACC. NO. 2535/ 2; Original; ff2).

24 *Jumada II* 1266 AH (7 May 1850)

410. *Parwana* of Raja Ram Bakhsh regarding fixation of Rs. 300/- in kind on the basis of production as salary for Hira Lal *mansabdar sarrishta* of Raja Dilsukh Ram from *Farwardin* corresponding to 1 *Rabi* II 1266 AH till the end of *Shahrivar* Ilahi corresponding to 10 *Shawwal* Ilahi 1266 AH in lieu of *taalluqa* Sad-o-Panj and the revenue of the salt of Machli Bandar out of the total *mahsul* of 1259 *Fasli*. Directs for the payment of his salary according to the yearly yield and obtain authoritative receipt so that it could be adjusted in the account in the office of audit and revenue.

The document in Persian *nastaliq* bears *sarnama Alif* and writer's seal on the cover and departmental endorsements with the jist of the document.

(ACC. NO. 2535/ 3; Original; ff2).

4 *Rajab* 1266 AH /21 *Baisakh* 1257 *Fasli* (16 May 1850)

411. *Zamanatnama* executed by Saiyid Bahadur Ali son of Saiyid Asad Ali resident of village Dumri *pargana* Bhailawar District Bihar in respect of a *theka* of 8 *dams* out of 2 *annas* of the entire 16 *annas* of the *ahl-i maash* obtained by his son Fazl Ali for a period of six years from 1256 to 1261 *Fasli* (1848 to 1853 AD) from Bibi Amiran and that he has paid advance amount of Rs. 35/-. States that land revenue installments up to *phaghun* 1257 *Fasli* was not deposited before the *ahl i maash* by the *thekedar*. Consequently a case was filed by Harnam Singh, *Karpardaz* of the said *Mst.* in *Muhkama Commissionery* claiming Rs. 25/ 4 as outstanding land revenue against his son (the *thekadar*) and his properties has been seized and also has made request to auction his property. Conceding the dues, the *thekedar* has made a request to return his seized property and he (the wrier) gives an undertaking that all the installment due from *Aas* up to *phalgun* 1257 *Fasli* amounting to Rs. 25/ 4, after deducting a sum of Rs. 17/-which has already been paid, the remaining sum of Rs. 8. 4/- would be paid by him. Further agrees to pay the *malguzari* installments due from *Rabi* 1258 till 1261 *Fasli* to the *ahli maasha* yearly in installment regularly without fail.

The brittle document in Persian *shikasta* executed on one Re. stamp paper bears *sarnama innahu.*

(ACC. NO. 2531/32; Original; f1).

12 *Rajab* 1266 AH (24 May 1850)

412. *Arzdasht* of Qasim Ali *muafidar* resident of Sandila. States that he has been in assignment of 52 *bighas* of land as *muafi* in lieu of Rs. 156/- at *qasba* Musapur towards

Mahswana in Muzaffarpur Ballia *illaqa* of Chaudhari Subhan Ata *pargana* Sandila the realization of which he had been spending on the expenses of *azadari* (of Imam Husain). Complains that in 1256 *Fasli* (1848 AD) the said Chaudhari paid him only Rs. 25/- on account of *mahsul* and in 1257 *Fasli* (1849 AD) he paid him nothing and that the Chaudhari is creating hurdles in the *muafi* land. Requests to issue an order to Raja Kundan Lal for the issuance of a *hukmnama* to Khwaja Husain Bakhsh, *naib chakladar* to summon the Chaudhari and direct him not to interfere in his *maafi* land and to pay him the pending realization of the year 1255 *fasli* enabling him to arrange the *majlis* of *azadari*. The document also contains orders of Saiyid Naqi Ali Khan to Husain Bakhsh for the redressal of the case.

The document in Persian *Shikasta* bears *sarnama innahu*.

(ACC. NO. 1608; Copy; f1).

19 *Rajab* 1266 AH/ 6 *Jaith Budi* 1906 *Samvat* (31 May 1850)

413. *Parwana* to Lala Mahu Lal. Referring to a *Rubakari* of the court on the petition of Khazani Mal But (?) informs that Lala Bahadur Singh *thanadar* of Bansur who was found guilty for taking bribe of Rs. 10/- has been suspended and he (addressee) has been appointed in his place. Directs him to take over the charge of the said *thana*. Also informs that his salary has been fixed Rs. 25/- beside the expenditure of a cab.

The document in Persian *shikasta* bears *sarnama Alif* and a dim seal in Hindi and Persian.

(ACC. NO. 275; Copy; f1).

2 *Jaith Budi* 1907 *Samvat* (12 June 1850)

414. *Rahnnama* executed by Kishan Sahai son of Gokul Chand, Chaudhari resident of *qasba* Rewari adjacent to *suba Dar al-Khilafa* Shahjahanabad in respect of 391 *ziras gaz-i Ilahi* along with 3 *kothas*, 1 *kothari* without any co- sharer in *muhalla* Sarai Balbhadra which was under his occupation for a sum of Rs. 200/- to Lal Ram Sarup, Ram Singh and Ram Saran, sons of late Lalji Pal. Promises to refund the amount within one year together with the interest of the actual amount at the rate of 10 *annas* per month and 10 *annas* of Rs. 100 of rent amount to the mortgagee. The amount of interest would be adjusted with it .

The document in Persian *shikasta* bears the signature of the witnesses and the reverse contains the physical description of the mortgager.

(ACC. NO. 2567/ 6; Copy; f1).

14 *Shaban* 1266 AH (25 June 1850)

415. Parwana of Raja Ram Bahadur Bakhsh to Raja Rang Rao. Informs that *taalluqa Nurgaon pargana* Nakhungaon *sarkar* Kallam *suba* Barar Payanghat has been granted as *inam-i altamgha* from the total *paibaqi mahal* to the *pujaris* generation after generation for the expenses of *puja, langar, Sadabarat (?)* organised for the *darbar* of Sri Gurdey Singh situated at *Dar al-Surur* Burhanpur from the beginning of 1260 *Fasli* in consultation with Bal Chand. Directs them to relinquish the same to the aforesaid pujaris.

The document in Persian *nastaliq* bears *sarnama Alif* and the cover contains the name of Raja Rang Rao (the addressee)and the seal of Raja Ram Bakhsh with the jist of document and departmental endorsement.

(ACC. NO. 2617/ 24; Original; ff2).

21 *Shaban* 1266 AH (2 July 1850) — 416. *Qabala-i bai* executed by *Mst.* Bibi Iqlim wife of Mir Akram Ali and *Mst...* wife of Mir Talib Husain. State that they have sold their one *bigha* out of 3 *bighas* land to Man Singh for Rs. 12/ 8/-. Acknowledge the receipt of the amount in full.

The document in Persian *shikasta* bears *sarnama Alif* and several seals and signatures of witnesses.

(ACC. NO. 2403/ 56; Original; f1).

16 July 1850 — 417. Letter to Nawwab Sahib (Resident). Acknowledges receipt of his letter regarding the border dispute and the incident that occurred on the cite of the dispute at *mauza* Paleri of *ilaqa* Tonk and Dankoh of *ilaqa* Jaipur due to false reporting/ manipulation by the *Amin* of Raj Sawai Jaipur. Also refers to the complaint made against the *amins* of *ilaqa* Tonk and unfair dealing / misappropriation by the *zamindars* of *mauza* Dankoh and his (addressee) instructions to him (the writer) to play as arbitrator towards the settlement of the dispute after making inquiry from the *amins* of the two states. Argues to obtain the permission of the Governor General with regard to the appointment of an official *Amin* before proceeding further. Adds that he has already made a request to Colonel John Loo at the department of the Agent at Rajasthan to appoint an *amin*.

The document in Persian *shikasta* bears *sarnama Alif* and signature of the writer.

(ACC. NO. 2701/21; Original; f1).

27 July 1850/ 16 *Ramazan* 1266 AH — 418. *Rubakari* issued from the office of the Resident at Lucknow under the session of Lt. Colonel Saleeman. Orders that a copy

of the said (*rubakari*) may be sent to the King of Oudh requesting him to provide a detailed list of all the officials holding *jagir* as well as the list of the decedents of late Haider Husain Khan furnishing information about the salary of every individual along with the certificates issued by the King to every individual. Also directs to send a copy of the same to Irtiza Husain Khan, the chief of the family for information.

The document in Persian *shikasta* bears *sarnama Alif.*

(ACC. NO. 2733/ 54; Copy; f1).

17 *Ramazan* 1266 AH (27 July 1850)

419. *La-dawa/ Farigh Khati* executed by Pai Reddy, *Muqaddam* of village Mamarpalli in respect of sale of a farm land situated in Siwar in *mauza* Atarlapalli, which is his ancestral property inheriting from Moti Begam for a sum of Rs. 2,500/- and that the amount was received by him in full. Declares that any claim by him or any of his relatives in this regard in future would be null and void.

The bilingual document in Persian *shikasta* and Kannada bears *sarnama Alif.*

(ACC. NO. 2536/ 20; Original; f1).

19 *Ramazan* 1266 AH (29 July 1850)

420. *Parwana* clarifying that Kandur Venkatachari Appavar *zunnardar* has been in assignment of 4 *anna* per diem from olden times and on perpetual basis in lieu of *Sad-o-Panch* while he (the addressee) pays him only for four months. Directs him to pay the *zunnardar* for the entire year and obtain authoritative receipt so that it could be adjusted in the accounts of *sad-o-panj* accordingly.

The document in Persian *nastaliq* bears *sarnama Alif* with the jist of the document.
(ACC. NO. 2535/ 1; Original; ff2).

26 *Ramazan* 1266 AH (5 August 1850) 421. Receipt of a sum of Rs. 548/ 3 received from Ganga Prasad Bihari Lal *mustajir* of Shahpur, Kamalpur which has been deposited in the royal treasury, under the charge of Maslih al-Sultan, Anjum al-Daulah Bahadur through Dabir al-Daulah Bahadur as income for 1257 *Fasli* (1849 AD).

The document in Persian *shikasta* bears *sarnama Alif* and the seal of the Court of *Sultan-i Alam* (i. e. Wajid Ali Shah, the Nawwab of Awadh) and the public treasury of *Sultan-i Alam*, besides endorsements in Devnagri.
(ACC. NO. 200; Original; f1).

21 *Zilqada* 1266 AH (28 September 1850) 422. *Parwana* of Raja Ram Bakhsh to Raja Lachmi Narain. Informs that 8 *annas* % from the kut income of the salt of Machli Bandar has been granted to Lal Khan father of Karim Khan while Amawant Medha Naik, Benivant Soma Naik, Jaswant Chunnu Naik, son of Ram Das Kasrata Naik and other *banjaras* were granted Chauki Acham Shiah as per the *danpatra of the said Naik. Expresses anxiety on the highhandedness of the naib of* Chauki who shows reluctance in providing income of the grant to the *banjaras* and taking in services of the sons of late Khan. Instructs him to restore the confidence of the *banjaras* and the *naib* of Chauki should be forced to release the income to Madar Khan and Jahan Khan, sons of late Khan and their services should be utilised for the kut income of the salt as usual.

The document in Persian *nastaliq* bears *sarnama Alif* with the seal of the writer and jist of the document on the reverse.

(ACC. NO. 2535/ VII; Original; ff2).

30 September 1850 423. Letter of J. Thomason (Lieutenant Governor of North West Province) to Begam Sahiba. Condoles with her upon the death of Saeed al-Nisa Begam. Also congratulates her as the successor of the deceased.

The document is written in Persian *nastaliq*.

(ACC. NO. 1685; Original; f1)

5 *Kartik sudi* 1907 *Samvat* (9 November 1850) 424. *Bainama* executed by Bhag Chand son of Tej Bhan, resident of *(qasba)* Bindraban regarding the sale of 10 *bighas* and 17 *biswas* of garden land having fruitful and otherwise trees besides well, *kotha, sehdari* etc. situated in *qasba* Bindraban (details given in the text) to Sri Ram Chander Jeo Gosain of Thakur Sri Gobind Dev Jeo, resident of Bindraban for a sum of Rs. 1500/- only. Also states that he has received the amount in full.

The document in Persian *shikasta* executed on a stamp paper of Rs. 12/- bears *sarnama Alif* and the symbol of signature of the executant and signatures of the witnesses in Persian and Devanagri. It also contains departmental endorsements on the reverse with the seal of the Court of District Mathura.

(ACC. NO. 2697/ 22; Original; f1).

7 *Muharram* 1267 AH (12 November 1850) 425. Letter of Muhammad Wazir Khan to Nasir Ali Khan. Acknowledges receipt of the letter requesting for the expenses and for the guards in view of the proposed visit

for three or four months. Informs that at present Rs. 50/- is being sent for the expenses of the proposed journey. Assures to send more money if required. Besides despatches 5 *sawars* and one troop of sepoys along with two *harkaras*.

The document in Persian *shikasta* bears *sarnama Innahu* and the seal of the writer.

(ACC. NO. 2701/22; Original; f1).

16 November 1850 426. *Rubakar-i Kachehri-i Adalat-i Faujdari, Zila* Gadha Jabalpur under the session of Captain Alexander Scan, Deputy Commissioner in a case filed by Nand Lal Rathore, the plaintiff against Darpal son of Mukundi. Referring to a *rubakari* of the Deputy Collector, Sihpura, dated 6 November (1850) directing Tholwa, Buri and Maha Brahman to appear in the court in connection to the theft of 3 buffalos and one ox valuing Rs. 59/ 1/- *kaldar* and that the stolen property is in the possession of Maha Brahman and to send a letter to the Raja of. Riwan through the Agent

The document in *Urdu shikasta* bears seal of the Resident al Baghelkhand

(ACC. NO. 2762/ 11; Copy; f1).

12 *Muharram* 1267/ 17 November 1850 427. *Parwana* of Muhammad Wazir Khan to Hafiz Muhammad Ibad Allah, *amil* of *pargana* Tonk. Referring to the severe draught in the region of *Qasba, amla, pargana* Tonk that has affected the barley crop of the region severely and has yielded less, encloses the papers of previous *bandobast* pertaining to the similar circumstances to look into. Directs him (the addressee) to inform after assessing the situation properly.

The document on its reverse contains the reply of Ibad Allah Khan dated 16 *Muharram* 1267 and also contains orders for Lala Shambhu Nath to enquire into the matter thoroughly.

The document in Persian *shikasta* bears *sarnama Alif* and the seal of the writer.

(ACC. NO. 2701/23; Original; f1).

26 *Muharram* 1267 AH (1 December 1850)

428. Receipt of a sum of Rs. 156/ 15/-received from Ganga Prasad *mustajir* of Shahpur, Kamalpur through Dabir al-Daulah Bahadur as installment of 1258 *Fasli* (1850 AD) which has been deposited in the royal treasury under the charge of Maslih al-Sultan Anjum al-Daulah Bahadur.

The document in Persian *shikasta* bears *sarnama Alif* and seal of the court of *Sultan –I Alam* (Wajid Ali Shah, Nawwab of Awadh) and the Public Treasury of *Sultan-I Alam* besides endorsements in Devnagri.

(ACC. NO. 1201; Original; f1).

1267 AH (1850-51 AD)

429. Petition of Muhammad Abd-al Qadir to.... Expressing his gratitude to the favours shown to his father Muhammad Nasir al-Din Khan submits that since the death of his father he is facing hardships in providing livelihood to numerous members of the deceased family and to pay the debt of his father as the stipend as well as the *ilaqa* assigned to his father has been withdrawn. Requests for the restoration of the allowance enjoyed by his father in his favour as he has to support a large family. Prays for the perpetuity of the addressee. The document also consists of a *qasida* in praise of the addressee.

The illuminated document in Persian *nastaliq* bears *sarnama Alif.*

(ACC. NO. 2403/ 92; Original; f1).

Undated 430. Letter to Bakhshi Gur Narain. Referring to the royal order directs him to be in complete agreement with Sardar Katan Singhji and execute the royal orders in accordance to the wishes of the chieftains thereof and submit every day report.

The document in Persian *shikasta* bears *sarnama Innahu*. The date is not forthcoming as the document is slightly damaged.

(ACC. NO. 2398/ 42; Original; f1).

Undated 431. Letter from Khalsa Darbar (to the Resident). Expressing pleasure on the friendly relation subsisting between the two states hopes that it would be further strengthened. Acknowledges the receipt of his (the addressee) letter. Refers the visit of *Jamadar* Brij Lal communicating the demand of 800 camels for the addressee. Informs that a servant was provided to Brij Lal and *parwanas* have been issued to the officials of Amritsar, Lahore and Band Dadan Khan for the purchase of the camels and instructions have also been issued not to create any obstacle on account of tax etc.

The illuminated document in Persian *shikasta* bears *sarnama Ba-fazl-i-Sri Akal Purakhji*.

(ACC. NO. 234; Original; f1).

Undated 432. Letter from Khalsa Darbar (to the Resident). Expresses pleasure on the friendly relations between Sri Akalpurakhji and the Company. Informs that Sardar Ajit Singh Laduwala attended the marriage of his son Kanwar Naunihal Singh and has returned to his state.

The illuminated document is written in Persian *Shikasta* bears *sarnama Ba-Fazl-i Sri Akal Purakhji*.

(ACC. NO. 230; Original; f1).

Illustrations

Sr. No. 19 (Document No. 2533/ 42)

Sr. No. 40 (Document No. 2403/ 20)

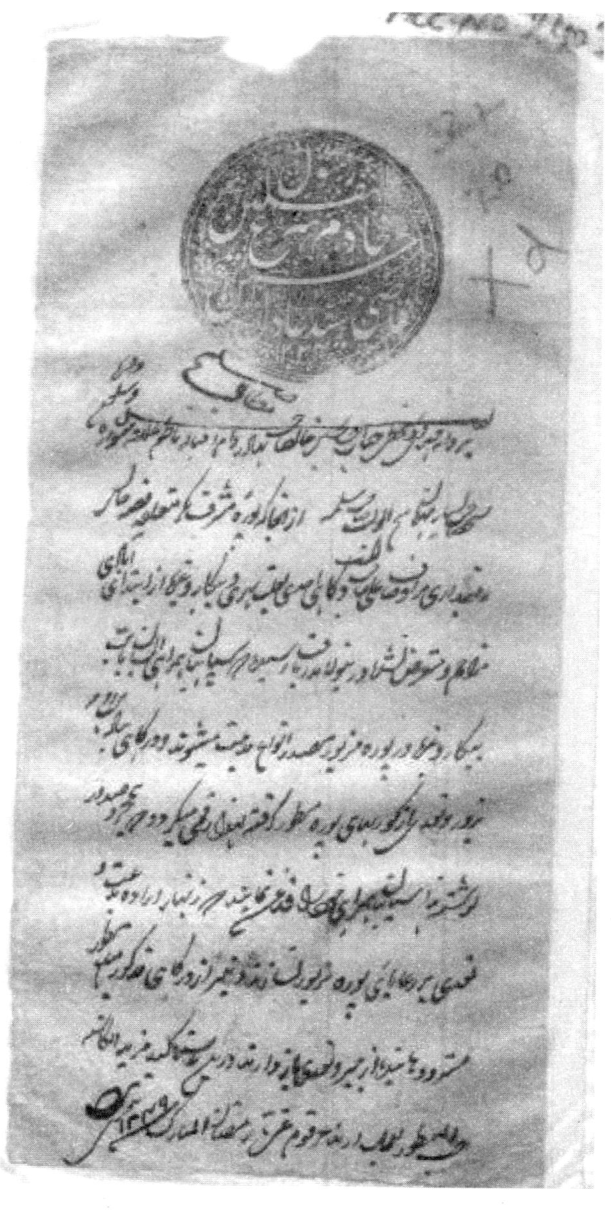

Sr. No. 46 (Document No. 2403-22-1)

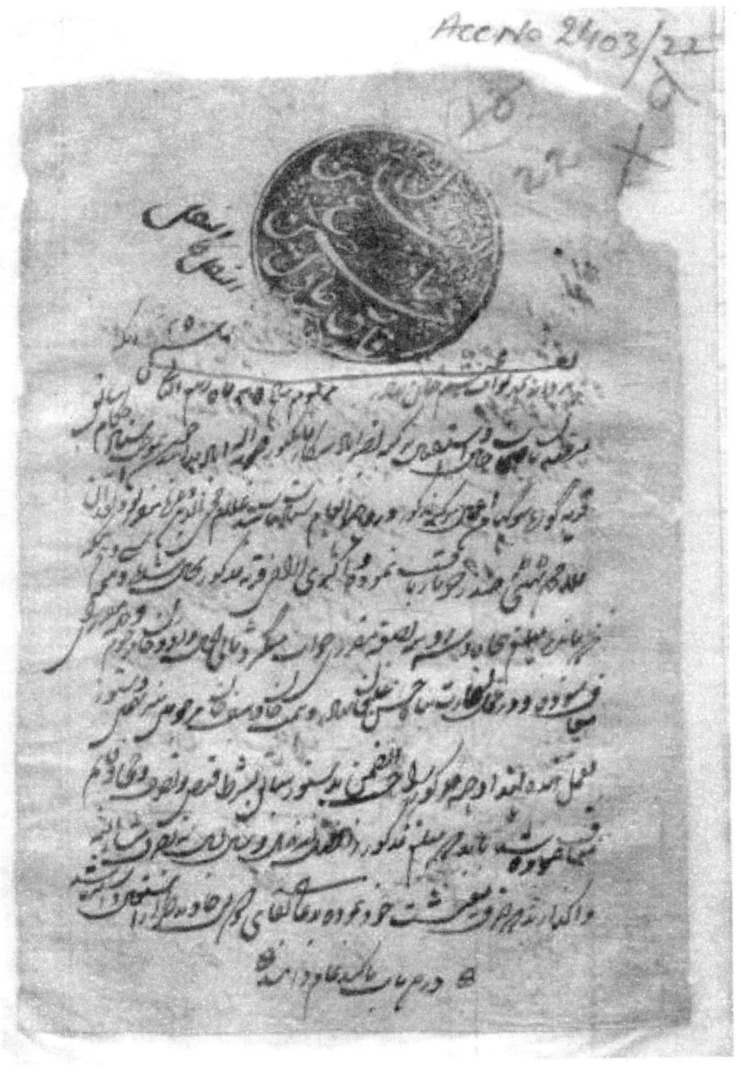

Sr. No. 46 (Document No. 2403-22-2)

Sr. No. 87 (Document No. 2695/ 40 part)

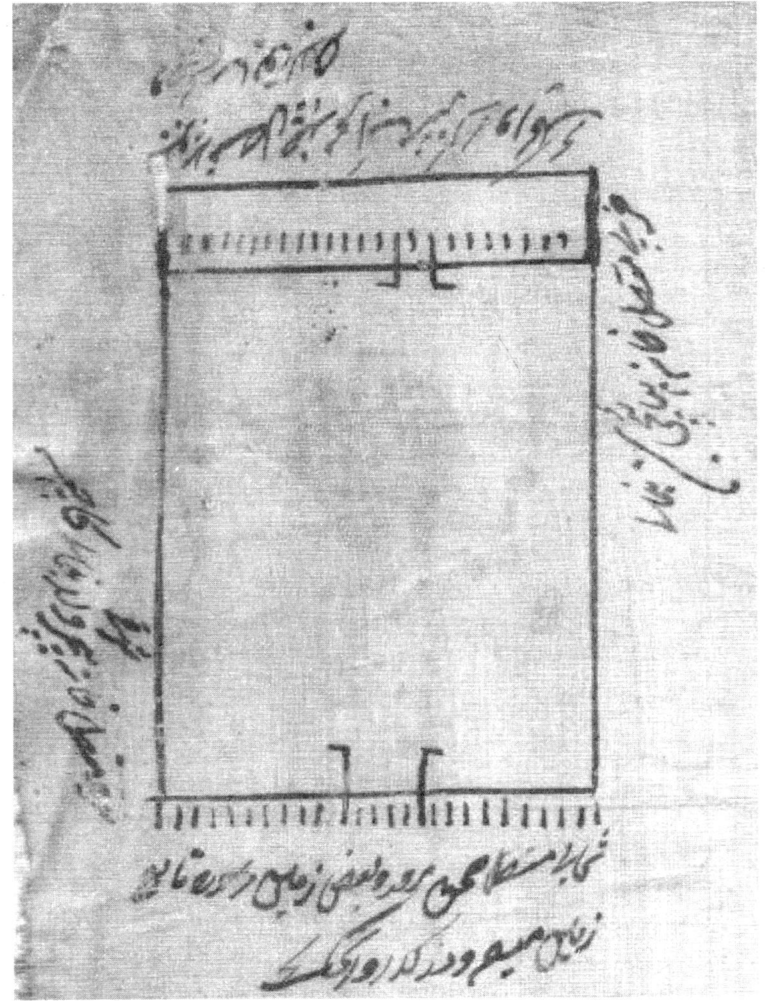

Sr. No. 87 (Document No. 2695/ 40 part)

Sr. No. 189 (Document No. 2536/ 30)

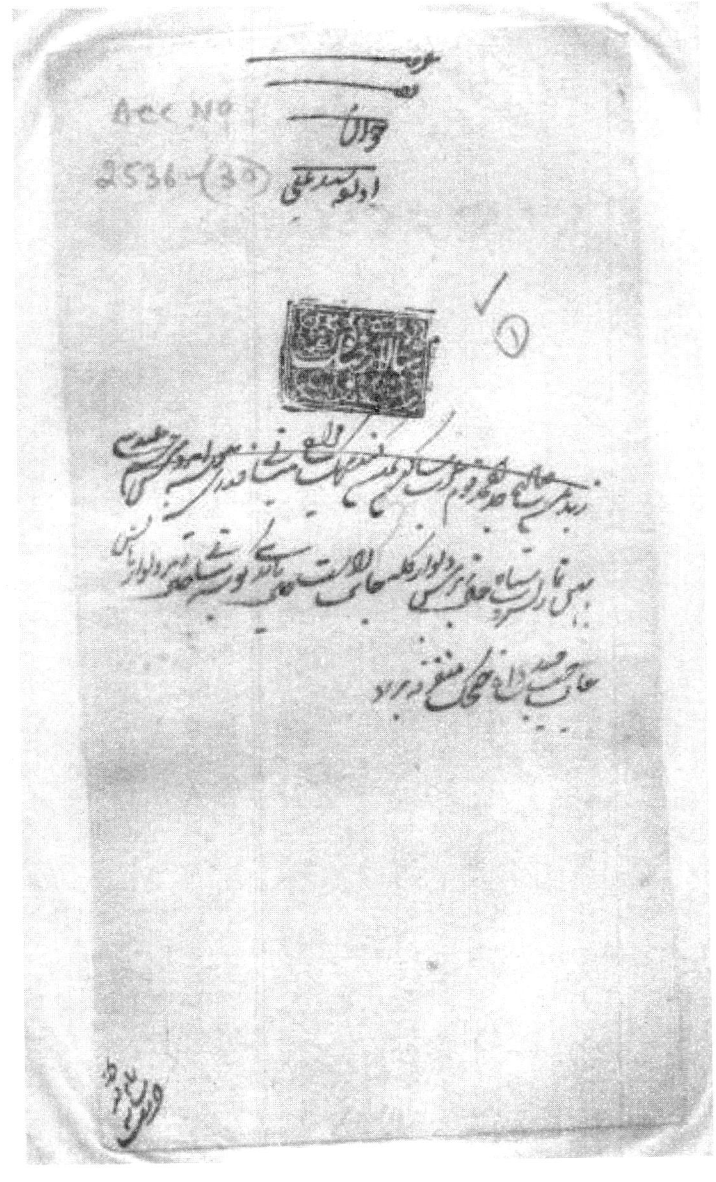

Sr. No. 390 (Document No. 2701/20)

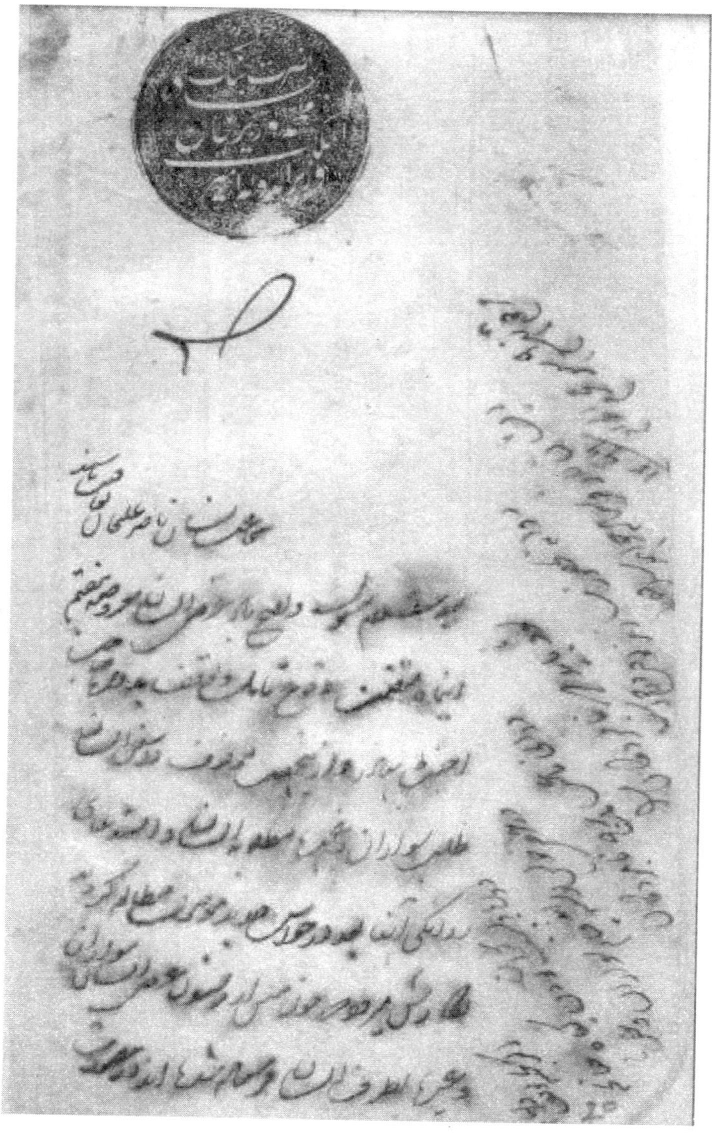

Glossary

(A – Arabic, B – Bangla, H – Hindi, P – Persian, S – Sanskrit, T – Turkish, U –Urdu)

Adalat-i Aliya (P/A): The court in which affairs, quarrels and cases regarding personal property are tried.

Adalat-i Diwani (P/A): Civil court, a court of civil jurisdiction.

Adalat-i Faujdari (P/A): A court of the *faujdar* or chief of the magistracy and Police of a district; the subordinate or district criminal court.

Ahalkar (P): People of business, officers of a court.

Ahar (H/S): A small pond or reservoir for collecting water for irrigation.

Ahl-i Maash (P/A): Possessor of a means of subsistence; holder of a rent free tenure.

Aimma (A): Land granted by Mughal government either rent free or subject to a quit -rent to learned and religious persons of Islamic faith.

Aimmadar (P): Holder of land granted for religious or charitable use.

Akhbar (A) (plural of *khabar*): News, the written intelligence of the proceedings of Native courts and Princes by their appointed agents.

Altamgha (T): A royal grant under the seal of some of the Mughal emperors.

Amanat (A): Deposit, charge, anything held in trust money deposited in court.

Amil (A): An officer of government in the financial department especially a collector of revenue.

Amin: A confidential agent, a trustee, a commissioner, an arbitrator; an officer appointed to take charge of an estate and collect the revenue.

Amin-i Sadr-i Ali (P/A): Principal *Sadr Amin* to whom lies an appeal from the decisions of the *amin* and who decides suits to unlimited amount.

Amla (P/A): Establishment of an office, Ministerial staff, workers, operators, executors, public officers.

Amurdad Ilahi: The fifth month of Ilahi Calendar founded by Emperor Akbar on the pattern of Iranian Solar Calendar. It is also the name of the 7th day of the month.

Arazi (P/A): Measured land applied especially to detached portion of land which either rent free or have been recovered from the retrocession of rivers.

Ariyatnama (P/A): An engagement to return any article or property which has been given on loan or in trust.

Arzdasht (P): A written petition.

Arzi (P): A petition, a respectful statement or representation.

Ashrafi (P): Gold coin, *mohur* rated at sixteen rupees silver.

Awarja (P): A diary, a daybook, an abstract, account of receipts and disbursement.

Azadari: Mourning on the 10th Muharram.

Bainama (P): A deed or certificate of sale.

Bakhshi (P): In-charge of a military administration as well as intelligence, a collector of house tax.

Bakhshishnama (P): A deed of gift.

Bandobast (P): Agreement, settlement of revenue to be paid by the *zamindars*, renter or farmer to the Government, or by the tenant to the *zamindars*.

Banjara (H): A grain and cattle merchant.

Baqqal (A): A grain merchant, also a caste in India.

Bazyaft (P): Resumption either wholly or in part of an alienated lands and again subjecting them to revenue assignment.

Begar (P): Forced labour for which no compensation was paid.

Bhaint (H): A complementary gift.

Bhandar (H/M): A treasury, a store, a feast given to a number of religious mendicants or *Gosains*.

Bhog (S): Food and other edibles offered to idol.

Bhograk (S): Food offered to an idol.

Bigha (H): A measure of land. The *bighas* as a unit was consisted of a square *jarib* (60x60 *gaz*) and with the introduction of the standard *gaz-i Ilahi* the standardized *bigha* consisted of 3600 square *gaz-i Ilahi* or nearly 5/8th of the acre.

Biswa (H): One- twentieth part of a *bigha*.

Biswansi (H/M): The fraction of *biswa*, usually the one twentieth part of a *biswa*.

Chabutra (H): A platform of earth as masonry raised slight above the surface of the ground. This name was given to the office of the *kotwal* or head police officer.

Chak (H): A portion of land derived off, a patch of rent free lands.

Chakla (H): A large division of a country comprehending a number of *parganas*. This division was introduced by Emperor Shahjahan.

Chakladar (P): Superintendent or proprietor, or renter of a *chakla*.

Chaudhary (H): The headman of a caste, the headman of a village.

Chauki (H): Station of police or of customs, a guard, a watch, a police post.

Chaukidar (P): Watchman, guard, a village watchman.

Chauth (H): Assessment equal to one fourth of the actual government collections demanded by the Marathas from certain chiefs of India who derived protection from their plunder because 'no plunder no payment' theory of Frank Perlin defines this phenomenon in a clear crystal manner.

Chela (H): A servant, a slave, a disciple.

Chitthi (H): A short letter, any letter or note conveying an order or document.

Daftar-i Istifta (P/A): Office of the legal consultant (*mufti*).

Dakhil Kharij (A): Mutation, a transfer of land or property under one name to another name in a deed or register.

Dakhl (A): Entering in an account, taking possession.

Dam (P): Copper coin.

Danpatra (H/S): A document for giving donation.

Danpatra (H/S): A donation box.

Dar al-Qaza (A): House of Justice.

Darbar (P): A court, a royal court. An audience or levee.

Dargah (P): A Muslim shrine, the tomb of some holy reputed persons.

Dar-o bast/ Darbast (P): The whole of a district or estate.

Darogha (P): Superintendent, specially of the Police, custom or excise.

Dastak (P): A permit, pass, passport, license.

Dastak-i Barkhast (P): A permit of dismissal.

Dastak-i Khas Bardar (P): An attendant carrying the arms of his lord one armed with firelock.

Dastawiz (P): A voucher, a document anything in writing producible in evidence.

Dastawiz-i Qubuliyat (P): A deed of acceptance.

Dastgardan (P): A loan without any voucher on a verbal promise to pay.

Dastur al-amal (A): Rule of practice, orders and rules of Government.

Deh / Deha (P): Village.

Deshmukh (H): A hereditary revenue village officer.

Deshpandeya (H): Record keeper or accountant.

Devotar (H): Rent free land in the name of Hindu deities usually granted for the maintenance of a temple or a religious site.

Dharmarth (H): Anything given for charitable or pious purpose.

Dunbala (Tel) An order for giving up the government share of the produce in the cultivation.

Fard (A): A sheet of paper, a document, a statement.

Fard-i Mahal: Statement of a fiscal unit.

Farigh Khati (P): A written receipt and acquaintance, a deed of dissolution of partnership or from partnership, a deed of release from all demands; a bill of divorcement.

Farman (P): A mandate, an order, a command, an imperial order, a patent. The term applied to every royal missive that issued from the sovereign on the chancellery bearing the imperial *tughra* and seal.

Fasli (P): Belonging to the harvest or season when cultivated, or lands productive of crops assessed according to the value of the crops.

Fatwa (A): Religious decree, legal opinion.

Fulus (A): A small copper coin of varying weight and value.

Gaddinashin (P): A chief, a principal, a prince one who sits on a throne.

Gaz-i Ilahi (P): A measure of length, a yard ,the basic measure of length which slightly exceeded 32 inches was introduced by Akbar.

Ghat (H): A landing place on the bank of a river, quay or wharf where customs are commonly levied.

Ghazi (A): A champion, especially one who fights against infidels.

Girvinama (P): Mortgage deed.

Gumashta (P): An agent, a steward, an officer employed by *zamindars* to collect their rents by bankers to receive money and by merchants to carry on their trade at different places.

Hakim (A): A ruler, a governor, a supreme administrative authority in a district.

Haqq-i Naibana (P): Right of a vice or a vice chief.

Harkara (H): Carrier of news, a messenger, courier, an emissary.

Hasilat (A): Actual realization of revenue of assessed lands.

Haveli (P): A house of brick or stone, house dwelling, habitation.

Hazir Zamini (A): Security, whether personal or pecuniary for the appearance of a person charged with any debt or offence.

Hiba Bilmuawaza (A): A deed of gift with a token of compensation.

Hulya (A): Descriptive roll.

Hissadar (P): A sharer, a share holder, one who pays his share of the revenue either to a *zamindar* or the state.

Hukmnama (P): A written order from a superior.

Hundwi/Hundi (H): A bill of exchange, money order, draft, cheque, bond.

Huzur-i Tahsil (A): Collection of revenue by the chief fiscal officer of the Government.

Ibranama (P): A written acquittance or relinquishment of claim.

Ijaranama (P): A lease, any document under which a lease or farm is held.

Ilaqa (A): Dependency, a district, a jurisdiction, an estate.

Imambara (P): A building in which the festival of *Muharram* is celebrated.

Inam (A): A gift, a benefaction in general or a gift by a superior to an inferior.

Inam-i Altamgha (T): A grant of rent-free land under royal seal as a reward for services rendered, or for religious or charitable purposes.

Iqrarnama (P): Deed of agreement.

Ishtiharnama (A): A written notice or proclamation.

Istifa-i Theka (P/A): A deed of relinquishment such as usually executed by *zamindars* on giving up their lands.

Jagir (P): Revenue assignment, land and villages given by government as a reward for services or as a free, a rent free grant.

Jagirdar (P): The holder of a *jagir*.

Jagir-i Zat (P): An assignment for personal support or sometimes requiring personal services.

Jalkar (H): Profits or rents derived from the water, lakes, ponds or the like with the right of fishing, and of cultivating the beds if dry.

Jama (A): Assessed land revenue; the total amount or rent or revenue payable by a cultivator or a *zamindar*, Government demand, aggregate assessment or an estate.

Jamabandi (H): Settlement of the amount of revenue assessed upon an estate, village assessment of revenue.

Jamadar (P): The chief or leader of any number of persons, a police, customs or any army officer.

Jihat (A): Taxes on certain traders, duties on manufacture.

Kachehri (H): An office; a court of justice, a place where any public business is transacted.

Kahar (H): Palanquin bearer.

Kaifiyat (A): Statement, description, account particulars.

Kalali (H): A wine seller, a tavern keeper, anything relating to spirituous liquors or tax upon them, excise.

Kamdar (P): A man of business, an agent, a steward, a representative especially in revenue matters.

Kardar (P): An agent, especially of the government.

Karinda (P): An agent, a manager, an attorney, an officer.

Khalsa Sharifa (A): Land or villages held immediately by the Mughal Government and of which the state is the manager, the royal exchequer.

Kham Bighas (P): The revenue of a village before any deductions are made for cost of cultivation, charges of collection, village disbursement.

Khandi (B) A portion of the lands of an estate.

Kharif (A): The autumnal harvest, the crops which are sown before the commencement of rains (April-May) and reaped after their close (October-November).

Khasabardar (P): An attendant carrying the arms of his lord, one armed with a fire lock.

Khiraj (A): Tax, tribute.

Kulhububat (P): All grains and others, but applied to cesses or imposts extra to the regular assessment.

Kulkarni (M): One of the principal village functionaries under the *patel* (q.v.), the village registrar and accountant, whose duty is to keep accounts between the cultivators and the government.

Lakhiraj (A): Rent free land, land exempted from paying revenue to the state for some particular reason.

Lambardar (P): Village headman, representative of the village community, a title of a person in a village who represents the community in their financial dealings with the Government and who is registered in the collectors ledger by a number as well as by name.

Langar (H): An anchor, an alms house.

Madad-i Maash (P): Grant of means of subsistence in general, also assignment of revenue for the support of learned or religious persons.

Mahajan (S): A great or eminent man, a banker, money-dealers, or merchant.

Mahal (A): A division of *taalluqa* or district yielding revenue according to assessment, an estate, an apartment, a fiscal unit of a *pargana*.

Mahant (H): The head of a religious establishment of the mendicants orders of the Hindus.

Mahr (A): A marriage portion of gift settled upon the wife before the marriage.

Mahr Mu'ajjal (A): The amount of *mahr* paid promptly or immediately.

Mahr Muwajjal (A): Deferred to some specified time, if no amount of dower is agreed upon at the time of marriage, the wife is entitled to a customary provision.

Mahsul (A): Collected, levied, revenue duty, public income from any source as lands, customs excise and like the produce or return realized from anything.

Mahsuldar (P): The collector of land revenue.

Mahsul-i Qaza (P): Fee of justice.

Mahzar (A): A general application, a representation, a statement laid before a judge, or a document attested by a number of persons professing to be cognizant of the circumstances of the case and submitted with their signatures to the court.

Majalis (A) (plural of *majlis*): An assembly, a court.

Mal-i-Zamini (P): Security for payment of money.

Malguzar (P): Revenue collector, a person responsible to Government for the payment of the revenues assessed on a village with whom the land settlement has been made, landed proprietor who pays Government demand into the treasury.

Malguzari (P): Revenue assessment, the payment of land revenue.

Mal-i Sair (A): Revenue from customs and other sources exclusive of land.

Mal-i Wajib (A): The authorised land revenue and taxes fixed or proper revenue.

Malik/Malika (A): A master, an owner, a proprietor, a cultivator possessing a hereditary or proprietary right in the land he cultivates.

Malikana (A): Pertaining or relating to the *malik* or proprietor as his right or due.

Mallah (A): A sailor, a boat man, a maker of salt.

Mal-o-Asbab (A): Goods and provisions.

Mal-o-Jihat (A): Land revenue and other taxes.

Man (Maund): A measure of weight of general use in India but varying in value in different places i.e. containing 4o *ser*.

Manpan (M): An honorary rights or privileges attached to official rank, the right of the village hereditary officers etc.

Mansabdar (P): A noble holding a *mansab* or military rank.

Mashaikh (A)(plural of *sheikh*): Elders, holy person, heads of religious fraternities among the Muslims.

Mauza (A): A village.

Mihr Ilahi (P): The name of the 7th Persian month.

Milk/ Milkiyat (A): Proprietary right, landed possessions.

Milkiyat -i Malguzari (P): Revenue assessed on a village.

Mohalla (U): Division of a town, a quarter, a ward.

Muafi (A): Rent free land grant, exemption.

Muafidar (P): One holding anything exempt from tax, the holder of rent free lands.

Muchalka (P): A written bond, a deed or a draft of any binding or undertaking, an agreement under a penalty to observe the condition of any deed or grant.

Muhafiz-i Daftar-i Kachahri-i Nizamat (P): Keeper of the records, the native officer of a court charged with the case of pubic papers.

Muhr-i Kachahri-i Khas (P): Seal of the royal court.

Muharrir (A): Clerk, scribe.

Muhkma-i Sadr al-Sharia (A): Department of the head of the law.

Muhtarfa (A): A tax or taxes levied on traders and professions on the artificers of a village or their implements.

Mujra-i Ikhrajat (A): Any authorised deduction, a pension, an allowance.

Mukhtar (A): An agent, a representative, attorney, chosen, selected.

Mukhtar-i Kar (P): Attorney.

Mukhtarnama (P): A deed appointing a representative, a power of attorney.

Munshi (H): A writer, a secretary.

Munsif (A): An arbitrator, a judge applied under the British Government to a native civil judge of the first or lowest rank.

Muqadddam (A): A superior officer of the revenue in a village, village headman, collector of revenue.

Muqaddami (P): Relating to the office, duties, or rights of a *muqaddam*, dues paid to him by the cultivators or when the revenue is collected by the state.

Mustajir (A): A tenant, hirer, farmer, a lessee, also farmer of revenue appointed to make collections on the part of a *zamindar*.

Mutasaddi (A): A general designation for official clerk, an accountant

Muzare (A): Husband men; tillers of the land.

Naib (P): A substitute, a deputy a representative, a lieutenant.

Naib Chakladar (P): Deputy/assistant superintendent of a *chakla* (q.v.).

Naib Tehsildar (P): Deputy/assistant collector of rents.

Naik (H): A Leader, a chief in general, also the head of a small body of soldiers, a title borne by the chiefs among several hill tribes.

Nankar (P): Lit. bread for work; assignment of land for subsistence in lieu of some services, an allowance of money or land to *zamindars*, *chaudharis*, *qanungos* etc. as maintenance.

Nankar Naqdi (P): A person getting allowance in cash for his maintenance.

Naqib (A): A servant who announces his master's approach and repeats his titles, a kind of herald or chamberlains.

Nazim (A): Governor, an administrator, the superior officer or Governor of a province, charged with the administration of criminal law and the police.

Nazr (A): A present, an offering especially from the inferior to a superior, to a holy man or to a prince.

Nazrana (P): Offerings, fees paid to government as an acknowledgment for a grant of land, a kind of tribute.

Nazr-i Peshgi (P): A fees paid to the State or to its representative on succeeding to an office or to property; (lit. advance money).

Nikah (A): Marriage, legal marriage, matrimony.

Nikahnama (P): A marriage contract signed/verified by a *qazi*, marriage certificate.

Nishan (P): Order or a missive of a prince, princes or the sons of princes.

Niyaz-i Dargah (P): An assignment of revenue to a sacred shrine or any religious establishment.

Nizam (A): An administrator, a governor; also a title of the ruler of Hyderabad.

Nizamat (P): Office of a *nazim* or provincial governor charged with the administration of criminal law and the police.

Pai Baqi (P): The revenue from lands so reserved not yet alienated and of lands which having been alienated had been resumed and paid revenue until a fresh assignment has been made.

Paimana (P): A measurement.

Parcha-i Wilayat (P): Cloth, clothing a piece of cloth.

Pargana (M/H): A district, a province, a tract of country comprising many villages.

Parwana (P): An order, a written precept or command; a letter addressed to a subordinate officer.

Parwangi (P): Command, order, permission, leave.

Patel (H): The head man of village, who has the general control and management of the village affairs. He is also the chief medium of communication with the officer of the Government.

Patta (H): A deed of lease; a document given by the collector to the *zamindars* or cultivator or under-tenant, specifying conditions on which lands are hold and the value of proportion of the produce to be paid to the authority or person from whom the lands are held. The *patta* also stated revenue demand upon an Individual cultivator or a village.

Patta-i Theka (P): A contract or farming lease, a deed assigning lands in farm for stipulated condition.

Patwari (M): A village accountant responsible to keep all papers connected with lands, rental, demand and collection of the village.

Peshkar (P): An agent, a deputy, a manager in general for a superior or proprietor, or one exercising in revenue or custom affairs.

Piada (P): A footman, foot soldier.

Pokhar (H): Small pond.

Potadar/Fotadar (P): A banker, a treasurer, a cashier; an officer in public establishments for weighing money and bullion and examining and valuing coins.

Pothi (H): A book, especially a manuscript book.

Pujari (H): A priest in a temple, one who conducts public worship and receives the offerings either on his own accounts or that of the proprietors of the temple.

Pura (S): A town, a city.

Qabala (A): Any deed of conveyance, or transfer of right of property, any contract of bargain or sale, a bond, a bill of sale, title deed, written agreement.

Qabala-i Rahn (P): A deed of mortgage.

Qabala-i Nilami (P): Deed of sale, public sale or auction.

Qabuliyat-i Theka (P): To take on contract, written agreement (to pay rent), the counterpart of a lease.

Qabz al-Wusul (A): A deed of acknowledgement or a receipt; a document acknowledging the receipt of money or their valuable.

Qaladar/Qiladar (P): Governor of a fort, Commandant of a garrison.

Qanungo (P): Local revenue official to record any supply information concerning the revenue receipts, area statistics, revenue rates and customs and practices; registrar of a *pargana* (q.v.) or the hereditary registrar of landed property in a *pargana*, a superintendent of village accountants.

Qasba (A): A small town or large village.

Qasida (A): A poem, a long ode, encomium.

Qaul Nama (P): A written deed o contract or engagement, the written voucher granted to the revenue payers specifying the terms of their payments and amount.

Qaul-o-Qarar-i Patta (P): Agreement or deed of lease executed in favour of a lessee, a document given by the collector to the *zamindar*, or by some other receiver of revenue, to the cultivators or under tenant.

Qubuliyat Nama (P): A deed of agreement, or a document in which a payer of revenue whether to the Government, the *zamindar* or the farmer, expresses his consent to pay the amount assessed upon his land.

Rabi (A): The spring harvest, the crop which are sown towards the close of the periodical rains, (in September-October) and reaped after February-March.

Rahnnama (P): A written contract of a mortgage, a deed of pledge.

Rasad / Rasadbandi (P): A store of grain provided for or sent to an army.

Razi Nama (P): A deed of agreement or concurrence, a deed of compromise by which the plantiff or prosecutor acknowledges that he has been satisfied by the defendant.

Riaya (A): A subject but especially applied to the agricultural population.

Rozina (P): A daily maintenance, a daily pension, a daily allowance to poor or religious persons.

Rubakar (P): Proceeding with, before the constituted authorities, as in a court of justice.

Rubakar-i Kachahri (P): The written record of a case stating the particulars and the grounds of the decision drawn up and authenticated by the judge in the company's court.

Rudad Nawis (P): Narrative or record of proceedings, statement of facts or occurrences, report of a subordinate officer deputed to inquire into any affair.

Ruqqa (A): A letter, a note, a draft, a bill.

Rusum (A) (plural of *rasm*): Fees, perquisites taxes, commission or allowances upon articles bought and sold made to the purchaser or the servant or agent of the buyer or seller.

Sadaat (A) (plural of the *Saiyid*): A lord, a chief; a designation assumed by a number of Muslims who pretend to be descended from

Husain son of Ali and grandson of Prophet Muhammad (PBUH).

Sadabrat (*Sadavarti*) (S): Distribution of provisions daily to passers by mendicants.

Sadr-i Ala (A): Chief *Sadr* or *Sadr al-Sudur.*

Sadr-i Juz (A): Provincial *Sadr.*

Shahna (A): A watchman, a person employed to watch the crops and prevent any fraudulent abstraction of the grain, a body of guards.

Saham (A) (plural of *Sahm*): A lot, a portion, the share of a person entitled to a part of the inheritance.

Sahukar (H): A banker, a dealer in money and exchanges, a merchant in general.

Sair Jihat (A): A tax on boats, an inland toll, duties on manufactures.

Sanad (A): A Royal ordinance, mandate or decree, a patent, grant, document, warrant, any royal deed or appointment under which another acts, an order, a written authority for holding either land or office.

Sarbarahkar (P): An officer of the Government skilled in business or management of affairs.

Sardrakhti (P): Tax on trees.

Sarkar (P): The government, the state, tract of a territory under Muslim rule, corresponding to a district or a division under British rule.

Sarnama (P): The sacramental superscription.

Sarishta (P): A record office, account, registry office.

Sarishtadar (P): A keeper of records, a registrar, superintendent of a court of justice or collectors office with the charge of the public records and official documents.

Sawar (P): A rider, horseman, It also indicates the number of horsemen to be maintained by the holder of a *mansab* introduced by Emperor Akbar in the late 16th century.

Sazawal (T) : A native collector of revenue, an agent appointed by a landowner or lesser to compel payment of rent by tenant or leaseholder.

Sehbandi (P): A soldier employed in collecting revenue, an establishment of peons.

Sewak (S): A servant, a slave, a worshipper.

Sewapuja (S): Service, attendance upon an idol, worship, adoration.

Shahriwar Ilahi (P): The name of the 6th Persian month.

Shariat (A): Literary means path, i.e. the path of the Prophet or the Islamic law.

Shikasta (P): A broken and tortuous writing.

Shikmi (P): As a revenue term it applies to a subordinate tenure in which the holder pays his revenue or his share of it through some other persons to the Government, not direct.

Shiwala (*Sivalaya*) (H): A temple of Siva.

Shuqqa (A): A royal letter or missive, a letter from a superior.

Siri (M) Arable land originally excluded from the village assessment either a fallen in consequence neglect of cultivation of forfeiture.

Siyaha (P): Register, An account book, an inventory.

Siyaha Nawis (P): An accountant, one who keeps the rough day book.

Suba (P): A province comprising many districts.

Taahud (A): Agreement, settlement, stipulated rent, a lease, or deed of lease.

Taalluqa (A): A district, a dependency, division of a province.

Taalluqadar (P): One who holds a *taalluqa,* land holder, possessor of an estate.

Tahqiqat-i Qanun (P): Inquiry, investigation ascertaining the truth of a matter.

Tahsildar (P): An official presiding over the *tahsil* of a district, incharge of a *tahsil,* a collector of rents.

Tahsil-i Kachahri (A): The office or the court of a *tehsildar.*

Tamassuk (A): A bond, a note of hand written acknowledgement of engagement.

Tamassuk Nama (P): A receipt executed in favour of any such party which has to discharge same obligation in respect of money.

Tamlik Nama (P): A deed of transfer ,whether of gift or conveyance.

Tankhwah (P): Salary, cash or in form of land assignment.

Tappa (H): A small tract, subdivision of a *pargana* also used to indicate the relative position of a field or properties.

Taqsim (A): A complete record of the measurement both cultivable and uncultivable land.

Taufir (A): Increase, an augmentation of revenue or excess above an intended amount of assignment which, when realized in a *jagir*.

Taziadari (P): Making of a *tazia* at *Muharram*, the observance of *Muharram*.

Thakur (H): An idol, a deity.

Thana (H): A military post or a police station.

Thanadar (P): Police officer, incharge of a *thana*.

Thathera (H): A brazier, a worker in tin and copper.

Theka (H): A lease, a contract by which a person engages to pay a fixed amount of revenue on an estate or district.

Thekadar (P): A farmer, a lease holder, one who receives the rent from the cultivators and pays stipulated amount to the proprietor.

Tirtha/(Tirth) (S): A holy place of pilgrimage.

Topkhana (P): An arsenal, an artillery park a place where military stores are kept.

Tosha Khana (P): A store room, a ward rob chamber in which objects of curiosity or value, not in daily request are kept.

Tuyul-i Khas (A): Land held in *jagir* by a member of a royal family, an appendage.

Ulama (A) (plural of *Alim*): Learned men, scholars, theologians.

Ulufa (A) (plural of *Alf*): Subsistence, supplies furnished gratuitously to great person on a journey by the villages on their route.

Waguzasht (P): Released from attachment, relieved from assessment, remitted.

Wajh-i Rusum (A): Salary, allowance, wages, hire, fees, perquisites, customary payments and gratitude.

Wakalat Nama (P): Power of attorney, letter of authority.

Wakil (A): A person vested with authority to act for another, an ambassador, a representative, an agent or an attorney.

Warasat Nama (P): A deed or document, either in proof of the distribution of an inherited property.

Wasiatnama (P): Deed of will.

Wasilbaqi (A): Collection and balance, an account showing the amount of revenue realized and the remainder outstanding.

Wasiqa (A): A compact, an agreement, a bond, a written obligation.

Wujuhat-i Zamindari (P): Allowances, extra collections by *zamindars* for personal expenses.

Yaddasht (P): A note, a memorandum, a diary; a petition a certificate.

Zamanat Nama (P): A deed of surety by which a person makes himself answerable for the debts of another.

Zamindar (P): Landlord, holder of land, landed proprietor; farmer

Zamindari (P): The office and rights of *zamindar,* the tract of land constituting the possession of a *zamindar.*

Zanbura (P): A small cannon usually mounted on a camel, accompanying the king.

Zat (A): Personal rank, which was generally coupled with the *sawar* introduced by Akbar in his *mansabdari* system.

Zila (A): A district, under British administration, a tract of country constituting the jurisdiction of a commissioner or circuit judges.

Ziladar (P): An officer who has the charge of the revenue of a *zila,* a provincial governor.

Zira (A): A measure of length, a yard.

Zunnardar (P): A Brahmin Hindu, one who wears a sacred thread.

Index

(All references are to the serial numbers)